STRANGER IN A STRANGE LAND

STRANGER IN A STRANGE LAND

ENCOUNTERS IN THE DISUNITED STATES

GARY YOUNGE

THE NEW PRESS

NEW YORK
LONDON

Requests for permission to reproduce selections from this book should be mailed to:
Permissions Department, The New Press, 38 Greene Street, New York, NY 10013

Co-published by The Guardian and The New Press, 2006
Distributed by W. W. Norton & Company, Inc., New York

LIBRARY OF CONGRESS CATALOGING-IN-PUBLICATION DATA

Younge, Gary.
  Stranger in a strange land : encounters in the disunited states / Gary Younge.
    p. cm.
  Includes bibliographical references and index.
  ISBN-13: 978-1-59558-068-9 (pbk.)
  ISBN-10: 1-59558-068-9 (pbk.)
  1. United States—Politics and government—2001– 2. Iraq War, 2003– 3. United
States—Race relations. 4. United States—Civilization—1970– 5. National characteristics,
American. 6. Bush, George W. (George Walker), 1946–Public opinion. 7. Public
opinion—United States. 8. Younge, Gary—Travel—United States. I. Title.
  E902.Y68   2006
  973.931–dc22   2005058043

The New Press was established in 1990 as a not-for-profit alternative to the large,
commercial publishing houses currently dominating the book publishing industry.
The New Press operates in the public interest rather than for private gain, and is
committed to publishing, in innovative ways, works of educational, cultural, and
community value that are often deemed insufficiently profitable.

www.thenewpress.com

Composition by Westchester Book Composition

Printed in the United States of America

2 4 6 8 10 9 7 5 3 1

Contents

Introduction

When I arrived in New York from London in January 2003 to take up my post as *The Guardian*'s New York correspondent, the United States appeared to be in the grip of a monumental autistic episode. The terrorist attacks of September 11, 2001, seemed to have left it incapable of empathy with the outside world.

The previous year, global opposition to the impending war in Iraq had grown alongside a tacit understanding that it would probably happen anyway. In the United States people were intellectually preparing themselves. The top five nonfiction titles on the *New York Times* bestseller list for that first month were: 1) *Bush at War*; 2) *The Right Man* (Bush's former speechwriter relives his first year in the White House); 3) *Portrait of a Killer* (Patricia Cornwell on Jack the Ripper); 4) *The Savage Nation* (a rightwing radio talk show host saves America from "the liberal assault on our borders, language and culture"); and 5) *Leadership*, by former Republican New York mayor, Rudolph Giuliani.

Britain stood virtually alone among its Western European neighbours in its desire to anticipate and replicate the Bush administration's every move. Reporting from the United Nations during my first few months felt like living in a parallel universe where mind and muscle operated completely independently. While most diplomats were trying to avert the war, the U.S. and British armies were amassing huge numbers of troops in the Persian Gulf and steeling themselves for war.

It was into this cauldron of destiny, demagoguery and despair that I sought to translate, explain and explore the U.S. for a British audience. As a child of empire—my parents left Barbados in the early sixties for England, where I was born—I was ambivalent about both the growing tides of both Euro-bashing and anti-Americanism on either side of the pond.

I came less in the tradition of Alexis de Tocqueville than that other great chronicler of American civilization, Trinidadian socialist C.L.R. James. Not so much transatlantic as black Atlantic. Coming from a nation that had interned the Irish and massacred the Mau Mau, the only thing I found exceptional about Abu Ghraib was that the perpetrators there had been caught on camera.

"A person is smart. People are dumb, panicky, dangerous animals and you know it," says Tommy Lee Jones in the film *Men in Black* when asked why he hides the existence of aliens on earth from ordinary people. There was no reason to believe that the American people would be any different in that regard from Western Europeans when they had their privilege challenged and their lives threatened.

Time and again while on the road I would experience just how warm, wonderful and occasionally warped Americans can be.

In Montgomery, Alabama, the cradle of the Confederacy, I was driven the wrong way up a one-way street by a young white woman high on life and martini whom I had only just met.

By day I was covering Rosa Parks's memorial services. By night I accompanied the young woman from gay bar to nightclub, drinking plenty and talking drugs as though the cast of *Letter to Brezhnev* had ended up in the Deep South. In Salt Lake City, the main town in the most conservative state in the union, I would wait for the mayor in a Hispanic biker bar watching slides of scantily-clad women writhing around on motorcycles beamed onto the wall. In Mississippi three elderly people threatened to shoot me when I asked directions. A few months later in the same state a policeman would threaten to jail me for "giving him a look."

I've always found America exciting but, for better and worse, never exceptional. Its efforts at global domination seemed like a qualitative and material plot development in the narrative of European empire rather than a break from it. Even as the French lambasted Secretary of State Colin Powell's presentation to the U.N. Security Council, protesters in Abidjan, the capital of the Ivory Coast, waved American flags and placards saying: "Bush Please Help Ivory Coast Against French Terrorism." There was precious little moral high ground to go round. Yet everyone, it seemed, was making a stake on it.

So it was with great bemusement that I found myself having to absorb abuse from white, rightwing Americans, who harked back to the Declaration of Independence of 1776 the Second World War to justify military aggression in Iraq.

They badgered me as though their own reference points represented the sole prism through which global events could possibly be understood. As if the struggle for moral superiority between Europe and the U.S. could have any relevance to someone whose ancestors were brought to the Americas as slaves and whose parents and grandparents lived through the war under European colonization.

"If it wasn't for us you would be speaking German," they would say. "No, if it wasn't for you," I would tell them, "I would probably be speaking Yoruba."

However, the sanctimony with which many liberal Europeans criticized the Bush administration was no less galling or historically illiterate. Their critique of U.S. foreign policy was often sound. But the haughtiness with which they delivered it was way off key. When their governments or citizens slam America for its brutality and imperialist pretensions, all too often they fail to do so with sufficient self-awareness or humility to see what to the rest of the world is obvious: that their nations have acted in an equally pernicious fashion whenever they have had the opportunity.

But while I was ambivalent about the players in this transatlantic battle, I was never indifferent to the outcome. Journalists should be honest and fair, but the idea that they can be objective is nothing less than insidious. The notion that there is a bald set of facts out there that once collected will lead us to an abstract and timeless truth is misleading and arrogant.

I came not with an agenda but with a view: that while America's imperial intentions represented a sequel to European colonialism, that did not make those ambitions any more morally defensible or the world any less precarious. While Europeans had no grounds to be pious the whole world had every reason to be concerned. September 11 had revealed the potential destructiveness of religious fundamentalism.

The Bush administration's subsequent actions indicated that national-ist and economic fundamentalism could wreak at least as much havoc and harm.

"We are the sum of the things we pretend to be," wrote Kurt Von-negut. "So we must be careful what we pretend to be." Pretend to be objective and you end up being disingenuous about your own preju-dices, influences and instincts—the real driving forces for the editorial choices we make. It is our duty not to indulge them but neither should we ignore them.

Not long after I arrived in America, I realized that one political misconception, above all, had dominated. While I was well aware that there were many Americans who were opposed to the Bush agenda (my wife being one of them), I had no idea that their number amounted to a significant critical mass. This was not a ludicrous mis-reading of the situation. I arrived just a few months after the Republi-cans had cemented their control of both the House and Senate. Bush's approval ratings were high and opposition to the war was soft com-pared with every other country in the world apart from Israel.

But as the war faltered and the economy stalled, opposition mounted. The growth and crystallization of this opposition took place for the most part under the radar. The mainstream news media either underreported it, misreported it or derided it until the moment when it became impossible to ignore. But it was always there.

America was, in short, bitterly divided. By the end of my first year, a *Time*/CNN poll showed 47 per cent of Americans said they were likely to vote for George Bush and 48 per cent said they would not; 79 per cent of Republicans said they believed he was a president you could trust, 75 per cent of Democrats said they thought he wasn't; 68 per cent of Democrats believed he had been "too quick to interject his own moral and religious beliefs into politics," 67 per cent of Re-publicans believed he hadn't. Break down the response of almost any question along party lines and the nation appeared irrevocably split—separate in outlook but roughly equal in size. Bush did not create these cleavages. Indeed he had to steal the 2000 election because of them. But he had clearly exacerbated them.

To the foreign ear, while the opinions of these two camps differ sharply, they share the same tone and tenor of debate. I have found liberals in America every bit as bombastic, preachy and doctrinaire as conservatives. Patriotism, meanwhile, infects the entire culture. Doves are just as anxious to display their patriotic credentials as hawks. Many peace activists are happy to sport "Support the Troops" bumper stickers on their cars and anti-war demonstrators carry banners saying "Peace Is Patriotic," "Love My Country, Fear My Government" or "Peace Is the American Way." And the left is as capable as the right of infantilising the American public with the claim that they are being duped by extremists and are therefore incapable of discerning their own interests.

But while the styles often seemed eerily similar, the substance could not have been more radically different. With no common ground and even the most basic facts and sources polluted by partisan enmity, it was at times difficult for straightforward conversations to take place. At an impromptu MoveOn.org meeting near my home in Brooklyn, I raised polling evidence that suggested that Democratic presidential hopeful John Kerry had to reach out more to his base only to be told that we couldn't trust polls because they were run by corporations. Likewise the issue of lack of weapons of mass destruction and the deteriorating situation in Iraq were, if the right were to be believed, the products of a conspiracy of disinformation by the "liberal media."

"You'll never convince me that there's no connection between Saddam Hussein and al-Qaida. Never," said Burton Kephart, who lost his son Jonathan in Iraq.

"What is the connection?" I asked.

"Terrorist activity," he said.

This dislocation between left and right, fact and fiction, became most apparent during the 2004 presidential election, which pollster John Zogby had branded the Armageddon election. "Each side predicts the end is near if the other side wins."

In the six weeks before polling day I drove from Boston, home of Kerry, to Midland, Texas, where Bush spent much of his childhood, stopping off in swing states along the way. Schlepping through the suburbs of Derry, New Hampshire, on a hot Sunday afternoon in September, I got a whiff of this impending apocalypse. I followed Pam and Patrick Devaney as they went to seek out progressive voters, armed with water, granola bars and talking points. Derry was a swing town in a swing state and the Devaneys were reluctant but determined novices. "I'm not comfortable doing this, but it has to be done," said

Pam. "Our democracy is at stake. This is the most important election in my lifetime."

Just ten days later I met the Kephart family in Oil City, Pennsylvania. The Kepharts were fundamentalist Christians and for them Armageddon was no metaphor. "I fear for this country if Kerry wins," said Mr. Kephart. "God has a plan for the ages. Bush will hold back the evil a little bit. He is a God-fearing man. He believes in praying to a God who hears his prayers. He's a leader."

Little more than a week after that, I watched the third presidential debate with about forty students in Iowa City. The Republicans sat on one side and the Democrats on the other. Sometimes the Republicans would cheer at a phrase or facial expression of one of the two candidates, and the Democrats would look bemused. A few minutes later the Democrats would do the same, leaving the Republicans similarly confused.

They were not just watching the candidates on a split screen. They were viewing the entire event as though from a split screen, each side hermetically sealed from the other. That pretty much summed up my trip thus far. Back in New Hampshire, Rick Sapareto, a Republican, said he was backing Bush because "I'm very concerned that my boys may end up fighting a war in fifteen years because we failed to take action."

Lisa O'Neill, who lives just a few minutes away, was supporting Kerry for almost precisely the same reason. "I have an eleven- and thirteen-year-old who could be drafted if this carries on," she said. When I called them both the day after the first debate each one thought his side had won.

That has seemed to be how just about every event, from Hurricane Katrina to the war, has been consumed. "National unity was the initial response to the calamitous events of September 11, 2001," argued the Pew Research Center in a report, *The 2004 Political Landscape: Evenly Divided and Increasingly Polarized.* "But that spirit has dissolved amid rising political polarization and anger. In fact, a year before the presidential election, American voters are once again seeing things largely through a partisan prism."

The nature of these divisions was all too easily oversimplified as between the red and blue states or Republicans and Democrats, but it was both far more profound and complex than that. At its heart it appeared to be a conflict over what the country was for, and it did not fit easily into a binary code. Indeed, sometimes the conflicting strands seemed to exist even within the same people.

Gena Edvalson, a lesbian whose partner Jana is pregnant, says her neighbours in Salt Lake City, Utah, couldn't be nicer. "They're going to have a baby shower for us," she says. "But that won't stop them from legislating the hell out of us." The steelworker who refused to give his name, in Canton, Ohio, thought Bush was stiffing the working man but would vote for him anyway because of Kerry's stance on abortion. The wealthy white Republican, Jude Waninski, was a strong supporter of Nation of Islam leader Louis Farrakhan. The evangelical protestors outside the Alabama supreme court waved Confederate flags and sang "We Shall Overcome" as they protested the impending removal of the granite block of the Ten Commandments.

Trying to explain this division whenever I went back to Britain was not easy. "How can you stand living there?" was a common question to which I would usually answer: "How can you stand living here?"

For there was nothing that you could say about American foreign policy that you couldn't say about Britain's. Indeed as the U.S.'s principal ally in Iraq, Tony Blair had arguably made Bush's foreign policy possible by making the claim that America had crucial allies easier to sell.

"At this very moment," wrote C.L.R. James in the 1950s, "despite the enormous power of the American government, its spokesman, the man on whom it depends and has depended for years to give some dignity and colour to its international politics is an Englishman, Winston Churchill." More than fifty years later the same could be said of Blair.

But while in America there was a clear and growing political opposition, in Britain that opposition was both confused and demoralised. True, Britain produced the biggest demonstration in its history to oppose the war on February 15, 2003. But equally true was that, unlike those who attended the much smaller demonstration that I was on in New York, most of the people at the demonstration in London had voted for the man prosecuting the war and would do so again two years later. In America there was hope of an electoral change (however slight in direction and meagre in difference) that energised huge numbers whereas in Britain there was resignation that this was what we were stuck with. That was not to say that the situation in Britain was necessarily worse—simply that in the U.S. there was real hope that both the domestic and international situation could be turned around, while in the U.K. there was mainly cynicism.

However, though this hope found real expression during the U.S. presidential election, few believed the outcome would satisfy it or repair the huge gash in the fabric of national life.

The fact that it's a big country, which like any complicated and interesting place is full of contradictions, is axiomatic. But it is rare to see a political culture and counterculture so enmeshed, confused and evenly balanced (numerically at least) that it is impossible to tell which is which. It's fairly obvious who has the power; it is much harder to work out who has the influence.

What follows is a series of columns, essays and news reports from and about the U.S. that document my efforts to understand this country through what I believe to be one of the most difficult and crucial eras in its recent history. Most date from the time I started living here. Journalism, it is said, is nothing more than a rough draft of history. Some of these pieces are rougher than they might be. Writing for a country which is five hours ahead means waking early, writing fast and filing at midday while the story is still moving. Writing for a foreign audience often demands painting the big picture, of which nuance is always a casualty. Where we have caught errors of fact we have corrected them. But the indecorous phrases, contradictions and errors of judgment remain.

STRANGER IN A STRANGE LAND

Part I

WAR

Actually, Random Lawlessness Ruled on September 10th, Too

September 17, 2001

To land in America from Britain used to feel like Dorothy moving from Kansas to Oz. You went from black and white to Technicolor and the transition horrified and fascinated in equal measure. Before you had left the airport it would be clear that people somehow walked faster and talked louder. Somehow, regardless of their size or yours, they seemed to take up more space—a sight and sound that was simultaneously impressive and imposing.

But that was long, long ago. A time when aeroplanes were a means of transportation rather than weapons of mass destruction and the twin towers of Lower Manhattan symbolised the invincibility of global capitalism rather than its vulnerability. It was an era whose distance from ours is measured not in time but events—less than seven days but more than a million repeated images and thousands of lives have passed since then.

To arrive this weekend was to touch down in another country altogether. It is a painful sight. A nation of hushed tones, of pacing aimlessly in circles. Several states away, in Cincinnati, Ohio, the airport is almost deserted—planes and people all in the wrong places. Business travellers, five days late in a country where minutes once mattered. At the meeting of five departure gates that would once have been overrun with a thousand passengers, just one airport employee sits, reliving the drama on CNN.

The area of rubble that was the World Trade Center is now la-
belled Ground Zero; the hour at which it began to crumble feels like
year zero. But just as there is a physical relationship between the towers and the debris, so too is there a connection between the international political climate before the attacks and after. The world last
Monday was a very different place.

A boatload of refugees from Afghanistan lingered off Australia's
borders, finally heading for a detention centre on the island of Nauru.
Afghanistan, a country now deemed sufficiently sinister to warrant an
international military attack, was not then regarded as being oppressive enough to justify offering refuge to those from it who sought asylum. When 433 people tried, they were demonised by the Australian
government as scroungers. That refusing them contravened international and domestic law seemed neither to bother the Australian government, nor most of its citizens.

An ocean away, at an antiracism conference in Durban, western
powers would not apologise for slavery. The few countries who now
seek to lead a coalition founded on the moral indignation of last Tuesday's atrocities held out against the many who wanted them to accept
their historical responsibility for treating people like chattel. Push
your point, said the powerful, and we will leave.

Just up the road in Zimbabwe, Britain finally looked as though
it had brokered a welcome deal with president Robert Mugabe. But
while the west, rightly, condemned his regime for the lawless, chaotic
and deadly seizure of land from a privileged minority, it continued to
defend the lawless, chaotic and deadly seizure of land by a privileged
minority in the Middle East.

All this looks as nothing compared to the thousands of body bags
now piled up in New York, but it does provide a snapshot of what
global politics had been reduced to. Whatever the west wanted, it
eventually got (except from China). Whether in trade, diplomacy, politics or war, the west used its wealth and muscle to force its interests
on the rest of the world. The west, led by the United States, had become not only the global policeman, but the world's judge, jury and
executioner.

Worse still, like the most shameless corrupt copper, the west not
only made the rules but decided which ones it could break as well.
Serbia is a cogent example. When the west could not reach a global

consensus to curtail Serb aggression, it simply bypassed the rest of the world's concerns and bombed the Balkans in contravention of international law. When it wanted to see Slobodan Milosevic in the dock in the Hague, it waved a chequebook in the direction of the Serb authorities, and he was grabbed. They day after Milosevic was handed over, the U.S. released $1.28 billion in aid to rebuild the nation it had bombed.

Meanwhile the Pentagon, which was attacked last Tuesday, remains the most implacable opponent of the international criminal justice system, refusing the idea that an American could ever be indicted as a war criminal. Republicans recently promoted a bill in Congress permitting the president to use force to free any American ever "captured" by the Hague prosecutors.

The relationship between these facts and last week's atrocities is contextual, not causal. Those who believe that America got what it deserved as a payback for its former ills lack the very humanism which they argue has been missing in America's foreign policy. But, similarly, those eager to stifle any critical understanding as to why these attacks happened lack the faculties to begin to imagine how to make the world a safer place.

This time last week the world was already in a state of maverick lawlessness. The moral, economic and political parameters were set by the powerful and imposed on the powerless, and shifted according to their interests. That the west's two favourite pariahs—Saddam Hussein and Osama bin Laden—were once on the payroll is not ironic but logical. The attacks on New York will not halt that trend but more likely entrench it. With reservists on call and the army on standby, the U.S. is ready, waiting and willing for war. Talk shows reveal a popular mood: shoot now and ask questions later. It is a brave but rare voice that chooses to dissent in this atmosphere.

Elsewhere, things are not much better. Asked last week whether the Israeli government was exploiting the carnage in New York to justify its activities in Palestine, which had left a nine-year-old girl dead, the former Israeli ambassador to Washington said: "We do not need justification. We will fight not only the terrorists but those who harbour them." But America's response to those attacks could expose just how much political capital it has expended by going it alone in the past.

6 STRANGER IN A STRANGE LAND
Last week the U.S. enjoyed the support of the full range of global opinion, from Colonel Gadafy to Ariel Sharon, in its grief. But as it moves to avenge the attacks, the coalition that it seeks to back its military action is ready to crack. Some of the U.S.'s western allies will not want to risk joining it on the list of terrorist targets for the sake of what could well be a gratuitous act of revenge. Others, particularly in the Arab world, will come under considerable domestic pressure not to back Israel's sponsor in the midst of an intifada.
Last Tuesday's attacks might feel like year zero. But as New Yorkers return to their desks today, others around the world are also remembering life this time last week. And many do not like what they see.

We Are All Victims Now

October 15, 2001

So we have come a full and bloody circle. As the American firefighters quench the flames and clear the rubble from the remains of the twin towers in Manhattan, the U.S. military, with British assistance, creates more rubble and starts more fires all over Afghanistan. The FBI has warned of more terror attacks in the next few days. In New York and Florida people live in fear of another anthrax attack. The al-Qaida terrorist network has warned Muslims in Britain and America not to fly. Meanwhile, winter in Afghanistan promises a humanitarian disaster of epic proportions. What started at ground zero is ending up as a zero-sum game.

Even by its own standards, Operation Enduring Freedom is proving a disaster. Taking western leaders at their word, its stated aim is to defeat terrorism. A reasonable test of their war aims, therefore, would be to ask whether their actions have made a terrorist attack more or less likely. More plainly speaking: do you feel more secure today than you did last Saturday? Americans don't seem to. Police forces and armies are on the highest state of alert possible. In London on Saturday night, hundreds of people were evacuated from restaurants and pubs after a chemical scare and Canterbury Cathedral was cleared of worshippers yesterday after a man dropped some white powder.

Every plane in the sky, every police siren on the road and every bullet-proofed bobby on a beat make me think it will be our turn next.

Such dark thoughts have been circling in the back of my mind since the original attacks just over a month ago; since the bombing started they are now at the forefront. The events of September 11 exposed the vulnerability of the west to an attack carried out by a few determined men. The bombing of Afghanistan merely exacerbated it. Following the atrocities people were only afraid of flying; now they are worried about opening their mail too. The system seems fragile because everyone is tense. Today any unstable individual can knock a few hundred points off the Dow Jones index, win themselves a place on prime-time TV and earn a military-assisted impromptu landing simply by making a dash for a cockpit.

Meanwhile opposition to the bombings has destabilised a nuclear power, Pakistan, which now wavers between a military dictator and militant mullahs. This precariousness, not to mention the terrorist attacks in Kashmir, is troubling its antagonistic nuclear neighbour, India. And that is before we get to the terrified ex-pats in Saudi, the riots in Indonesia and the uneasy calm in Egypt. With every smart bomb that goes astray and hits a residential areas (how smart can these bombs really be?) we know that more people will take to the streets. We wait for al-Jazeera to broadcast the first picture of a mosque in flames and then watch the sparks fly all the way to Gaza.

True, these are early days. Bush has promised a year more of this if need be. So the short-term panic would, arguably, be worthwhile if one seriously thought that it was a long-term solution to terrorism. But nobody really does. Terrorism is not like foot and mouth which, with enough culling, quarantine and road blocks, you can snuff out. It is, depending on the time, the place and the cause in which it is committed, an expression of either the absence of dialogue, the failure of negotiation or a determination by a few to undermine the popular will—and sometimes a mixture of all three at once. It can, for short periods of time, be contained but it cannot be extinguished. Either way it is its political character that distinguishes it from other acts of social violence.

That does not make it better or worse but different and as unlikely a candidate for eradication as other political evils such as racism or corruption. That does not mean that we shouldn't try. It does mean you have to be clear in your objectives, realistic in your expectations and subtle in your means. The bombing of Afghanistan cannot lay claim to any of those attributes. If they kill Osama bin Laden they will create a martyr; if they capture him America will find itself on trial; if he remains on the loose they will have failed.

This is not just a question of the west losing the propaganda war. The problem is not with the marketing, but the product. In order to take out the al-Qaida network and get Bin Laden, America needs the full support of the Arab world. The backing has only been lukewarm, because of America's appalling record in the Middle East. Three weeks ago it was considered a mixture of heresy, naivety and plain bad taste to raise the issue of American foreign policy; now it is widely accepted that without a just settlement in the Middle East, networks like al-Qaida will always be able to prey on disaffection in the Arab world.

But the damage has, literally, largely been done. Those here who wilfully confuse anti-war with anti-American, context with cause and explanation with justification in order to polarise debate and deride dissent, now have their wish. Those who did not back the bombing, they say, are appeasers or apologists for the Taliban. They laid out a choice between backing western imperialism on the one hand and Islamic fundamentalism on the other. A growing number in the Muslim world look at the record of both in their area and are opting for the latter. It is thoroughly depressing that they believe that those are the only two options available.

Nonetheless they have been pretty much the only two presented. From the outset Bush has been putting the world "on notice" and warning: "You're either with us or you're against us." Both he and Blair act as though there are only two possible responses to the terrorist attacks. Either you bomb one of the poorest, most famine-stricken countries in the world to smithereens, or you do nothing. There are few who believe that those responsible for the attacks should go unpunished. But mention the United Nations or an international court of human rights and their eyeballs start rolling. They want something done "now." They talk as though "now" is its own point in time—not connected to other atrocities America committed years ago or the consequences that will endure ahead. The South Africans waited years for their truth and reconciliation committee; a million Rwandans died in the 1994 genocide yet it was a full year before the trials of the suspects began. America holds fire for twenty-six days before lashing out at Afghanistan and is praised for its patience. If this is restraint, define rash; if this is justice, then define revenge.

In the meantime every bomb they drop turns what was an unpopular, dangerous outsider into a hero among a significant and growing minority of the Muslim world. With the west's help Bin Laden has managed to present himself as the largest immovable object against American cultural, political and economic hegemony. This is disastrous for all of us. Not only are Bush and Blair not defeating terrorism, they are creating a generation of terrorists for the future. With enemies like these, Bin Laden does not need friends.

Shades of Grey

March 28, 2003

Under Swedish law, anyone who receives a state pension and lives abroad has to present themselves to the embassy every year to prove that they are still alive. In December last year, just after the U.N. Security Council had passed a unanimous resolution ordering Iraq to disarm, Hans Blix, the chief U.N. weapons inspector, turned up at the Swedish consulate in New York.

"What are you doing here?" the consul general asked the man who was fast becoming one of the most famous faces in the world. "Well, I'm retired, so I have to get my paper to prove that I'm still alive," said Blix, apparently oblivious to the fact that he was by now the owner of one of the most famous names on the planet.

The very idea that Blix, the man the world had charged with the responsibility of adjudicating between war and peace, felt the need to confirm his earthly existence tells us a great deal about the characteristics that have guided him in recent times.

Formal, self-deprecating, proper and precise, Blix has spent the last few months buffeted by the transatlantic diplomatic storms and emerged with the few hairs he has left on his head in place. Not for him an emotional response to the horrors of war that he believes, at least for now, could have been avoided. Offer him a range of adjectives to describe his mood at the breakdown of talks—even as he argued that further inspections could still produce results—and he picks only "sadness" and "disappointment," not "anger" and "frustration."

"Sadness because now it was a matter of using force and destruction," he says. "Disappointment because I thought it was too early breaking off the attempts to achieve disarmament. I thought there should have been a little more patience."

But time was one thing the Americans would not give him. "From the end of January, beginning of February the Americans were losing patience," he says. "Even though I was reporting on some improvements and some positive features, I think that they were moving towards the other conclusion."

With the British and Americans insistent that Iraq had weapons of mass destruction, even if they didn't know where they were, Blix felt that there was little he could do to prove otherwise. "The big difference between us and the U.K. and U.S. was that all the intelligence agencies were convinced that there were weapons of mass destruction, whereas I had not seen evidence.

"We would say, 'Iraq should present any anthrax,' while the U.S. and U.K. were inclined to say, 'Iraq should present the anthrax.'"

Such was Blix's dilemma. Every few weeks this mild-mannered, even-tempered Swede would take centre stage as the honest broker in an increasingly ill-tempered and divided debate. A civil servant in a chamber of entrenched partisans. When called to the table, he would emerge, plodding purposefully towards his seat. A small, tubby man with grey hair and a grey suit—a shade of grey in a room full of black and white.

Diplomats, soldiers, Iraqi civilians and national governments hung on his every word seeking to discern some nuance, inflection, emphasis or denial that might presage an uncertain future. Markets fell and rose on his inflection. The Americans and the French would seize on various aspects to justify their positions. And throughout it, Blix maintains, he tried to keep his eyes on the prize. "We saw our job all the time as a technical, independent and impartial work that was taking place in a political minefield," he says. "People would say, 'You were playing into the hands of the hawks,' and I would say, 'We aren't playing at all.'"

And yet, for all his attempts at denial and avoidance, from the outset Blix has often become the issue. The Americans were not keen on his appointment as head of the U.N. monitoring, verification and inspection commission. They expressed doubts about the quality of his work after he concluded, during the eighties, that Iraq was not trying to build a nuclear weapon. But when inspectors went in after the Gulf war, they found an aggressive nuclear weapons programme in place and Saddam only around six months away from acquiring a bomb.

"It's correct to say that the International Atomic Energy Agency was fooled by the Iraqis," he says. Leading hawk and deputy U.S. defence secretary Paul Wolfowitz even got the CIA to investigate him—a fact that makes Blix laugh. "That wasn't serious. Everything they wanted to know they could have got from the State Department."

Only a few weeks ago the Americans accused him of hiding information that would have been helpful to their case regarding drones and cluster bombs. Here Blix comes the closest he probably gets to being angry. "This was advanced as an argument against us as a battle for votes. But I think it was unfair, unjustified sniping."

If his trip to the Swedish embassy tells us something about his character, then his favourite phrase when navigating these byzantine negotiations is informative about his philosophy. "The noble art of losing face," he says, "will one day save the human race."

Yet despite the fact that there was little nobility displayed in the negotiations and that large numbers of the human race are perishing through military action despite his efforts, he does not regret picking up the phone to Kofi Annan four years ago while on an Antarctic cruise with his wife and coming out of retirement to take on the job. "I was taken out of the refrigerator, literally," he said recently. "I have my career behind me."

The life ahead of him appears somewhat solitary. He lives in New York; his wife is in Sweden. At seventy-four, he confesses to living the life of a "monk." His only indulgences are Bordeaux and Oriental carpets; his main hobbies, preparing Scandinavian fish dishes and making his own marmalade. This is a man who spends his leisure time reading political biographies and U.N. documents.

His office, on the thirty-first floor of the United Nations, with a striking view of the Chrysler Building, is decorated with aerial pictures of Baghdad. "A lot of these buildings have probably been bombed now," says his press spokesman, dashing his pen across vast swathes of the city, pointing out the government ministries.

Blix believes there was nothing he could have said that would have convinced the Americans not to go to war at this time. "They would have wanted a clear-cut guarantee that [the Iraqis] did not have weapons of mass destruction," he says. "I could not have given them a guarantee that if they had waited a few months more there would have been results."

Could anyone have given them a guarantee?

"Not at this stage. Now we'll see if occupation does it. If we had come out and said on the basis of what we had and said, 'We can solve this in three months,' they would have said, 'You're not credible.' "

So what was the point of it all, then? Of all the shuttling backwards and forwards, the weighing of words and the delivering of reports when so soon after his first report war seemed inevitable?

Blix's response is a masterpiece of the diplomatic understatement for which over a few short months he became a byword: "While we were disappointed that it didn't continue and that it came to war, I think we have shown that it was feasible to build up a professional and effective and independent inspection regime . . . it's just too bad it didn't work."

The Limits of Generosity

April 7, 2003

"The aristocracy of birth and the aristocracy of religion have been destroyed," announced a member of the revolutionary French parliament in 1794. "But the aristocracy of the skin still remains. That too is now at its last gasp and equality has been consecrated."

And so, to rousing applause, three new representatives—one black, one mulatto, and one white—were welcomed from the Caribbean island of San Domingo, now made up of Haiti and the Dominican Republic. The man who had overthrown that aristocracy of skin in Haiti was Toussaint L'Ouverture, the leader of the most successful slave rebellion in history. The French revolution had already established the notion of liberté, egalité, fraternité; Toussaint's uprising would test just how universal the rights of man really were, and just how enlightened its European sponsors would be.

With revolutionary France as an ally, he led his nation against British and Spanish invasion. But what has been consecrated can also be desecrated. When France went from revolution to reaction under Napoleon Bonaparte, it also went from being an ally of San Domingo's black-led government to being an enemy. Toussaint was captured and shipped to France on Bonaparte's orders.

For some, even then, Toussaint was a cause célèbre. "There is not a breathing of the common wind that will forget thee," wrote William Wordsworth of the imprisoned leader. "Thou has great

allies; thy friends are exultation, agonies and love and man's uncon-
querable mind."

Two months later, on April 7, 1803, Toussaint died in a French
prison. It was not just a man Bonaparte was trying to kill or even a nation he was eager to conquer. It was the very notion of liberation itself
he was trying to crush.

"The freedom of the negroes, if recognised in St. Domingue and
legalised by France," he told one of his ministers, "would at all times
be a rallying point for freedom-seekers of the New World."

Two hundred years to the day after Toussaint's death, as U.S.
troops wonder why the Iraqis they have bombed in southern cities are
not rushing out to embrace them, his legacy feels more relevant than
ever. He fought slavery so that he could enjoy freedom, not so that he
could swap a domestic slave master for a colonial one. He welcomed
foreign solidarity, but understood that only the people of San
Domingo could be the architects of their own liberation.

As U.S. troops encircle Baghdad for the final swoop, you get the
impression that, in the eyes of U.S. president George Bush and British
prime minister Tony Blair, freedom is not a banner to which oppressed people flock, but rather a state that must at times be inflicted
on the reluctant. To them the Iraqi people cannot be trusted to be subjects in their own emancipation and so must resign themselves to be
objects in the "liberation" the carpet bombers have in store.

The most generous explanation they have advanced for why we
have yet to see any dancing in the streets of Basra is that so long as
war is in play, Saddam may be alive, and the Ba'ath party exists, ambivalence offers the best promise of survival pending an uncertain
outcome.

"They cannot be sure in their own minds yet that we mean what we
say," Blair said. "In their own minds, they have to be very circumspect
until they're sure the regime's gone."

This is generous only because it endows the Iraqi people at least
with memory and cognitive faculties rarely assigned to brown-skinned
people under occupation. The Shia remember rising against Saddam
in 1991, with U.S. encouragement, only to be abandoned and massacred by the regime.

Extend that generosity back a few more years, however, and Iraqis
will also remember that those who seek to disarm Saddam today

armed him yesterday—that those who come to liberate them today enslaved them yesterday, suppressing international criticism as Saddam gassed and tortured. Extend their memories beyond Iraq's borders and they may also remember Jenin or the massacres at Sabra and Shatila and wonder how the countries who bankroll oppression in Palestine can bring freedom to Iraq.

But the limits to this generosity are imposed by the west's own poor memory. Led by the United States of Amnesia, the past is an inconvenience. Instead, we live in the ever-evolving present and its ever-changing enemy.

More consistent and more repugnant is the missionary position, which is best articulated by the home secretary, David Blunkett. Like a nineteenth-century crusader, Blunkett genuinely believes that while Iraqis don't know what's best for them right now, they will understand, after they have been conquered, colonised and thoroughly humiliated, that all of this murder and destruction is in their best interests.

"We know that for the moment we will be seen as the villains," he said. But he promises that views would change "once this is over and there is a free Iraq, with a democratic state, building the affluence that can come from an educated people with enterprise and capability."

At that stage, he said, "the population as a whole will say that we want a free country, we want a state to live in where we can use our talent to the full."

The trouble is, if Iraq is to be truly free, there will be no place for Americans or British troops to occupy it. There is no doubt that Iraqis want rid of Saddam. But it does not follow that they want to be ruled by an American viceroy. That is a choice imposed on them by Bush and Blair in defiance of international will. But it is not, nor has it ever been, the only option. Having been "liberated" from a domestic tyrant, the Iraqis will then have to liberate themselves from a foreign one.

The notion that the British or Americans will withdraw as soon as democracy is restored defies all understanding of history and is betrayed by the very actions and methods of the soldiers on the ground.

"It's a similar situation to Northern Ireland," said platoon sergeant Barry Little, who spent five and a half years there. "It's a terrorist threat more than an enemy threat."

The parallel is as instructive as it is disconcerting. For once Saddam's regime is definitively crushed, ordinary Iraqis may well pour out onto the streets just as there were accounts of Catholics greeting British troops when they arrived in Northern Ireland in 1969. But the antagonism that underpinned the British presence in the province soon reasserted itself. The result was a war that spanned more than twenty-five years and claimed hundreds of lives, underpinned by economic inequality, social injustice and the loss of civil liberties throughout the U.K.

Toussaint's life taught us that liberation cannot be imposed from above, let alone be imported from outside, and that the rights of man are universal or they are meaningless, and they are irrepressible once they are understood.

"In overthrowing me, you have cut down in San Domingo only the trunk of the tree of liberty," he told his French captors as he was led away. "It will spring up again by the roots, for they are numerous and deep."

The United States, Race and War

August 11, 2003

As America's most eloquent minister for war, Tony Blair has often taken it upon himself to placate criticism of United States military aggression abroad by pointing to its social achievements at home. And there can be few greater American accomplishments, in his mind, than race.

Quite how he came to this ill-informed conclusion, and why he would choose to share it, is not entirely clear. He rarely mentions race domestically—the last time there were riots in the north, he didn't even venture up there to see what had sparked them. So when he raises it about America, it exposes both his weakness on the subject in Britain and his ignorance of its dynamic in America.

In the Labour Party conference speech in 2001 where he made the case for the bombing of Afghanistan, he hailed a meritocracy that could produce a black secretary of state. "I think of a black man, born in poverty, who became chief of their armed forces and is now secretary of state, Colin Powell, and I wonder frankly whether such a thing could have happened here," he said.

Leave aside for the moment that Powell was not born into poverty; the truth is that as prime minister Blair could appoint a black person to the post of foreign secretary any time he wants. The fact that it took him five years to put Paul Boateng in a far lowlier position in his own cabinet is down to nobody but himself.

A few weeks ago, addressing Congress to justify the war on Iraq, he was at it again. "Tell the world why you are proud of America," he implored. "Tell them when the 'Star-Spangled Banner' starts Americans get to their feet, not because some state official told them to but because, whatever race, colour, class or creed they are, being American means being free."

He might have asked himself how far his policies on asylum seekers, ID cards and immigration (not to mention the reckless language and bigoted logic of his home secretary, David Blunkett) have put back the day when black, Asian and Muslim Britons might feel similarly comfortable with their own national identity.

But what is most staggering about his use of race in his tributes to Uncle Sam is not that the accomplishments he supports in America are the very ones he is so busy stifling at home. It is that the very cause in which he raises them—war—has the least backing among those whose experience he uses to marvel at America's greatness: black people.

It is not difficult to see why. If America's achievements in race relations are exemplary then someone forgot to tell African Americans—that section of the population most likely to be unemployed, poor, without health care, imprisoned, executed and arrested. And if war is the best way to remedy these ills, nobody told them that either.

Even at the height of the popularity of the war against Iraq in April, a Pew Research Center poll found only 44 per cent of African Americans supported it, the lowest level of any group surveyed. Overall, 66 per cent of Americans favoured military action, with support at 77 per cent among whites and 67 per cent among Hispanics.

Black Americans obviously shared the shock and loss of September 11. But most did not share the righteous indignation because the notion that they could be the victims of a mindless act of deadly violence in their own country was not entirely new. "Living in a state of terror was new to many white people in America," said writer Maya Angelou. "But black people have been living in a state of terror in this country for more than 400 years."

Indeed, the very man who claims to be fighting the war to make the world safe for democracy—President George Bush—came to power because black Americans in Florida were systematically denied the right to vote.

Such hypocrisy may be news to Blair. But it is no revelation for

African Americans. It is not just this war that irks them. They have
been more sceptical than whites about every war during the past century because it has long been a staple truth of American foreign policy
that the United States would claim to be fighting for rights abroad that
it refused to extend to black people and others at home.

Nor is it news to the American government. After the Second
World War, tackling domestic racism was as much a foreign policy
decision as anything else. A civil rights committee, appointed by
President Harry Truman, reached the following conclusion: "We cannot escape the fact that our civil rights record has been an issue in world
politics . . . They have tried to prove our democracy an empty fraud and
our nation a consistent oppressor of underprivileged people."

It would be almost another twenty years before black Americans
would be assured of the right to vote. Tied to a country by geography
and nationality, yet denied full allegiance to it by politics and history,
African Americans have developed a habit of looking askance when
their leaders reach for their guns in the name of the greater good.

But while they were the least likely to support these wars, since Korea they have been the most likely to end up fighting them. In fact, the
American military is more reliant on the poor, and therefore non-
whites, than ever before—pushed by poverty and pulled by the promise of learning a trade. In 1973, 23 per cent of the military was from
racial minorities; in 2000 it was 37 per cent. The demographic group
most overrepresented in the military is the same one that polls show
have least enthusiasm for the conflict—black women.

But if black Americans' resistance to U.S. foreign policy is understandable, it is not uncomplicated or unqualified. If their opposition to
the war has been greater than white Americans, their support for it has
also been greater than the predominantly white populations of Europe. Two of the principal people responsible for the prosecution of
the war—Powell and Condoleezza Rice—are black.

Herein lie the contradictions in what the late black intellectual
W.E.B. DuBois referred to as black America's "double consciousness."
Bar the native Americans and a handful of Pilgrims, they are the most
longstanding racial group in the country. There are few who can lay a
greater claim to being American than African Americans. Yet there are
few who can point to as much systematic prejudice at the hands of
America.

"It is a peculiar sensation, this double consciousness," wrote DuBois. "One ever feels his twoness—an American, a Negro; two warring souls, two thoughts, two unreconciled strivings; two warring ideals in one dark body, whose dogged strength alone keeps it from being torn asunder."

It is a nuance that Blair clearly does not see and, given his backward racial policies in Britain, would not understand even if he did. For when they stand for the "Star-Spangled Banner," they salute what they believe to be the nation's promise, not what they know to be its practice. And they are the least likely to believe that declaring war on foreign nations is the best way to fulfil that promise, because they have first-hand experience of how selective the ideals can be of those who fight them.

Don't Mention the Dead

November 7, 2003

When the silver casket lid went down on Artimus Brassfield a reflexive, convulsive sob echoed through Ebenezer Ministries. In the seconds it took for the coffin to be draped with the American flag, Pastor Seon Thompson reminded the congregation that this was a celebration of his life. By the time the drummer had given them the beat for "He's Gone to Be a Soldier in the Army of the Lord," they had found their voice.

Brassfield, twenty-two, also went to be a soldier in the Fourth Infantry Division of the American army. By all accounts, throughout his short life there were only two things he really wanted to do—play basketball and join the army. And so the tank driver from Flint, Michigan, was playing basketball at a military base in Samiri, Iraq, on October 24 when a mortar struck and killed both him and twenty-six-year-old José Mora instantly.

Brassfield was so determined to enlist that he took the entrance test three times. But while he enjoyed serving in the forces, his letters home suggest he had mixed feelings about serving in Iraq. His concerns were personal, not political. The weather was too hot and he was homesick. He asked his mother not to send him chocolate as it would only melt, and he looked forward to buying a truck with Michigan plates and eventually opening his own barber's shop.

"I'm pretty blessed to be in Saddam's home town, Tikrit," he wrote in an e-mail to his father. "It's very nice here other than the fact that we're in Iraq and there ain't no escaping it." In a letter to his mother, he tells her: "Be thankful to the Lord that we are American because I don't see how these people live like this."

Brassfield was buried with full honours, the purple heart and bronze star presented to his wife, Andrea. In the distance, the bugle played. It was not clear whether it was just a man puffing his cheeks or really playing. Since last month the military has been using "ceremonial buglers" at some military funerals—a tape that can be inserted into the bugle and sounds like the real thing. "We've got 1,800 veterans dying each day, and only 500 buglers," said Lieutenant Colonel Cynthia Colin, a defence department spokeswoman. "We needed to do something to fill the void."

The mother of Donald Wheeler, who was killed eleven days earlier by a rocket-propelled grenade, sent her condolences to the Brassfields. "I hope you never wonder whether or not your son's death was in vain," she wrote. "He died for my freedom and your freedom too. What a hero!"

The Brassfields have no doubt that Artimus was a hero. His father, Cary, who served in the military himself, says he is proud that his son served his country, but he is not sure his heroism was put to good use: "Evidently the war is over and yet we still have people dying every day. He was a sitting duck. Who is going to be the next person? I don't want to say my patriotism is diminishing. But I'm losing confidence in the purpose of us being there."

Artimus's aunt, Karmen Williams, believes President Bush should withdraw the troops now. "He needs to say enough is enough, just bring our boys home."

For years political orthodoxy had it that America would no longer know days like these. Not because it was shy about going to war, but because after Vietnam it was determined not to incur large numbers of casualties in doing so. The U.S. military would bomb from a great height or use proxies to enforce its will. Public opinion would endorse the country's involvement in most military conflicts, so long as the nation did not have to endure the sight of its young men and women coming home in body bags. As Henry Shelton, the chairman of the joint chiefs of staff, said in 1999, a decision to use military force is based in part on whether it will pass "the Dover test"—public reaction to bodies arriving at the country's only military mortuary in Dover, Delaware.

Dr. Joseph Dawson, a military historian at Texas A&M university, says the American public's response to casualties is qualified by what they believe the soldiers are fighting for. "If the cause seems significant enough then Americans will bear the loss," he says, pointing to the huge death tolls in the Second World War and the Civil War. "But if the cause no longer appears to be significant they will not. It's still rather too early to read public opinion about this cause."

But now almost every day there is a funeral like Artimus's somewhere in the country. With victory already declared, two-thirds believe the number of casualties are unacceptable and more than half believe that the U.S. will get bogged down in Iraq, according to a *Washington Post* poll earlier this week.

The shooting down of the Chinook helicopter on Sunday ended the deadliest week in the war and intensified pressure on the president to address the issue of casualties directly. "We're now encountering deaths at rates we haven't seen since Vietnam," says David Gergen, who worked in the Nixon, Ford, Reagan and Clinton administrations. "And I think it's important for the country to hear from the president at times like these and for the families to know. I think the weight is on the side of clear expression," he told the *New York Times*.

At the opening of the upgraded Dover mortuary last week, Senator Joseph R. Biden said: "The idea that this facility is opening at a time when body bags are coming home is not a glad time. Thank God [the centre] is here, but I wish we didn't need to build it. Everyone thought this was going to be like Gulf War I, that Johnny and Jack would be home by Christmas."

On December 21, 1989, President George Bush senior was holding a press conference about the U.S. intervention in Panama as the first American fatalities from the conflict were arriving at Dover.

With General Manuel Noriega still at large and half of America believing the military intervention could not be regarded a success while he remained so, it was a politically sensitive time. At the beginning of the briefing the president had told reporters he was suffering from neck pain. At the end he did a duck walk to illustrate his stiffness. That's when "the goof-a-meter went off the charts," as one correspondent put it.

Unbeknown to the White House, three major news networks had moved to a split screen. While the president shared his light-hearted moment with the press corps on one half, America's dead were arriving in caskets on the other. It was a public relations disaster. White House spokesman Marlin Fitzwater described the coverage as "outrageous and unfair" and vowed to express his "extreme dissatisfaction" to the channels concerned.

Less than a year later the White House decreed a ban on traditional military ceremonies and media coverage marking the return of the bodies of U.S. soldiers to Dover. It was an abrupt shift in policy for what had become a national wartime ritual. Along with yellow ribbons and flag waving, the scenes from Dover were part of the American war experience.

For the next twelve years the ban was largely ignored, even after it was extended to all military bases during the last days of the Clinton administration. But this March, shortly before the war began, the Pentagon handed down a directive that made it perfectly clear it expected the policy to be heeded.

Bush writes to each family, but his friends say he was offended by what he regarded as Clinton's occasionally gushing public performances, which he felt turned private grief into political gain. The trouble for Bush is that the public liked Clinton for his ability to empathise. Bush's apparent reluctance to publicly identify with the dead is beginning to look like a desire to disassociate himself from the failure of the mission. When news of the downed Chinook came through on Sunday he stayed in his ranch and let Defence Secretary Donald Rumsfeld meet the press.

"The public wants the commander-in-chief to have proper perspective and keep his eye on the big picture and the ball," says Dan Bartlett, the White House communications director. "At the same time, they want their president to understand the hardship and sacrifice many Americans are enduring at a time of war. And we believe he is striking that balance."

Others disagree. They say the growing number of casualties is the ball, which is precisely why the Pentagon enforced the ban on coverage at Dover. "You can call it news control or information control or flat-out propaganda," says Christopher Simpson, a communications professor at Washington's American University. "Whatever you call it, this is the most extensive effort at spinning a war that the department of defence has ever undertaken in this country. Casualties are a very important media football in any war [and] this is a qualitative change."

Either way, implementing the ruling has had an effect. For the first time since war in the television era, the sight of flag-covered caskets arriving to the salute of military colleagues and the tears of mourning relatives are no longer part of the national narrative. Bush has not attended the funeral of a single soldier slain in the war and refers to the casualties only in general terms. Without Dover, there can be no Dover test.

The bald numbers of the death toll dominate political debate and public disquiet. But the human impact behind those statistics has been scattered to communities throughout the country. The bodies travel from a global conflict to local crises without apparently touching the national consciousness. Even on a regional level the deaths receive scant attention. Detroit is only sixty miles from Flint, but Artimus's death made neither of the city's two papers.

"This is the fifth soldier in Flint to have died," says Ken Palmer, a reporter for the *Flint Journal*, "and the third since the president declared the war was over. The first couple had a real impact. But now I think people are becoming numb."

Yesterday, Cary Brassfield woke up to the news that two more soldiers had died in Iraq and the administration promise that its campaign in Iraq will be unrelenting. "The ones that are speaking do not have the same stakes that we have," says Artimus's father. "They have their political careers. But our homes are being torn apart."

Get Mad—and Get Even

November 17, 2003

The U.S. president, George Bush, looks pretty baffled at the best of times. But after an hour-long meeting with "moderates" in Bali during his whistle-stop tour of Asia last month, he cut a particularly confused figure. For reasons he could not quite grasp, his self-professed vision of America as a benign superpower spreading democracy through the Middle East was received with polite scepticism, even among those nations and leaders he considered allies. "Do they really believe that we think all Muslims are terrorists?" he asked. "I've been saying all along that not every policy issue needs to be dealt with by force."

The difference between how Bush and his administration perceive the world and almost everybody else experiences it would be comic if the consequences were not so tragic. It is not the product of a misunderstanding but carefully crafted, wilful ignorance. Once, when asked how he gets his information, Bush said: "The best way to get the news is from objective sources. And the most objective sources I have are people on my staff."

Nonetheless, the fact that both he and his staff have finally realised that the difference between their perception and reality actually does exist is a small breakthrough. "On a trip like this he can get a glimpse of it, but only a glimpse," said one senior official who attended several of the meetings in Asia. "Of course, when you are moving at warp speed, there isn't a lot of time to think about what you are hearing."

Given that Bush's state visit to Britain, which starts tomorrow, will be conducted at a more leisurely pace, we can only hope that the huge demonstrations that greet him will give him more than a glimpse of where this "perception gap" might have come from.

Travel, if you let it, can broaden the mind. So from the time Bush lands, it is important that he is aware that while the British prime minister may be his ally in the war against Iraq, the British people are not and, barring a short spell at the outset of the fighting, never have been. That is why the upcoming demonstrations around Bush's visit are not only necessary but demand our full support. The threat of them alone has shifted the focus of the visit from the two leaders' proposed declaration of a quick exit from Iraq to the question of why they ever entered in the first place.

Meanwhile, America's preparation for them shows just how much they value our special relationship and what kind of democracy they like to export on their travels. Among other things, U.S. armed special agents have asked for diplomatic immunity in case they kill a protester; to patrol the skies with Black Hawk helicopters; and include a tank, equipped with a gun that can kill a dozen people in one go, in their presidential cavalcade. While these requests have been turned down much of central London will still be closed down to create a "sterile zone" so that Bush's belief that he has the support of the British people will not be contaminated. If ever there was an example of a guest taking liberties, this is it.

But if Bush's visit provides the motivation for the demonstrations it would be a mistake if it also monopolised their message. For to be effective the protests should not mark a reflexive response to the arrival of an unpopular foreign dignitary, but reflect an expression of the popular will that has been forced on to the streets because our own parliament's inability to adequately represent us.

If the leader who is coming is a problem, the leader who invited him is no less so. As the man who led the charge to war, Bush is a worthy target of our ire. As the man who followed him and in so doing lent the war what little legitimacy it ever had, Blair is even more so.

We did not elect Bush (it is a moot point whether anybody did) and can do little about him but hope that the Democrats get it together to beat him next year. We did elect Blair, and if these demonstrations are going to be about anything more than ire, then it is our responsibility to get rid of him.

For if the demonstrations show our strength in numbers they also reveal a weakness in application. We have shown that we can get mad; we have yet to show that we can get even. This is a global problem, not a local one. The vast majority of humanity did not want this war to happen, and it happened anyway. Even in those countries that are prosecuting it, including America, opinion polls showed that most were opposed to military action without U.N. approval.

If that were not bad enough, we now know that in order to gain even minority support they had to lie about weapons that do not exist, using intelligence that could not be trusted. So we have a war we did not want, led by people we can no longer believe. And yet it remains to be seen whether anyone will be held accountable or forced to pay an electoral price. So, while the problem may manifest itself on a global scale, the solution is essentially local. Leaders like Blair, who use their association with Bush to strut the world stage with hubris, must be shown the meaning of humility at home. Having found a way to demonstrate our frustration, we must now find a way to make it count.

In fact, it is a challenge more pertinent to Britain than anywhere else. For unlike Bush, Silvio Berlusconi, Jose Maria Aznar or John Howard, Blair—ostensibly—comes from the left. So, unlike the anti-war demonstrators in the United States, Italy, Spain or Australia, most of those who oppose the war also supported the man who is prosecuting it. And unless they come up with an alternative, they may well end up doing so again.

It is in this one crucial respect that America remains a far more hopeful place than Britain. For there is little confusion in the American anti-war movement about whom the enemy is and what needs to be done about him. Their protests are having real consequences in the Democratic race for the presidential nomination, where anti-war candidates are making all the running and have lifted the level of debate to a far higher level than we are currently seeing in the Labour Party.

This is what makes the charges that the demonstrations are anti-American as ridiculous as they are predictable. Americans are not the problem: Bush is. The majority of Americans disapprove of his handling of the war. As the bodybags and the bill for occupation mount, so the opposition keeps rising. If anyone is bucking the tide of U.S. public opinion it is Blair and Bush, not the protesters.

Meanwhile, Bush comes to the same country that turned out in droves to welcome Bill Clinton when he walked through the centre of London with a smile and a wave and not a combat vehicle in sight. Bush is not synonymous with America any more than Blair is synonymous with Britain. We can make Bush uncomfortable; it is only Blair we can make unemployed.

Blame the White Trash

May 17, 2004

Two young women have achieved iconic status in U.S. President George Bush's battle between good and evil currently touring Iraq. And if the administration's propaganda machine is to be believed, one of them is good and the other one is evil.

One the side of good there is Jessica Lynch. When we first met her, in April last year, she was the plucky soldier who had been captured after a "valiant gunfight," slapped around and then rescued on camera in a "midnight ballet" by a daring posse.

Representing evil is Lynndie England. When we first met her she was smoking a cigarette and giving a thumbs up while pointing at the genitals of a naked, hooded Iraqi prisoner. She appears to be laughing; he appears to be masturbating.

Lynch was lauded as a national hero; England has been lambasted as a national disgrace. While no one has yet to describe England as the anti-Christ they have come close. In the words of one of her neighbours, she is the "anti-Jessica."

Lynch and England are real people—both young working-class women from West Virginia, one of the poorest states in the union. But in the hands of the Pentagon spinmeisters they are also constructs, rooted in gender and class. Lynch, we now know, never fired a shot and was well cared for while held captive. Of the Pentagon's spin machine she complained: "They used me as a way to symbolise all this stuff . . . I'm not about to take credit for something I didn't do."

Precisely the same is happening of England and, to a lesser extent, the other soldiers who have been court-martialled as a result of the atrocities at Abu Ghraib. They are being used to symbolise not all that is wrong with the war but the only thing that is wrong with it. While all the evidence, including new allegations that the defence secretary, Donald Rumsfeld, authorised physical coercion and sexual humiliation in Iraqi prisons, points to the American political establishment's active encouragement of the abuse, the White House keeps pointing at England and her six colleagues to bear the moral burden for their immoral war.

England's brutality is explained away not as the logical continuum of the occupation but as a contradiction to it. Increasingly, Bush's best hope is to take out the "trailer trash." They have cast not only the actions as disgraceful but the people accused of carrying them out as dispensable—collateral damage in the propaganda war at home, where the poor don't vote or contribute to any campaigns.

When Bush went on Arab television two weeks ago, he said the behaviour "does not represent the America that I know." But then, thanks to his connections, he has never had to serve in the army during a war. And England and her friends were never going to pledge for the Skull and Bones, the elite fraternity to which both Bush and Democratic challenger, John Kerry, belonged at Yale. They are neither wealthy nor well connected—he doesn't need to know them, although the irony is that if they did vote they would probably vote for him.

So long as the buck stops with England and her colleagues, the whole episode can be reduced to soccer hooligans in uniform—the white working class (one African American is accused, although he is featured rarely and appears in no photographs) running amok. Like arresting the Watergate burglars and leaving Nixon in the White House, convicting only them would suggest the abuse can be understood as the sporadic acts of a few offensive individuals. The higher up it goes, the clearer it becomes that they were in fact the systemic actions of an occupying institution.

There is no need to fetishise class in all of this. Their class on its own does not carry any moral value, guilt or innocence. But it is relevant to their agency in a top-down military command structure. In the words of one of their attorneys: "Do you really think a group of kids from rural Virginia decided to do this on their own?"

Like Lynch, England and her fellow abusers must, of course, take responsibility what they did and did not do. The beatings, humiliations and possibly murders carried out were vile, depraved and sadistic. Their claim that they were only following orders finds its chilling echoes in postwar Nuremberg. Similarly, England's defence that she was made to pose for the pictures is only relevant in so far as it implies more senior people were involved. If and when a fair trial determines the extent of their involvement—given the pictures, it is difficult for them to claim they were not involved—they should be given the severest of punishments.

Who they are is no defence for what they did. Indeed, who they are enabled what they did. It is one of the hallmarks of colonialism that the poorest, least powerful citizen of an occupying nation can wield enormous power in an occupied territory. A former chicken-plant worker like England can humiliate virtually any Iraqi she wants precisely and only because she is an American in Iraq. Once she returns to America she reverts to the bottom of the pile.

But they have choices, however limited. It was the former car mechanic from rural Pennsylvania, Joseph Darby, who blew the whistle after senior brass had tried to hush the whole thing up by slipping a disc under an investigator's door.

However, who they are does explain what is now being done to them. Their poverty has made them easier to dismiss. After viewing more pictures and tapes of their actions, Republican senator Ben Campbell said: "I don't know how these people got into our army."

To find out he need go no further than Sabrina Harman, one of the soldiers under investigation. "I knew nothing at all about the military except the fact that they would pay for college," she told the *Washington Post*. For the most part they joined to get paid, not because they believed in the war on terror. Indeed the most overrepresented demographic group in the military—African American women—is the same group least likely to support the war in Iraq.

In the case of England and Harman, their gender has also made them easier to demonise. Last week, rightwing firebrand Ann Coulter told one radio station: "This is yet another lesson in why women shouldn't be in the military . . . Women are more vicious than men."

Others claim that their involvement in sexual abuse is deviant. "Somehow, I could more readily understand women committing physical torture against prisoners of war," writes Jill Porter for the *Philadelphia News* last week. "But this kind of sexual oppression? It seems to me like a kind of treason. I look at the smirking women in the photos and wonder: how could they?"

It is a good question. Where did these people get the idea that the Arabs need not be treated humanely, that international law does not apply to them and that humiliation and intimidation are the best way to get what they want? This may not represent the America Bush knows. Sadly, it is the one with which the rest of us are becoming all too familiar.

Never Mind the Truth

May 31, 2004

Seeing the U.S. national security adviser, Condoleezza Rice, testify before the 9/11 Commission on CNN in April was a challenge in eye-ear coordination. While she eloquently spelled out the Bush administration's strategy for the war on terror, the tickertape of rolling news spewed out grim news from the front across the bottom of the screen. Your ears took in the official narrative: "We are in control and shaping a positive future for the Middle East." Your eyes traced the brutal reality: "This is a bloody mess and innocents are dying."

At the very moment when Rice said that the invasion had removed a source "of violence and fear and instability in the world's most dangerous region," the tape read: "Iraq's interim interior minister Nuril Al-Badran announces his resignation; interior ministry is in charge of police forces."

At the point when she told the commission that invading Iraq was one of "the only choices that can ensure the safety of our nation for decades to come," the wire services reported: "Iraqis say air strike killed dozens gathered for prayers."

Politics has, to an extent, always been about the triumph of symbols over substance and assertion over actuality. But in the case of Iraq this trend seems to have reached its apogee, as though statements by themselves can fashion reality by the force of their own will and judgment. Declaration and proclamation have become everything. The question of whether they bear any relation to the world we actually live in seems like an unpleasant and occasionally embarrassing intrusion. The motto of the day both in Downing Street and the White House seems to be: "To say it is so is to make it so." These people are rewriting history before the ink on the first draft is even dry.

The most obvious example was President George Bush's speech to the nation last week, as he struggled to define the mission in Iraq. "On June 30 the occupation will end and Iraqis will govern their own affairs," he said. To understand what will happen at the end of the month it would make more sense to turn the sentence inside out so that it says the opposite: "On June 30 the occupation will continue and Iraqis will not govern their own affairs."

To the charge that this is leftwing axe-grinding, look no further than the lead editorial in the *Economist*, which supported the war. "To those who complain that in this case the sovereignty of the Iraqi government is going to be pretty bogus, the answer of Messrs Bush and Blair ought to be the honest one. Of course it is. In Iraq's present context, sovereignty is just a word on paper, and not even the most important one."

Only yesterday the Iraqi governing council members complained of "massive pressure" to endorse Adnan Pachachi, America's choice for president of the interim government, even though most of them favoured another candidate, more critical of the United States. The U.S., which has the final say in the matter, threatened not to recognise the council's choice. Given that the U.S. chose the members of the council, one can only imagine how they will get on with a truly independent, democratically accountable group of representatives.

Sadly, we are not about to find out. What will in fact happen on June 30 is that a former CIA operative, Iyad Allawi, who was picked by the U.S. with little involvement from the United Nations, will head a puppet regime. This "sovereign" country will have 138,000 U.S. troops on its soil, not to mention soldiers from Britain and elsewhere, and its "sovereign" leader will have no control over what they do. "U.S. forces remain under U.S. command and will do what is necessary to protect themselves," says Colin Powell.

Tony Blair for once disagreed. "If there is a political decision as to whether you go into a place like Fallujah in a particular way, that has to be done with the consent of the Iraqi government and the final political control remains with the Iraqi government," he said. But by the next day he was back in his box. "We are both absolutely agreed that there should be full sovereignty transferred to the Iraqi people, and the multinational force should remain under American command," he told the Commons.

In so doing he revealed two of the golden rules in this new era of politics by pronouncement. First, so long as you say things boldly and confidently, they do not have to make any sense. Second, whatever announcement you make last negates all announcements you've made before.

Indeed, Blair, of whom Doris Lessing, the novelist, once said: "He believes in magic. That if you say a thing, it is true," is the high priest of this dark art. Here are a few corkers he pulled out of the hat in the past two years.

"There is no doubt at all that the development of weapons of mass destruction by Saddam Hussein poses a severe threat, not just to the region but to the wider world," he said in April 2002. Just four months before he bombed Iraq he said: "Nobody in the British government is in favour of military action against Iraq." And then there is my favourite, from this April. "We have been involving the U.N. throughout," by which we can only presume he means bugging the offices of the secretary general.

The least kind, and yet most obvious, explanation for why these statements have no resemblance to the truth would be that Blair keeps lying. A more generous interpretation would be that he is a hopelessly wishful thinker.

In fact, wishful thinking has been the entire intellectual and political thrust of the "liberal hawks"—the lefties who backed the war. They wished that the U.N. would pass a second resolution, that Saddam had weapons of mass destruction, that the Iraqi people would come out and greet western soldiers, that the Bush administration had noble intentions and that Blair could exert influence over the U.S. in the Middle East. Some of us wished that they would get real.

For one of the most pernicious baseless assertions in recent times is the notion that there is any such thing as a "liberal hawk." There isn't. People are not liberal just because they say so. For the term to have any meaning at all they have to share some common ground on which the bombing of Iraq has no place. There was no progressive case for bypassing the will of the U.N. and international law and bombing a country that posed no immediate threat to any other. There was a liberal dilemma about how you confront vicious dictators. But in the case of Iraq it no more led to war than the liberal dilemma over how to solve crime leads to capital punishment.

Having seen their wish-list shredded by the neoconservatives in the Pentagon and the White House, some now wring their hands and wonder where it all went wrong, while others become ever more bullish and bizarre in defence of a stance long since discredited.

Liberals never provided a case for this war. There was "liberal" cover for it. A fact for which conservatives are delighted and those co-opted by them should be ashamed.

A Fantasy of Freedom

January 24, 2005

There is one tiny corner of Cuba that will forever America be. It is a place where innocent people are held without charge for years, beyond international law, human decency and the mythical glow of Lady Liberty's torch. It is a place where torture is common, beating is ritual and humiliation is routine. They call it Guantanamo Bay.

Last week, the new United States secretary of state, Condoleezza Rice, listed Cuba, among others, as "an outpost of tyranny." A few days later President Bush started his second term with a pledge to unleash "the force of freedom" on the entire world. "The best hope for peace in our world is the expansion of freedom in all the world," he said.

You would think that if the Americans are truly interested in expanding freedom and ending tyranny in Cuba, let alone the rest of the world, Guantanamo Bay would be as good a place to start as any. But the captives in Guantanamo should not ask for the keys to their leg irons any time soon. Ms. Rice was not referring to the outpost of tyranny that her boss created in Cuba, but the rest of the Caribbean island, which lives in a stable mixture of the imperfect and the impressive.

In short, while the United States could liberate a place where there are flagrant human rights abuses and over which they have total control, it would rather topple a sovereign state, which poses no threat, through diplomatic and economic—and possibly military—warfare that is already causing chaos and hardship.

Welcome to Bush's foreign policy strategy for the second term. His aim is not to realign the values at Guantanamo so that they are more in line with those championed by the rest of the world. It is to try and realign the rest of the world so that it is more in keeping with the values that govern Guantanamo, where human rights and legal norms are subordinated to America's perceived interests.

Under this philosophy, the Bush administration understands the words "tyranny" and "freedom" in much the same way as it understands international law. They mean whatever the White House wants them to mean. Bush is happy to support democracy when democracy supports America, just as he is happy to dispense with it when it does not. Likewise, when tyranny is inconvenient, he will excoriate it; when it is expedient, he will excuse it.

Take Uzbekistan, one of the most repressive regimes in Central Asia. In April 2002, a special U.N. rapporteur concluded that torture in the country was "systematic" and "pervasive and persistent . . . throughout the investigation process." In the same year, Muzafar Avazov, an opposition leader, was boiled alive for refusing to abandon his religious convictions and attempting to practise religious rites in prison. In 2003, Bush granted a waiver to Uzbekistan when its failure to improve its human rights record should have led to its aid being slashed. In February 2004 the U.S. secretary of defence, Donald Rumsfeld, visited the country's dictator, Islam Karimov, and said: "The relationship (between our countries) is strong and growing stronger. We look forward to strengthening our political and economic relations."

Yet the U.S. continues to shower the country with aid, docking a mere $18 million last year (around 20 per cent of the total) after expressing its "disappointment" that Mr. Karimov had not made greater strides towards democracy. Pan down the shopping list of tyrannical states in Ms. Rice's in-tray (Iran, Burma, North Korea, Zimbabwe, Belarus and Cuba) and you will find no mention of Uzbekistan. Why?

Because Uzbekistan, with an estimated ten thousand political prisoners, hosts a U.S. military base that offers easy access to Afghanistan and the rest of the region.

So for every tenet that Mr. Bush claimed last week to hold dear, it was possible to pick out a country or place he is bankrolling or controlling that is in flagrant violation, and where he could improve

conditions immediately if he wished. The point here is not that the
U.S. should intervene in more places, but that it should intervene consistently and honestly or not at all.

Bush's inauguration speech was packed with truisms, axioms, plati-
tudes and principles that appear reasonable at first glance. The trouble
is they are contradicted by the reality he has created and continues to
support.

As he delivered his address, you could almost whisper the caveats.

"America will not pretend that jailed dissidents prefer their chains
(apart from in Abu Ghraib and Guantanamo Bay), or that women welcome humiliation and servitude (apart from in Saudi Arabia) or that
any human being aspires to live at the mercy of bullies (apart from
Uzbekistan and Israel)."

Such hypocrisy is not new. When Mr. Bush said "Our goal instead
is to help others find their own voice, attain their own freedom and
make their own way," nobody imagined he was referring to the Boli-
vian peasants fighting oil price hikes and globalisation or the landless
Venezuelans taking over farms.

The agenda for a second Bush term represents not a change in direction but an acceleration of the colossal and murderous folly that he,
and most of his predecessors, have pursued.

The damage that this selective notion of liberty inflicts on the rest
of the world should by now be pretty clear. According to the independent website Iraqbodycount.net, reported civilian deaths in Iraq have
already reached between 15,365 and 17,582 since the war started,
while the recent study for the Lancet estimated the death toll at
100,000 at least, and probably higher; meanwhile, the number is growing remorselessly. Next weekend's elections in Iraq—which take place
in the midst of a war against foreign occupiers, with most candidates
too scared to campaign, the location of polling sites kept secret until
the last minute and key areas unable to participate—have become not
an example of democracy but an embarrassment to the very idea of
democracy.

Meanwhile, a global poll for the BBC last week showed the U.S.
more isolated than ever, with people in eighteen out of twenty-one
countries saying that they expect a second Bush term to have a negative impact on peace and security.

What is less clear is whether most Americans understand that this isolation leaves them more vulnerable to attack. Ms. Rice last week promised "a conversation, not a monologue" with the rest of the world. But as the situation in Iraq shows, conversations that start with "D'you want a piece of this?" rarely end well for anybody.

Both Osama bin Laden and the Taliban have shown that the tyrants the U.S. supports today can easily turn against it tomorrow while fostering resentment among their victims. Yet the idea that the U.S. is a civilising force endowed with benevolent intentions is still as prevalent within the U.S. as it is rejected outside it.

Indeed, Tony Blair seems to be the only foreign leader who still holds to the mixture of wishful thinking, wilful ignorance and warped logic behind the idea that Bush is leading humanitarian interventions at the barrel of a gun.

When questioned about the prospects for Bush's second term, the British prime minister was upbeat. "Evolution comes with experience," he said. The fact that Bush does not believe in evolution has long been known. Only now are we discovering how little Blair learns from experience.

No Home Fit for Heroes

April 2, 2005

Like Martin Luther King, Herold Noel had a dream that was "deeply rooted in the American dream." It did not involve anything as lofty as racial harmony or the brotherhood of man. Herold was after something far more basic. "I wanted to have a white house with a picket fence, without drugs and all that," he says. "That was my dream. I grew up in the ghetto, and in the ghetto you will see a ten-year-old smoking weed. That's what I was raised around, and I wanted a better life for me and my kids. I didn't want to be like Puffy and pour $1,000 bottles of Cristal on the floor. I just wanted to throw a barbecue in my own backyard."

So Herold joined the army. "The army offered me a better life," he says. It was his passport out of the ghetto. He signed up in September 2000, "to check it out." "I didn't really expect to be in a war before I joined, but when Bush came to office, I knew there would be one."

Sure enough, in January 2003, Herold went to the Middle East and eventually to Iraq, where he worked as a fuel handler. He didn't think much of the politics involved in his mission. "I let the politicians handle that." To the extent that he did think about it, his views did not go beyond basic revenge for the terrorist attacks of September 11. "My views were, we're fighting for our country, because they're bombing our country. We're going to go and fuck these guys up, because they fucked up our country. I was fighting for our freedom."

But in August 2003, Herold returned to the United States to find the personal dream he had been struggling for more elusive than ever. Herold had gone abroad to fight for his country and came back to find he was homeless. First he went to shelters, but he had his war medals stolen and felt harassed. By the middle of January, the twenty-five-year-old father of four found a place to sleep not behind a white picket fence but in the back of his red 1994 Jeep Cherokee. He had sent three of his children to live with their grandmother in Florida. Meanwhile, his wife and toddler son were poised to join him in the car. The sister-in-law with whom they had been staying was about to move to a smaller apartment. "Now I'm fighting a different kind of war, but it's still a war for survival," Herold says.

Two years into the war in Iraq, and a growing number of isolated cases, such as Herold's, of U.S. veterans from the war on terror returning home to a life of virtual destitution have emerged. So far, the numbers are small. A couple of dozen unemployed veterans enrolling in a job-training programme at a New England shelter for homeless veterans; three men seeking help in Ohio; a handful showing up in a survey in Minnesota; thirty looking for assistance at the Black Veterans for Social Justice Center in Brooklyn.

According to the National Coalition for Homeless Veterans, the total is sixty-seven nationwide. That figure amounts to a small fraction of the one hundred thirty thousand who have already served and come home. And yet those who work with homeless veterans already see this as a terrible sign. "We fear that we are going to see this big wave," says Linda Boone, director of the National Coalition for Homeless Veterans. "It's too early for that yet, but it could happen. People have these yellow ribbons saying Support the Troops. They support them when they're in the war, but it's when they take off the uniform that things get bad."

Nicole Goodwin, twenty-four, found herself shuttling her one-year-old daughter Shylah between New York's homeless shelters last year after she returned from Iraq. "I thought my story was one in a million," she says. "But it's not. There are around forty in New York alone; we're pushing for a congressional hearing."

The director of Special Projects Veterans Affairs at Ohio Valley Goodwill says the worst is yet to come. "It hasn't been dramatic up to this point, because it's just beginning. We haven't learned a damned thing since Vietnam."

"A true war story is never moral," wrote Tim O'Brien in *The Things They Carried*, his book about Vietnam. "If at the end of a war story you feel uplifted, or if you feel that some small bit of rectitude has been salvaged from the larger waste, then you have been made the victim of a very old and terrible lie . . . You can tell a true war story by the way it never seems to end. Not then, not ever."

Herold describes his experience in Iraq as "a living hell" that shows little sign of ending. "We saw dead bodies everywhere. People walked over dead bodies like they weren't there. Women and children played with AK-47s. When you see a crowd in Iraq, you know that something bad's going to happen when the sun goes down."

More than once, something bad nearly did happen to Herold. One time, he was filling a fuel tank when he came under fire. The tank fell on its side. It would have taken one good shot to pierce the tank and blow him up. "I couldn't see anything. One of the other soldiers broke my window and got me out of there. I thought I wasn't going to see my kids or nothing. I went through all that. I got religious over there. I thought somebody's got to be looking out for me."

Now Herold finds riding the subway difficult because he can't be around a lot of people. "I was a happy-go-lucky person. Now I'm angry and agitated. I get angry quick. I have bad dreams. I started hearing kids crying. I hear a lot of screaming, like there's a riot going on."

Vietnam hangs heavy on the American psyche. It is the moral weight against which any military adventure is measured: a flexible fable used as often by those who support war as by those who oppose it. Military veterans make up 9 per cent of the overall population and 23 per cent of the homeless. Most of those are from the Vietnam era, but on average they did not become homeless until they had been back home from Vietnam for between nine and twelve years. That was how long it often took for the mental health problems to take their toll in the loss of family, job and home. It is also why providers of services believe the early trickle of homeless veterans from the Iraq war could presage something far more dramatic.

The legacy of Vietnam shapes the public response to troops and veterans. Conscious that conscripted soldiers paid the price for a political mistake thirty-five years ago, Americans hold the troops sacrosanct— and this regardless of their politics. The nation is split over the war in

Iraq, but the metallic yellow ribbons saying Support the Troops give no indication of whether a person is for or against the war.

When Herold and Nicole's stories became public last year, the response was breathtaking. *New York Times* readers offered Nicole rooms in their homes, baby supplies and pledges of more than $17,000. A woman in California sent a cheque for $10, to be used for "a better life"; an anonymous donor sent a cheque for $1,000, with a note that said, "You risked your life in Iraq for your country . . . for all of us." Nicole was also offered a $12-an-hour job by a community housing company, which she took so that she could rent a one-room apartment in Harlem from the Coalition for the Homeless.

When Herold explained his situation on the radio, a caller offered him a job—he declined, saying that campaigning for veterans' housing is his job. A couple of weeks later, a benefactor paid his rent for a year for an apartment big enough to reunite his family.

So long as the homeless veterans are few, such kindness from strangers is possible. But a recent study published by the New England Journal of Medicine found that 15 to 17 per cent of veterans from Iraq meet "the screening criteria for major depression, generalised anxiety or PTSD." Of those, just 23 to 40 per cent are looking for help. Add mental illness to poor education and poverty, and many returning vets find themselves, like most of America's working poor, just one routine mishap away from destitution—medical bills for an unexpected illness, an inescapable repair to a house or harsh weather blocking your way to work.

In Herold's case, he was living in Georgia waiting to re-enlist in the army when his car engine blew up. Living in a place where you needed a car to get around, Herold had a tough choice: "It cost $2,500 to mend it, and I didn't have no $2,500. So it was either pay rent or get the car fixed. I had to pay the rent, but then we both lost our jobs because we didn't have a car. That's how come I came to New York with no job and no home."

Like Herold, Nicole has been diagnosed with post-traumatic stress disorder. Like Herold, she has yet to receive any state benefits. Nicole, who went to the same high school as former secretary of state Colin Powell, became homeless last year after she fell out with her mother. Given the living conditions, it was not surprising. She

came back from Iraq to a two-bedroom flat in the projects that served
as home to her mother, her two sisters, a four-year-old nephew,
Nicole and her daughter, Shylah. It took a week for the situation to
deteriorate to the point where she and her mother could not share the
same roof. "It wasn't any one thing," she says. "Just the same old same
old."

After a spell in shelters, she now has a place in Harlem. When I arrived, Nicole apologised for the mess. A smart young woman with
plans to go to university and study political science and journalism,
Nicole's outlook on life is generally upbeat. "They throw you a lot of
lemons and you have to make lemonade," she says. But since her return, she's had trouble sleeping and is struggling to cope. Sometimes
she feels numb. Walking down the street with Shylah recently, she almost got hit by a car. "I felt nothing," she says. "The only thought in
my head was that people die every day. In Iraq, there were so many situations that you couldn't help that I just got used to feeling that way.
The worst thing wasn't the war, it was coming back, because nobody
understood why I was the way I was."

The government body that is supposed to deal with these issues is
the Department of Veterans Affairs. But the VA is hopelessly over-
stretched, capable of helping just one hundred thousand of the five
hundred thousand homeless veterans each year. And they can hope for
little improvement. Recently the Bush administration offered generous benefits to those who died in battle, including an increase from
$12,420 to $100,000 to the families of fallen soldiers, plus an extra
$150,000 in life insurance. But for the living there were cuts in the
number of nursing care beds and plans to charge wealthier veterans
with non–service related problems an annual fee and double their pre-
scription payments.

"Congress has gone too far in expanding military retiree benefits,"
David Chu, a defence undersecretary, told the *Wall Street Journal* in
February. He went on to say the growth in veterans' benefits was
"starting to crowd out two things: first, our ability to reward the person who is bearing the burden right now in Iraq or Afghanistan . . .
[second] we are undercutting our ability to finance the new gear that is
going to make that military person successful, five, 10, 15 years from
now." It's an analysis that conflicts with the way Americans like to
think about themselves.

America's Promise is a standard history textbook, used by many of the nation's high-school students, which tells the story of the country from the ice age to the present day. At the end of 690 pages detailing, among other things, the genocide of the Native Americans, slavery, segregation, Vietnam, Watergate, the final paragraph reads: "The history of the United States is one of challenges faced, problems resolved and crises overcome. Throughout their history Americans have remained an optimistic people, carrying this optimism into the new century. The full promise of America has yet to be realized. This is the real promise of America; the ability to dream of a better world to come."

It is difficult to overstress just how deeply ingrained this belief is. The U.S. is the only country in the world where (apart from a few years in the mid-1970s) people consistently believe that the next year will be better than the current one. To many U.S. citizens, America is synonymous with "freedom," "democracy" and "opportunity." These are the ideals that many believe the nation is exporting to the Middle East in the present war; they are also the ideals that many believe they are defending at home.

Nicole and Herold were no different. As they talk about why they went to war and what they think of it now, they will waver between nationalistic pride and disappointment. Pride in what they believe America should be; disappointment in what it has actually been for them. Both volunteered for the army for their own particular reasons, but they were, in essence, conscripted by poverty. "I did it to get away from all the negativity in my life," says Nicole. "I didn't think I was going to get involved in a war. I didn't have a sense of direction and I thought the army would give me that."

Nicole is part of a trend that has seen a huge increase in minority women serving in the U.S. army in noncombat roles. Black women, who make up only 16 per cent of the civilian population, now outnumber white women in the army. "A survey of the American military's endlessly compiled and analysed demographics paints a picture of a fighting force that is anything but a cross-section of America," wrote the *New York Times* last year. "With minorities over-represented and the wealthy and the underclass essentially absent."

Both Herold and Nicole say they could not dwell on the rights or wrongs of this particular war. They were soldiers and this was their job. But events over the past few years have forced them to rethink.

"There's not a day goes by that I don't ask myself what was I fighting for," says Nicole. "There were no WMD. We were lied to, and it hurts me to think I went there for somebody's lie."

Herold thinks the war was primarily about money. "I thought I was fighting for a better world," he says. "I thought I was fighting so my kids and maybe their kids could go to Iraq on vacation if they wanted to. But if you're fighting this war for your own personal gain, that's another thing. If you're fighting for world peace, then I agree with it. It looks like we're fighting for somebody else's pocket. So that Halliburton can get rich."

Yet neither the meagre opportunities that forced them to join the army nor the dire conditions of their return can undermine their investment in the very American dream that progress and individual success are, if not inevitable, then universally possible. "I saw Jay-Z [the rap star] going to these beautiful places, and I believe that if Jay-Z could come out of the ghetto, then I could come out of the ghetto," says Herold.

Nicole goes further. "The ideals of this country are that anybody could come back to America and make a better life for yourself. It's a land of opportunity. In this country alone, if you put forth the effort, you can bear fruit."

Squaring these mantras with their material conditions, however, is becoming increasingly difficult. They are caught between a need to believe in America's Promise and the realisation that in some way it has failed to deliver. Abandoned by institutional indifference, but rescued by individual generosity, they remain intensely patriotic, though their understanding of what that means has shifted subtly. "I was fighting for freedom for the Iraqi people," says Herold, "but I never had that decent life myself."

"I think it's ironic that I could go and fight for freedom abroad and cannot find this kind of freedom in my own city," says Nicole. "What America thinks of as freedom and what I think of as freedom are two different things. I want to get a house, day care and go to school. My freedoms are small. But I can't give up," she adds. "That's what I learned when I was getting shot at—if millions of Iraqis couldn't stop me, my own country's not going to stop me."

Blair's Blowback

July 11, 2005

Shortly after September 11, 2001, when the slightest mention of a link between United States foreign policy and the terrorist attacks brought accusations of heartless heresy, the then–U.S. national security adviser Condoleezza Rice got to work. Between public displays of grief and solemnity she managed to round up the senior staff of the National Security Council and ask them to think seriously about "how do you capitalize on these opportunities" to fundamentally change American doctrine and the shape of the world. In an interview with the *New Yorker* six months later, she said the U.S. no longer had a problem defining its post–cold war role. "I think September 11 was one of those great earthquakes that clarify and sharpen. Events are in much sharper relief."

For those interested in keeping the earth intact in its present shape so that we might one day live on it peacefully, the bombings of July 7 provide no such "opportunities." They do not "clarify" or "sharpen" but muddy and bloody already murky waters. As the identities of the missing emerge, we move from a statistical body count to the tragedy of human loss—brothers, mothers, lovers and daughters cruelly blown away as they headed to work.

The space to mourn these losses must be respected. The demand that we abandon rational thought, contextual analysis and critical appraisal of why this happened and what we can do to limit the chances that it will happen again, should not. To explain is not to excuse; to criticise is not to capitulate.

We know what took place. A group of people, with no regard for law, order or our way of life, came to our city and trashed it. With scant regard for human life or political consequences, employing violence as their sole instrument of persuasion, they slaughtered innocent people indiscriminately. They left us feeling unified in our pain and resolute in our convictions, effectively creating a community where one previously did not exist. With the killers probably still at large, there is no civil liberty so vital that some would not surrender it in pursuit of them and no punishment too harsh that some might not sanction it if we found them.

The trouble is there is nothing in the last paragraph that could not just as easily be said from Falluja as it could from London. The two should not be equated—with over a thousand people killed or injured, half its housing wrecked and almost every school and mosque damaged or flattened, what Falluja went through at the hands of the U.S. military, with British support, was more deadly. But they can and should be compared. We do not have a monopoly on pain, suffering, rage or resilience. Our blood is no redder, our backbones are no stiffer, nor our tear ducts more productive than the people in Iraq and Afghanistan. Those whose imagination could not stretch to empathise with the misery we have caused in the Gulf now have something closer to home to identify with. "Collateral damage" always has a human face: its relatives grieve; its communities have memory and demand action.

These basic humanistic precepts are the principal casualties of fundamentalism, whether it is wedded to Muhammad or the market. They were clearly absent from the minds of those who bombed London last week. They are no less absent from the minds of those who have pursued the war on terror for the past four years.

Tony Blair is not responsible for the more than fifty dead and seven hundred injured on Thursday. In all likelihood, "jihadists" are. But he is partly responsible for the one hundred thousand people who have been killed in Iraq. And even at this early stage there is a far clearer logic linking these two events than there ever was tying Saddam Hussein to either 9/11 or weapons of mass destruction.

It is no mystery why those who have backed the war in Iraq would

refute this connection. With each and every setback, from the lack of
U.N. endorsement right through to the continuing strength of the insurgency, they go ever deeper into denial. Their sophistry has now
mutated into a form of political autism—their ability to engage with
the world around them has been severely impaired by their adherence
to a flawed and fatal project. To say that terrorists would have targeted
us even if we hadn't gone into Iraq is a bit like a smoker justifying their
habit by saying, "I could get run over crossing the street tomorrow."
True, but the certain health risks of cigarettes are more akin to playing
chicken on a four-lane highway. They have the effect of bringing that
fatal, fateful day much closer than it might otherwise be.

Similarly, invading Iraq clearly made us a target. Did Downing
Street really think it could declare a war on terror and that terror
would not fight back? That, in itself, is not a reason to withdraw
troops if having them there is the right thing to do. But since it isn't
and never was, it provides a compelling reason to change course before more people are killed here or there. So the prime minister got it
partly right on Saturday when he said: "I think this type of terrorism
has very deep roots. As well as dealing with the consequences of this—
trying to protect ourselves as much as any civil society can—you have
to try to pull it up by its roots."

What he would not acknowledge is that his alliance with President
George Bush has been sowing the seeds and fertilising the soil in the
Gulf for yet more to grow. The invasion and occupation of Iraq—
illegal, immoral and inept—provided the Arab world with one more
legitimate grievance.

Bush laid down the gauntlet: you're either with us or with the
terrorists. A small minority of young Muslims looked at the values displayed in Abu Ghraib, Guantánamo Bay and Camp Bread Basket—
and made their choice. The war helped transform Iraq from a vicious,
secular dictatorship with no links to international terrorism into a
magnet and training ground for those determined to commit terrorist
atrocities. Meanwhile, it diverted our attention and resources from the
very people we should have been fighting—al-Qaida.

Leftwing axe-grinding? As early as February 2003 the joint intelligence committee reported that al-Qaida and associated groups
continued to represent "by far the greatest terrorist threat to western
interests, and that that threat would be heightened by military action

against Iraq." At the World Economic Forum last year, Gareth Evans, the former Australian foreign minister and head of the International Crisis Group think tank, said: "The net result of the war on terror is more war and more terror. Look at Iraq: the least plausible reason for going to war—terrorism—has been its most harrowing consequence."

None of that justifies what the bombers did. But it does help explain how we got where we are and what we need to do to move to a safer place. If Blair didn't know the invasion would make us more vulnerable, he is negligent; if he did, then he should take responsibility for his part in this. That does not mean we deserved what was coming. It means we deserve a lot better.

Part II

RACE

Black Bloke

October 6, 1996
The Washington Post

Before I came to America from England three months ago, I asked an American journalist in London what kind of reactions to expect. "Well, when they hear an English accent Americans usually add about twenty points to your IQ. But when they see a black face they usually don't," he said. "You'll be an anomaly."

Recalling that the authors of the book *The Bell Curve* had claimed that black people have an IQ fifteen points lower than whites, I was heartened to think that even in the eyes of the most hardened racist I would still come out at least five points ahead.

After three months here I am left wondering whether "anomaly" quite covers the mixture of bemusement, amazement and curiosity I have encountered since I arrived. Often people just think I am showing off. This is especially the case with African Americans. All I have to do is open my mouth and they prime themselves to ask, "Who are you trying to impress with that accent?" They don't actually say anything. Their thoughts are revealed in the downward trajectory of the eyebrows and the curl of the lip.

Once I say I'm English, the eyebrows go back up and the lips uncurl. Now they are in shock. At times I have had to literally give the people I have met here a couple of minutes to compose themselves. "I had no idea," said a white woman near Baton Rouge, Louisiana, in a tone my grandmother might use if I came out as a cross-dresser.

Then there was the woman in the bank who called her colleagues over to hear my accent. "Listen to this, listen to this," she said. "Go, say something," she demanded, as though I was a circus marmoset.

Most people here who have not traveled much abroad seem astounded to learn that black people exist outside of America and Africa at all. Their image of England is what they see on television (*Fawlty Towers* and *Upstairs Downstairs*) and what they read in the papers (Lady Di and Mad Cow Disease). Whether that is the image that England wants to sell or the one that America wants to buy is not quite clear—my guess is that it's a mixture of both—but either way it doesn't leave much room for black people.

Once I have told someone I am English they are generally prepared to take me at my word, which is more than can be said about people I meet back home. A typical conversation goes something like this:

"Where are you from?"

"London."

"Well where were you born?"

"London."

"Well, before then?"

"There was no before then!"

"Well, where are your parents from?"

"Barbados."

"Oh, so you're from Barbados."

"No, I'm from London."

Although there have been blacks in Britain for centuries, they only came there in sizable numbers after the Second World War. During the 1950s and 1960s they came from Africa and the Caribbean—alongside those from the Indian subcontinent—to do the sorts of jobs that the indigenous white population wasn't eager to do.

My parents came to England from Barbados in the early sixties and I was born there. Like many immigrants they only planned to stay for a few years, work hard, earn some money and then return home. But like many immigrants they ended up staying, starting a family and building a life there. Blacks now make up about 3 per cent of the British population. Britain's sense of national identity is still trying to catch up. But in the meantime questions like "Where are you from?" are often interpreted to mean, "Please tell me you are not from here."

Which is why meeting so many Americans with names like Gugliotta, Biskupic and Shapiro is so refreshing. Almost everybody here is originally from somewhere else. Even the white people. And most people lay claim to another identity—Italian American, Irish American, Hungarian American—which qualifies their American identity but does not necessarily undermine it.

The same is true for black Britons. They are two separate words relating to two very distinct and often conflicting identities. If black people in Britain define themselves as British at all—I was seventeen before I would admit it publicly—then they will usually put "black" in front of it to show that they do not see themselves as fully British and are not always accepted as British. At the NAACP's annual convention, which I recently attended in Charlotte, North Carolina, there seemed to be only three higher authorities to which the speakers called upon—God, the Constitution and the American flag.

The NAACP may represent the "old school" of African American politics but throughout my time here I have yet to meet an African American who does not place some faith in these common reference points. Britain, in contrast, doesn't have a written constitution, is far less religious, and you wouldn't get a Union Jack (the British flag) within five miles of a political meeting full of black people, regardless of how moderate the organization may be.

This may change in time. But for now the difference seems stark. Black Americans who feel aggrieved can, and often do, look to the symbolism of their national flag as a form of redress. Black Britons see their flag not as a possible solution but as part of the problem. For Americans, this seems to breed a kind of confidence that allows a more open discussion of race issues than in my country. During my interview for the fellowship at the *Washington Post* that brought me here, I was asked what problems I faced as a black journalist in Britain. An Englishman would never ask that sort of question. It would be considered . . . well, rude.

I was amazed, on a day trip to Harper's Ferry, West Virginia, recently, to see an all-white group of cub scouts learning all about how John Brown fought alongside black abolitionists and the legacy of Frederick Douglass. White kids learning about black history on a day out during the summer holidays. At the time I felt like I had died and gone to heaven. Upon reflection it was much more like purgatory.

I know that one of the reasons that Americans discuss race so much is because there is so much to talk about. Both the present—affirmative action, the demise of the inner cities, poverty, church burnings—and the past—civil rights, slavery, segregation—offer no end of subjects that can and should be debated.

Nevertheless, in England, which has similar but nowhere near as acute social problems affecting the black community, race ranks alongside sex, politics and religion as a topic not to be brought up in polite conversation. At my newspaper in London I was once described to someone as "the short, stocky guy with an earring," even though I am one of only half a dozen black journalists in the building.

Here I look local and sound foreign—an object of intrigue in public places. At home I look foreign and sound local—and everybody tries hard not to notice. To say one is better or worse than the other would be too simplistic. The bottom line is that I will soon return to a racism I understand.

But I will miss those extra twenty IQ points for my accent.

Jesse Jackson: Power, Politics and the Preacher Man

April 17, 1999

To the sound of the sixties soul tune, "Hold On, I'm Coming," the Reverend Jesse Jackson takes the stage. He stands over six foot tall in a brown, pin-striped three-piece suit—the central character in his own production. At his feet is a mostly black audience; on the awning over his head are the words "Know before whom thou standest"; behind him is a portrait of Martin Luther King; ahead are the television cameras. Public adulation, scripture, a civil rights icon and media attention—signs and signifiers framing both the message and the man.

Clutching the lectern, grabbing the air, jabbing his finger and dabbing his brow with a bright white handkerchief, Jackson gives not just a speech but a performance. His confidence is contagious. When he punctuates his delivery with: "Can I have a witness here?" the crowd returns: "You say it." When he calls out: "Talk to me somebody," they reply: "That's right." One woman, standing somewhere between distraction and delirium, closes her eyes and waves her hand heavenwards in appreciation. With each staccato sentence Jackson's voice gets louder, as do the cheers of the crowd. "Release your mind. It's your power. It's your vote." He is on the South Side of Chicago, at the headquarters of the Rainbow/PUSH (People United to Serve Humanity) coalition, the organisation he founded almost thirty years ago and which has met almost every Saturday since then. But were it not for the bitter wind blowing off Lake Michigan this could be a Baptist service in a black church anywhere in the southern states.

Jackson leaves the audience while it is still on its feet, and with a small entourage heads for his office. The route takes him past several pictures of himself—some as a young man with King, some on his own—down some stairs and into pandemonium.

Rainbow/PUSH's offices have the air of a badly-run student union. The decor is tatty and worn. There is a bustle of excitement but little activity and the people hanging around outnumber those who are there to work by about three to one. A hint of the everyday chaos can be found in the messages taped to the walls. "Please respect our need to do our work at our desks," says one. "Do not feel free to use our desks or phones even if we are not present at the moment," says another.

In Jackson's office, the end result of that chaos is unravelling to the tune of a 1970s soul ballad (music seems to follow him almost wherever he goes). It is three days before citywide elections. A press release has gone out saying he will cast his vote over the weekend because he will be out of town on polling day. Jackson says he has other plans for the weekend and plans to vote on Monday away from the cameras. "Who told you this?" he asks Jerry, his press officer. Before Jerry can stammer an answer, Jackson interrupts. "Who told you to do that? Nothing goes on my schedule without checking it with me first. Nothing. This is your job, Jerry . . . It makes us look bad." All the charm and charisma with which he embraced the audience just minutes before has evaporated. Replacing it is an imperious and hectoring tone, as he strides around looking for someone on whom to offload his annoyance. Few people that he passes on the way from the office to his car escape a tongue-lashing.

And then we are off, in a sulk and a black limousine, cruising along Lakeshore Drive on our way to Chicago's CNN studios, where he is about to present his weekly show, *Both Sides*. Only the Detroit Spinners's "Ghetto Child" breaks the silence. Jackson is in the front, with his driver, frantically scribbling on small cards. From the back seat I ask about his views on the Stephen Lawrence case, but before I can finish he raises his hand, without turning his head.

"I'm busy now," he says, and carries on scribbling. A few hours later—after he has grilled a self-avowed racist preacher for the cameras—he will signal the interview is over by simply standing up, putting on his coat and making for the door.

Working with Jackson is not easy. "He has a complete inability to trust anyone who works beneath him," says one former colleague, "and at times that does become a real problem." He also has a foul temper. "He can be hugely insensitive," Richard Hatcher, his former adviser, said in Marshall Frady's biography of Jackson, entitled *Jesse*. "He can say and do things, almost without thinking, that are just terrible." Jackson loves humanity; it is people he has a problem with.

But his capacity for sheer graft is incredible. He calls newspaper editors in the middle of the night, records interviews with radio stations before his colleagues are awake, and usually seeks advice from a self-selected court of academics, activists and commentators around the country before his first meeting of the day.

"He might have twelve different phone conversations before he comes out of his bedroom in the morning," says one former adviser. "At times it can be infuriating because you don't know whether his ideas have been formed by a southern preacher or some left-wing academic." And all the time he bustles he is thinking, says Mark Stietz, his senior policy adviser during his 1988 presidential campaign, juggling several options simultaneously, from which he will eventually pluck a course of action at the last possible moment. "He can engage not just with many ideas but in many courses of action all at the same time and then, once he's made up his mind, he just runs with it and you've just got to catch up." This can be both a strength and a weakness. "I worked with the reverend for many years," says Donna Brazile, a former Jackson staffer. "They were the best years of my life. He was my mentor and my teacher, but I would never do it again. He'll be in a television studio or on a radio show and he'll say we're going to march in Philadelphia or Boston, and we'd know nothing about it. When you work with the reverend you have to be two days ahead of him and two days behind him all at once." As America starts scouring the nation for its next president, Jackson's position is not entirely clear. Vice President Al Gore has declared his intention to stand for the presidency; the minority leader in Congress, Richard Gephardt, has made it clear that he will not. Jackson is reported to have said he will not run, but at times he still sounds like a possible candidate.

"I have not made a decision," he says. "I am reluctant but there are several issues to consider. What are to be the factors for increasing voter registration, regaining the Senate, the Supreme Court justices, the House? Running may be the most effective way to do that. It may not. I don't know." Friends say there are also other more personal reasons for his reticence. He is annoyed by the way he has been mistreated by the Democratic Party machine, which has kept him at arms length even as he delivers them so many votes. The huge number of death threats during his last campaign—around three hundred, according to one account—may also act as a powerful deterrent.

The last time he ran for the presidency, in 1988, he comfortably beat both Gore and Gephardt. But a lot has happened since. In 1992, Clinton publicly sidelined Jackson after calculating that he could woo the black vote without him. After that both Louis Farrakhan, the Nation of Islam leader, and General Colin Powell, the former chief of staff, would emerge as claimants to be the dominant voice in black America.

Meanwhile Jackson was appointed Clinton's special envoy to Africa—sucked into the establishment with a gift from the president that, some believe, has forced him to tone down his opposition to Clinton's centrist drift. Using an extended baseball metaphor, he explains that Clinton has, on balance, been a good thing. "We have to judge politicians by their cumulative score. In one inning they make a great catch, in another they drop the ball. In one they score a home run, in another they strike out. But it is their cumulative batting average that we are interested in. In 1992 he dipped to political expediency but on the whole he's done well." Talk like this has left Jackson open to criticism from the left as well as the right. "I don't think he should stand in 2000," says Kevin Grady, a former aide from South Carolina. "Because I don't know what he'd stand for. Jesse doesn't stand for the poor any more. He's standing for himself." But the problem with his critics is not so much that they have often misjudged Jackson—many of their criticisms are valid—but that they have always underestimated him. During his 1984 primary campaign, pundits thought he had no money because he had no support; the truth, it transpired, was that he had lots of support but his supporters had no money.

Even after he came from nowhere to win 3.5 million primary votes (21 per cent of the total) they still said he was on his way out. His success, wrote George Will, the columnist, was like "a comet hitting the earth's atmosphere, burning brightly but fatally and soon to be a small cinder."

Four years later he doubled the number of votes and netted 12 per cent of white Democrats. When he wasn't selected for the vice presidency his political obituary was warmed up. When Clinton snubbed him in 1992 it was served. But last August, on the night Clinton was at his most vulnerable, having confessed to his wife, his daughter, the Grand Jury and the nation that he had misled them over the Monica Lewinsky affair, it was Jackson he called for—not to rally the troops but to give family counselling to the First Family in the White House.

Jackson went willingly and performed his pastoral duties, although he has told some that even this mission had a political motive. "He said if he does run for president he'll have to criticise the Clinton administration," says one friend. "And he thinks this will show that his attacks won't be personal but political. It's about issues and direction. He hopes he'll be remembered as the man who was most loyal when the president was most embattled." The fact that he was there at all is evidence of his enduring status. Polls show he is still the most popular politician amongst African Americans. History shows that since 1944 the Democratic Party has only once won the presidency—with Lyndon Johnson in 1964—with a majority of the white vote. Logic suggests that Jackson still matters.

Outside America this is well understood. When he travels abroad he is treated to the pomp and ceremony normally reserved for heads of state. His arrival is met with cavalcades and he is whisked off for talks, deals and handshakes for the camera among the U.S.'s enemies and allies. On the home front, however, he is still treated with suspicion. Jackson, his critics are always keen to point out, has never held public office. To be held democratically accountable or to have to consult those around him would feel like an imposition.

He does not just lead a civil rights organisation. He is the organisation. It is an adjunct of both his personality—its spontaneity, energy, passion and political direction are his own—and his family—his son, Jesse Jackson Jr., is both a congressman and his heir apparent in the movement. He takes advice from several quarters—but the decisions are down to him and him alone.

The benefits of this style of leadership are clear—when Jackson moves he moves fast, acts decisively and speaks with authority—but so are the drawbacks. Many, including a large number of African Americans, accuse him of being an opportunist. In much the same way as they used to criticise King, they say he simply flits from one crisis to another, throwing himself at the head of the march and in front of the microphones.

Even his closest allies believe that his greatest mistake since he founded the Rainbow Coalition has been his inability, or unwillingness, to turn it into a functioning, democratic, grassroots movement.

"The difference between the Christian and Rainbow coalitions is that the Christian Coalition actually exists," says one former aide. "He squandered the possibility to build an organisation or structure. He really does believe in fast-break politics. So he just parachutes into a community and sometimes it works and sometimes it doesn't. He's a tree shaker not a jelly-maker." "If he feels accountable to anything," says Robert Borosage, a senior adviser to Jackson in his 1988 campaign, "then he feels accountable to history. In that sense he is a lot like King." But Jackson is part of a political lineage that extends way beyond King. It is what Manning Marable, the African American intellectual, calls the "black messianic style"—a style with roots in the church, which, thanks to its independence from the white power structure, has been the focal point for black political resistance since slavery. "The principal social institution within every black community was the church," writes Marable in his latest book, *Black Leadership*. "As political leaders, the black clergy were usually the primary spokespersons for the entire black community, especially during periods of crisis . . . To some extent this tradition has been characterised by a charismatic or dominating political style." The result has been a culture of organisation in which political belief, like faith, became an absolute; dissent, like heresy, led to sanctions and even expulsion; and leaders have generally been a hybrid of preacher and politician— regarded by their core supporters not only as men of ideas to be engaged with, but as visionaries to be revered. "He used to teach us things not just from the Bible but about the Bible," says Brazile. "He says: 'This is a revolutionary document.'"

It is not only a legacy he has inherited. It was one he was born into. When sixteen-year-old Helen Burns announced that she was pregnant by her next-door neighbour, a married father of three called Noah Robinson, she was banished from the Springfield Baptist church which she had attended her entire life, and was virtually exiled from the local black community in Greenville, South Carolina.

It was 1941 in one of the most religious areas of the country, more than a decade before the U.S. Supreme Court's *Brown v. the Board of Education* decision put an end to official segregation—a bleak time and a bleak place to be black, female and unmarried with a new-born baby.

Helen was exiled for a period of her pregnancy, and it was only when she returned with her infant son and told her church "I have sinned" that she was allowed to return to the flock. But in many eyes she would never be fully rehabilitated. So Jackson was not only born in scandal but raised in poverty—a three-room shack with a tin roof without hot or cold running water.

It was a situation he would often refer to on the campaign trail. "You know, people'd always ask, 'Why is Jesse Jackson running for the White House?' They never seen the house I'm running from." As an only child in a house full of women—he lived with his grandmother, Matilda, and his mother—he grew into a precocious and lively little boy. "He thought a whole lot of himself right off the bat," says Vivian Taylor, a friend of Jackson's late mother. "You know, people saying he was so cute—he completely concurred with that." His mother married Charles Jackson when Jesse was three, although it was not until he was a teenager that he would change his name. Nothing throughout his childhood could stop him yearning for a father figure. Friends recalled how he would stand outside his father's house and watch his stepbrothers playing. "He almost worshipped Robinson," a childhood friend, Owen Perkins, told Frady. "He completely idolised the man." But despite a reconciliation with his father once his fame had been secured, Jesse the child would rarely have his affections returned.

Not only a bright student but a good footballer, Jackson earned a football scholarship and spent a year at the University of Illinois at Urbana-Champaign before dropping out and coming back down South to the historically black college of Greensboro A&T in North Carolina. He was there in the summer of 1960—a landmark year for both the civil rights movement and Greensboro A&T after four young men kicked off a decade of spontaneous student protests by staging an impromptu sit-in at the local Woolworth's luncheonette.

The demonstrations became national news, sparking similar sit-ins in segregated areas throughout the South and acts of solidarity in the

North. But it apparently had little impact on Jackson, who was studying sociology and did not get involved. "Throughout all that time I never saw him," says one of the original sit-in activists who did not wish to be named. "I don't know why but somehow it really wasn't his bag. I wonder whether it was really because it started without him and he knew he couldn't control it." He also had other things on his mind. One afternoon, as he lined up with other football players outside the canteen, he met Jacqueline Lavinia Brown. His first words were, "Hey girl, I'm going to marry you." But Jackie, even then far more outspoken and more left-wing than him, was at first put off by his possessive manner. They married on New Year's Eve, 1962, and within a few years had started a family.

By this time Jackson had found a place for himself at the head of the civil rights struggle in Greensboro, where he was elected student president. A few years later his active interest would take him to Selma, Alabama, where King was leading a march for the right to vote and where Jackson made his presence felt among King's entourage.

And so began a relationship with America's best-known civil rights leader which would provide Jackson with an apprenticeship for his future career. Employed by King's Southern Christian Leadership Conference (SCLC) to run Operation Breadbasket, Jackson impressed his elders within the movement with his enthusiasm and irritated them with his publicity-seeking.

Those close to King would complain at the way he tried to monopolise his mentor, co-opting him as both a father figure and political idol. They would also turn against him with great acrimony when, the day after King's assassination, Jackson appeared on television with a shirt he claimed was smeared in the slain leader's blood. His actions spawned a bitterness that would continue for many years, with both Coretta Scott King, King's widow, and Andrew Young, one of King's senior lieutenants, refusing to support Jackson's first presidential bid.

It was only a matter of time before Jackson would leave the SCLC and set up PUSH, bankrolled by a mixture of government grants, black businesses and the occasional maverick, including Hugh Hefner, the Playboy magnate. From this local base he steadily and self-consciously built a national profile. In 1984 he went to the voters in the primaries as the ultimate outsider. "The first time it was really about shock value," he says. "It showed there was a rebellion out there." His arrival on the national scene prompted several unsuccessful attempts to undermine him with accusations of financial impropriety and sexual infidelity. But it took his reference to New York as "Hymietown"—a term which deeply offended the Jewish community—to leave an indelible stain. Jackson believes his record speaks for itself: "I don't think the Hymietown incident reflects who I am. I have worked hard to build relationships between Jewish people and black people. I don't see that as a defining moment in my career." His success in 1984 made him a significant if unwelcome power-broker in the Democratic machine. He was unelectable but also unavoidable. Four years later, however, he had spread both his message and his political constituency beyond black voters and the left to the trade unions, women's groups and gay rights organisations.

At one stage in 1988, when there was a real prospect that he might be nominated, his campaign team was having trouble rising to the occasion. Press releases were not going out. Rallies were starting late: "We weren't ready for prime time," says Mark Stietz, "and Jesse was getting mad." Jackson called a meeting and slammed his team for their incompetence and buck-passing. "I've had enough of this 'Well, I tried, but he lied, so we died,' excuses," he said. "As soon as we get to 'we died' it doesn't matter if you tried or he lied because we are all dead already." Three days later, on the campaign trail, Jackson and his team were stranded on a runway in rural Iowa, without a phone, waiting for a plane they had forgotten to book. They were two hours late for one meeting and would have to cancel another.

"There we were in the middle of nowhere and Jesse was just standing on his own, so mad he couldn't even see," says Stietz. "It was my job to kind of try and defuse the situation, so I went over and asked him whether he had been saving that 'I tried, he lied, and we died' speech for the right moment, or if he just thought of it right there on the spot." Jackson's stern demeanour melted into a smile, as he turned to Stietz. "When I get the idea, the words they just come." Words come easily to Jackson. He has an ability to reduce political discourse to one powerful, lyrical, narrative that both entertains and inspires. Words to him are like clay to a skilled potter: raw material which he effortlessly and deftly manipulates to mould, shape and define something of aesthetic as well as practical value. "He's the most accomplished politician I have ever briefed," says Borosage. "He can take something he has no idea about, hear the briefing and then translate it into something that's real and that works and connects with ordinary people." Jackson is the master of the metaphor. That working-class whites and working-class blacks share economic interests even though they are divided by race, becomes: "When they close down your factory or foreclose on your farm, and they pull the plug and the lights go out, we all—we awlll—look amazingly similar sitting there in the dark." That white people owe their superior economic, social and political status to racial discrimination and have secured it by creating a system that excludes African Americans becomes: "When the playing field is even and the rules are public it always gets better. But when blacks are kicking up the field and people start making up the rules . . . that's when the problems start." And then come the mantras, the rhymes with reason that he makes his audiences incant: "Keep America strong, make America better, red and yella, brown, black and white, everyone is precious in God's sight; Hope not dope"; and his all-time favourite: "Respect me, protect me, never neglect me. I am somebody." Detractors belittle his political patter as little more than "jive talk"—glib one-liners for unsophisticated supporters. They insist his style is evidence of his own limited grasp of complex issues and, worse still, evidence of both demagoguery and opportunism. "The populist message is praised for its power and passion," wrote Charles Krauthammer, a *Washington Post* columnist. "Well, Mussolini and Peron had passion and a powerful message . . . Passion may be a rare political commodity in America. But it is cheap. And unhinged from fact, it is dangerous." So there he is—Jesse Jackson stripped bare before white America's cognoscenti—black and dangerous. Like Muhammad Ali he has negotiated a relationship with white America which excites and terrifies in equal measure and earned the respect of those African Americans who don't even agree with him; and like Ali he answers all questions about a comeback with the answer that he has never been away.

But Jackson is greater than the sum of his similes. Were he not black, or if racism in America did not exist, there is no saying what he might be doing. But he is and it does. And in the three decades since King's assassination he has remained the central character in the nation's troubled racial narrative. A protagonist who has frequently been accused of having lost the plot, but remains determined never to be written out of the script.

Claudette Colvin: She Would Not Be Moved

December 16, 2000

This much we know. On Thursday, December 1, 1955, Rosa Parks, a forty-two-year-old black seamstress, boarded a bus in Montgomery, Alabama, after a hard day's work, took a seat and headed for home. The bus went three stops before several white passengers got on. The driver, James Blake, turned around and ordered the black passengers to go to the back of the bus, so that the whites could take their places. "Move y'all, I want those two seats," he yelled.

The bus froze. Blake persisted. "Y'all better make it light on yourselves and let me have those seats," he said.

The three black passengers sitting alongside Parks rose reluctantly. Parks stayed put. Blake approached her. "Are you going to stand up?" he asked.

"No," said Parks.

"Well, I'm going to have you arrested," he replied.

"You may do that," said Parks, who is now eighty-seven and lives in Detroit.

It was an exchange later credited with changing the racial landscape of America. Parks's arrest sparked a chain reaction that started the bus boycott that launched the civil rights movement that transformed the apartheid of America's southern states from a local idiosyncrasy to an international scandal. It was her individual courage that triggered the collective display of defiance that turned a previously unknown twenty-six-year-old preacher, Martin Luther King, into a household name. It was a journey not only into history but also mythology. "She was a victim of both the forces of history and the forces of destiny," said King, in a quote now displayed in the civil rights museum in Atlanta. "She had been tracked down by the zeitgeist—the spirit of the times." And, from there, the short distance to sanctity: they called her "Saint Rosa," "an angel walking," "a heaven-sent messenger." "She gave me the feeling that I was the Moses that God had sent to Pharaoh," said Fred Gray, the lawyer who went on to represent her.

But somewhere en route they mislaid the truth. Rosa Parks was neither a victim nor a saint, but a long-standing political activist and feminist. Moreover, she was not the first person to take a stand by keeping her seat and challenging the system. Nine months before Parks's arrest, a fifteen-year-old girl, Claudette Colvin, was thrown off a bus in the same town and in almost identical circumstances. Like Parks, she, too, pleaded not guilty to breaking the law. And, like Parks, the local black establishment started to rally support nationwide for her cause. But, unlike Parks, Colvin never made it into the civil rights hall of fame. Just as her case was beginning to catch the nation's imagination, she became pregnant. To the exclusively male and predominantly middle-class, church-dominated, local black leadership in Montgomery, she was a fallen woman. She fell out of history altogether.

King Hill, Montgomery, is the sepia South. In this small, elevated patch of town, black people sit out on wooden porches and watch an impoverished world go by. Broken-down cars sit outside tumble-down houses. The pace of life is so slow and the mood so mellow that local residents look as if they have been wading through molasses in a half-hearted attempt to catch up with the past fifty years. "Middle-class blacks looked down on King Hill," says Colvin today. "We had unpaved streets and outside toilets. We used to have a lot of juke joints up there, and maybe men would drink too much and get into a fight. It wasn't a bad area, but it had a reputation." It is here, at 658 Dixie Drive, that Colvin, sixty-one, was raised by a great aunt, who was a maid, and great uncle, who was a "yard boy," whom she grew up calling her parents.

Today, she sits in a diner in the Bronx, her pudding-basin haircut framing a soft face with a distant smile. Her voice is soft and high, almost shrill. The urban bustle surrounding her could not seem further away from King Hill. She now works as a nurses' aide at an old people's home in downtown Manhattan. She turns, watches, wipes, feeds and washes the elderly patients and offers them a gentle, consoling word when they become disoriented.

"I make up stories to convince them to stay in bed." Her rhythm is simple and lifestyle frugal. She works the night shift and sleeps "when the sleep falls on her" during the day. She shops with her workmates and watches action movies on video. Until recently, none of her colleagues knew anything of her pioneering role in the civil rights movement. But go to King Hill and mention her name, and the first thing they will tell you is that she was the first. They remember her as a confident, studious, young girl with a streak that was rebellious without being boisterous. "She was a bookworm," says Gloria Hardin, who went to school with Colvin and who still lives in King Hill. "Always studying and using long words."

"She was an A student, quiet, well-mannered, neat, clean, intelligent, pretty, and deeply religious," writes Jo Ann Robinson in her authoritative book, *The Montgomery Bus Boycott and the Women Who Started It*.

Colvin was also very dark-skinned, which put her at the bottom of the social pile within the black community. In the pigmentocracy of the South at the time—and even today—while whites discriminated against blacks on grounds of skin colour, the black community discriminated against each other in terms of skin shade. The lighter you were, it was generally thought, the closer you were to whatever the power structure—and the more likely you were to attract suspicion from those of a darker hue. From "high-yellas" to "coal-coloureds," it is a tension steeped not only in language but in the arts, from Harlem Renaissance novelist Nella Larsen's book *Passing*, to Spike Lee's film *School Daze*. "The light-skinned girls always thought they were better looking," says Colvin. "So did the teachers, too. That meant most of the dark complexion ones didn't like themselves."

Not so Colvin. They had threatened to throw her out of the Booker T. Washington School for wearing her hair in plaits. As well as the predictable teenage fantasy of "marrying a baseball player," she also had strong political convictions. When Ms. Nesbitt, her tenth-grade teacher, asked the class to write down what they wanted to be, she unfolded a piece of paper with Colvin's handwriting on it that said: "President of the United States."

"I wanted to go North and liberate my people," explains Colvin. "They did think I was nutty and crazy."

One incident in particular preoccupied her at the time—the plight of her schoolmate, Jeremiah Reeves. Reeves was a teenage grocery delivery boy who was found having sex with a white woman. The woman alleged rape; Reeves insisted it was consensual. Either way, he had violated the South's deeply ingrained taboo on interracial sex—Alabama only voted to legalise interracial marriage last month (the state held a referendum at the same time as the ballot for the U.S. presidency), and then only by a 60–40 majority. "When I was in the ninth grade, all the police cars came to get Jeremiah," says Colvin. "They put him on death row." Four years later, they executed him.

It was this dark, clever, angry young woman who boarded the Highland Avenue bus on Friday, March 2, 1955, opposite Martin Luther King's church on Dexter Avenue, Montgomery. Colvin took her seat near the emergency door next to one black girl; two others sat across the aisle from her. The law at the time designated seats for black passengers at the back and for whites at the front, but left the middle as a murky no man's land. Black people were allowed to occupy those seats so long as white people didn't need them. If one white person wanted to sit down there, then all the black people on that row were supposed to get up and either stand or move further to the back.

As more white passengers got on, the driver asked black people to give up their seats. The three other girls got up; Colvin stayed put. "If it had been for an old lady, I would have got up, but it wasn't. I was sitting on the last seat that they said you could sit in. I didn't get up, because I didn't feel like I was breaking the law."

To complicate matters, a pregnant black woman, Mrs. Hamilton, got on and sat next to Colvin. The driver caught a glimpse of them through his mirror. "He asked us both to get up. [Mrs. Hamilton] said she was not going to get up and that she had paid her fare and that she didn't feel like standing," recalls Colvin. "So I told him I was not going to get up, either. So he said, 'If you are not going to get up, I will get a policeman.'"

The atmosphere on the bus became very tense. "We just sat there and waited for it all to happen," says Gloria Hardin, who was on the bus, too. "We didn't know what was going to happen, but we knew something would happen."

Almost fifty years on, Colvin still talks about the incident with a mixture of shock and indignation—as though she still cannot believe that this could have happened to her. She says she expected some abuse from the driver, but nothing more. "I thought he would stop and shout and then drive on. That's what they usually did."

But while the driver went to get a policeman, it was the white students who started to make noise. "You got to get up," they shouted. "She ain't got to do nothing but stay black and die," retorted a black passenger.

The policeman arrived, displaying two of the characteristics for which white Southern men had become renowned: gentility and racism. He could not bring himself to chide Mrs. Hamilton in her condition, but he could not allow her to stay where she was and flout the law as he understood it, either. So he turned on the black men sitting behind her. "If any of you are not gentlemen enough to give a lady a seat, you should be put in jail yourself," he said.

A sanitation worker, Mr. Harris, got up, gave her his seat and got off the bus. That left Colvin. "Aren't you going to get up?" asked the policeman.

"No," said Colvin.

He asked again.

"No, sir," she said.

"Oh God," wailed one black woman at the back. One white woman defended Colvin to the police; another said that, if she got away with this, "they will take over."

"I will take you off," said the policeman, then he kicked her. Two more kicks soon followed.

For all her bravado, Colvin was shocked by the extremity of what happened next, in full sight of the public. "It took on the form of harassment. I was very hurt, because I didn't know that white people would act like that and I . . . I was crying," she says. The policeman grabbed her and took her to a patrolman's car in which his colleagues were waiting. "What's going on with these niggers?" asked one. Another cracked a joke about her bra size.

"I was really afraid, because you just didn't know what white people might do at that time," says Colvin. In August that year, a fourteen-year-old boy called Emmet Till had said, "Bye, baby," to a woman at a store in the neighbouring state, Mississippi, and was fished out of the nearby Tallahatchie river a few days later, dead with a bullet in his skull, his eye gouged out and one side of his forehead crushed. "I didn't know if they were crazy, if they were going to take me to a Klan meeting. I started protecting my crotch. I was afraid they might rape me."

They took her to City Hall, where she was charged with misconduct, resisting arrest and violating the city segregation laws. The full enormity of what she had done was only just beginning to dawn on her. "I went bi-polar. I knew what was happening, but I just kept trying to shut it out."

She concentrated her mind on things she had been learning at school. "I recited Edgar Allan Poe, 'Annabel Lee,' the characters in *Midsummer Night's Dream*, the Lord's Prayer and the twenty-third Psalm." Anything to detach herself from the horror of reality. Her pastor was called and came to pick her up. By the time she got home, her parents already knew. Everybody knew.

"The news travelled fast," wrote Robinson. "In a few hours, every Negro youngster on the streets discussed Colvin's arrest. Telephones rang. Clubs called special meetings and discussed the event with some degree of alarm. Mothers expressed concern about permitting their children on the buses. Men instructed their wives to walk or to share rides in neighbour's autos."

It was going to be a long night on Dixie Drive. "Nobody slept at home because we thought there would be some retaliation," says Colvin. An ad hoc committee headed by the most prominent local black activist, E.D. Nixon, was set up to discuss the possibility of making Colvin's arrest a test case. They sent a delegation to see the commissioner, and after a few meetings they appeared to have reached an understanding that the harassment would stop and that Colvin would be allowed to clear her name.

When the trial was held, Colvin pleaded innocent but was found guilty and released on indefinite probation in her parents' care. "She had remained calm all during the days of her waiting period and during the trial," wrote Robinson. "But when she was found guilty, her agonised sobs penetrated the atmosphere of the courthouse." Nonetheless, the shock waves of her defiance had reverberated throughout Montgomery and beyond. Letters of support came from as far afield as Oregon and California. She still has one—a handwritten note from William Harris in Sacramento. It reads: "The wonderful thing which you have just done makes me feel like a craven coward. How encouraging it would be if more adults had your courage, self-respect and integrity. Respectfully and faithfully yours."

But even as she inspired awe throughout the country, elders within Montgomery's black community began to doubt her suitability as a standard-bearer of the movement. "I told Mrs. Parks, as I had told other leaders in Montgomery, that I thought the Claudette Colvin arrest was a good test case to end segregation on the buses," says Fred Gray, Parks's lawyer. "However, the black leadership in Montgomery at the time thought that we should wait."

Some in Montgomery, particularly in King Hill, think the decision was informed by snobbery. "It was partly because of her colour and because she was from the working poor," says Gwen Patton, who has been involved in civil rights work in Montgomery since the early sixties. "She lived in a little shack. It was a case of 'bourgey' blacks looking down on the working-class blacks."

"They never thought much of us, so there was no way they were going to run with us," says Hardin. Others say it is because she was a foul-mouthed tearaway. "It bothered some that there was an unruly, tomboy quality to Colvin, including a propensity for curse words and immature outbursts," writes Douglas Brinkly, who recently completed a biography of Parks. But people in King Hill do not remember Colvin as that type of girl, and the accusation irritates Colvin to this day. "I never swore when I was young," she says. "Never."

Everyone, including Colvin, agreed that it was news of her pregnancy that ultimately persuaded the local black hierarchy to abandon her as a cause célèbre. For Colvin, the entire episode was traumatic: "Nowadays, you'd call it statutory rape, but back then it was just the kind of thing that happened," she says, describing the conditions under which she conceived. She refused to name the father or have anything to do with him. "When I told my mother I was pregnant, I thought she was going to have a heart attack. If I had told my father who did it, he would have killed him."

A personal tragedy for her was seen as a political liability by the town's civil rights leaders. In his Pulitzer Prize–winning account of the civil rights years, *Parting the Waters*, Taylor Branch wrote: "Even if Montgomery Negroes were willing to rally behind an unwed, pregnant teenager—which they were not—her circumstances would make her an extremely vulnerable standard bearer."

"If the white press got ahold of that information, they would have [had] a field day," said Rosa Parks. "They'd call her a bad girl, and her case wouldn't have a chance."

Montgomery's black establishment leaders decided they would have to wait for the right person. And that person, it transpired, would be Rosa Parks. "Mrs. Parks was a married woman," said E.D. Nixon. "She was morally clean, and she had a fairly good academic training . . . If there was ever a person we would've been able to [use to] break the situation that existed on the Montgomery city line, Rosa L. Parks was the woman to use . . . I probably would've examined a dozen more before I got there if Rosa Parks hadn't come along before I found the right one."

"Facts speak only when the historian calls on them," wrote the historian E.H. Carr in his landmark work, *What Is History?* "It is he who decides which facts to give the floor and in what order or context. It is the historian who has decided for his own reasons that Caesar's crossing of that petty stream, the Rubicon, is a fact of history, whereas the crossing of the Rubicon by millions of other people before or since interests nobody at all."

Montgomery was not home to the first bus boycott any more than Colvin was the first person to challenge segregation. Two years earlier, in Baton Rouge, Louisiana, African Americans launched an effective bus boycott after drivers refused to honour an integrated seating policy, which was settled in an unsatisfactory fudge. And, like the pregnant Mrs. Hamilton, many African Americans refused to tolerate the indignity of the South's racist laws in silence. Nor was Colvin the last to be passed over. In the nine months between her arrest and that of Parks, another young black woman, Mary Louise Smith, suffered a similar fate. Smith was arrested in October 1955, but was also not considered an appropriate candidate for a broader campaign—E.D. Nixon claimed that her father was a drunkard; Smith insists he was teetotal.

But there were two things about Colvin's stand on that March day that made it significant. First, it came less than a year after the U.S. Supreme Court had outlawed the "separate but equal" policy that had provided the legal basis for racial segregation—what had been custom and practice in the South for generations was now against federal law and could be challenged in the courts. Second, she was the first person, in Montgomery at least, to take up the challenge. "She was not the first person to be arrested for violation of the bus seating ordinance," said J. Mills Thornton, an academic and civil rights expert. "But according to [the commissioner], she was the first person ever to enter a plea of not guilty to such a charge."

It is a rare, and poor, civil rights book that covers the Montgomery bus boycott and does not mention Claudette Colvin. But it is also a rare and excellent one that gives her more than a passing, dismissive mention. Either way, historians do not take the trouble to talk to her. Most Americans, even in Montgomery, have never heard of her. She has literally become a footnote in history.

For we like our history neat—an easy-to-follow, self-contained narrative with dates, characters and landmarks with which we can weave together otherwise unrelated events into one apparently seamless length of fabric held together by sequence and consequence. Complexity, nuances and shaded realities are a messy business. So we choose the facts to fit the narrative we want to hear.

While this does not happen by conspiracy, it is often facilitated by collusion. In this respect, the civil rights movement in Montgomery moved fast. Rosa Parks was thrown off the bus on a Thursday; by the Friday, activists were distributing leaflets that highlighted her arrest as one of many, including those of Colvin and Mary Louise Smith: "Another Negro woman has been arrested and thrown in jail because she refused to get up out of her seat on the bus for a white person to sit down," they read. "It is the second time since the Claudette Colvin case that a Negro woman has been arrested for the same thing."

By Monday, the day the boycott began, Colvin had already been airbrushed from the official version of events. Meanwhile, Parks had been transformed from a politically-conscious activist to an upstanding, unfortunate Everywoman. "And since it had to happen, I'm happy it happened to a person like Mrs. Parks," said Martin Luther King from the pulpit of the Holt Street Baptist Church. "For nobody can doubt the boundless outreach of her integrity. Nobody can doubt the height of her character, nobody can doubt the depth of her Christian commitment and devotion to the teachings of Jesus." Though he didn't say it, nobody was going to say that about the then heavily pregnant Colvin.

But Colvin was not the only casualty of this distortion. Parks was, too. Her casting as the prim, ageing, guileless seamstress with her hair in a bun who just happened to be in the wrong place at the right time denied her track record of militancy and feminism. She appreciated, but never embraced, King's strategy of nonviolent resistance, remains a keen supporter of Malcolm X and was constantly frustrated by sexism in the movement. "I had almost a life history of being rebellious against being mistreated against my colour," she said. But the very spirit and independence of mind that had inspired Parks to challenge segregation started to pose a threat to Montgomery's black male hierarchy, which had started to believe, and then resent, their own spin. Nixon referred to her as a "lovely, stupid woman"; ministers would greet her at church functions, with irony, "Well, if it isn't the superstar." Reverend Ralph Abernathy, who played a key role as King's right-hand man throughout the civil rights years, referred to her as a "tool" of the movement.

Those who are aware of these distortions in the civil rights story are few. Betty Shabbaz, the widow of Malcolm X, was one of them. In a letter published shortly before Shabbaz's death, she wrote to Parks with both praise and perspective: " 'Standing up' was not even being the first to protest that indignity. Fifteen-year-old Claudette Colvin was the first to be arrested in protest of bus segregation in Montgomery. When E.D. Nixon and the Women's Political Council of Montgomery recognized that you could be that hero, you met the challenge and changed our lives forever. It was not your tired feet, but your strength of character and resolve that inspired us." It is a letter Colvin knew nothing about.

Colvin is not exactly bitter. But, as she recalls her teenage years after the arrest and the pregnancy, she hovers between resentment, sadness and bewilderment at the way she was treated. "They just dropped me. None of them spoke to me; they didn't see if I was okay. They never came and discussed it with my parents. They just didn't want to know me." She believes that, if her pregnancy had been the only issue, they would have found a way to overcome it. "It would have been different if I hadn't been pregnant, but if I had lived in a different place or been light-skinned, it would have made a difference, too. They would have come and seen my parents and found me someone to marry." When the boycott was over and the African American community had emerged victorious, King, Nixon and Parks appeared for the cameras. "It's interesting that Claudette Colvin was not in the group, and rarely, if ever, rode a bus again in Montgomery," wrote Frank Sikora, an Alabama-based writer. After her arrest and late appearance in the court hearing, she was more or less forgotten. Later, she would tell a reporter that she would sometimes attend the rallies at the churches. "I would sit in the back and no one would even know I was there."

The upshot was that Colvin was left in an incredibly vulnerable position. A poor, single, black, teenage mother who had both taken on the white establishment and fallen foul of the black one. It is this that incenses Patton. "I respect my elders, but I don't respect what they did to Colvin," she says. "For a while, there was a real distance between me and Mrs. Parks over this. Colvin was a kid. She needed support." If that were not enough, the son, Raymond, to whom she would give birth in December, emerged light-skinned: "He came out looking kind of yellow, and then I was ostracised because I wouldn't say who the father was and they thought it was a white man. He wasn't." She became quiet and withdrawn. "I wasn't with it at all. All I could do is cry."

Robinson recalls: "She needed encouragement, for since her conviction as a law violator her head was not held so high. She did not look people straight in the eye as before." She received a scholarship to the local, historically black university, Alabama State, even though the college authorities were none too keen on having a "troublemaker" on campus. The tears kept coming. She dropped out. She could not find work in Montgomery because as soon as white people found out what she had done, they fired her. "I just couldn't get a job. I'd change my name so that I could work in a restaurant, and they'd find out who I was and that was it. I ran out of identities." Even when she did get work, it was humiliating. "I had this baby of my own and yet I had to leave him with my mother so I could babysit for white people who hated me."

In the space of a few years, a confident A-grade student had passed through the eye of a political storm and emerged a bedraggled outcast. "It changed my life," she says. "I became aware of how the world is and how the white establishment plays black people against each other." She believes, however, that they were right to choose someone such as Rosa Parks as a standard-bearer. "They picked the right person. They needed someone who could bring together all the classes. They wouldn't have followed me. They wanted someone who would shake hands and go to banquets. They wanted someone they could control, and they knew, as a teenager, they couldn't control me."

But she also believes that they were wrong not to support her in her time of need. "They weren't there for me when I tried to make a comeback. I thought maybe they would help me get a degree, or talk to someone about getting me work. I thought they could get me together with Rosa Parks and we could go out together and talk to children."

Similarly, Patton believes that the pragmatic decision not to put Colvin in the spotlight at first was probably correct, but that it does not excuse a wilful negligence to acknowledge her contribution afterwards. "I have no problem with them not lifting up Colvin in 1955. I have a problem with them not lifting her up in 1970. Rosa Parks could have said many times [in the intervening years], 'And there were others.'"

Colvin's life after Montgomery is a metaphor for postwar black America. As the struggle moved from civil rights to economic rights, Colvin followed the route of the great migration and went North to a low-paid job and urban deprivation. She left Montgomery for New York in 1958 to work as a live-in domestic and soon became accustomed to the differences and similarities between North and South. While the power relationship of maid and madam was the same, she encountered less petty racism and institutionalised indignity in the North. In the South, a live-in domestic would never dream of washing her own clothes with those of her employers. In laundry as in life, whites and coloureds could not mix. So when she came down one day to find her employer's dirty clothes dumped on top of hers with a polite request to wash them at the same time, she was shocked. "That's when I knew I was out of the South. That could just never have happened there."

At the start, she occasionally travelled back to Montgomery by bus with baby Raymond to see her parents and look for work in a place where her family could lend support, but no one would employ her. A year later, she fell pregnant again, and in 1960 gave birth to Randy. The pressure of making ends meet in the urban North with two infants and no family became too much. In what was a common arrangement at the time, she left Raymond and Randy with her mother in

Montgomery as she sought work in the North. Things got tough. A couple of times she even considered going into prostitution. "The only thing that kept me out of it was the other things that go with it. Stealing, drugging people. I figured that after the first time the physical thing wouldn't matter so much, but I couldn't get involved in all the other stuff."

At one and the same time, she had become both more independent and more vulnerable, and looking for some evidence for the gains of the civil rights era in her own life. "What we got from that time was what was on the books anyhow. Working-class people were the foot soldiers, but where are they now—they haven't seen any progress. It was the middle classes who were able to take advantage of the laws."

Her two boys took wildly divergent paths. Like many African American men, Raymond, the unborn child she was carrying during the heady days of 1955, joined the U.S. army. Like all too many, he later became involved in drugs, and he died of an overdose in her apartment. Like many others, Randy emerged successful and moved back down South, to Atlanta, where he now works as an accountant. Colvin has five grandchildren.

Earlier this month, Troy State University opened a Rosa Parks museum in Montgomery to honour the small town's place in civil rights history on its forty-fifth anniversary. Ray White, who was responsible for much of what went into the museum, called Colvin to ask if she would appear in a video to tell her story. She refused. "They've already called it the Rosa Parks Museum, so they've already made up their minds what the story is."

He suggested that maybe she would achieve some closure by participating. "What closure can there be for me?" she asks with exasperation. "There is no closure. This does not belong in a museum, because this struggle is not over. We still don't have all that we should have. And, personally, there can be no closure. They took away my life. If they want closure, they should give it to my grandchildren."

Not While Racism Exists

January 7, 2002

Standing at a hotel bar in Freetown, Sierra Leone, a few years ago with an unreconstructed Afrikaner and a white Briton whose racial politics I trusted even less, I was approached by a local, black hustler who put his arm around my shoulder, smiled and asked: "How's my nigger?" I turned swiftly, pointed my finger in his face and said: "Don't you ever, ever, call me that again." He walked away looking both baffled and upset and leaving me feeling both conflicted and annoyed.

Had I been on my own, or in all-black company, I might have asked him where he learned this word and advised him not use it with strangers. But the smirks on the white faces either side of me suggested far more was at stake. He had not embarrassed me (I did not care what they thought of me) but he had compromised me. If it was left unchallenged, I would have to listen to racist people using racist language and justifying it with the pretext that a black man had said it first. A word that I usually encounter only when white people use it in hate mail was about to be sanitised for their casual delectation. That was not an indignity I was prepared to endure.

There are few words as inflammatory or as confused as the word "nigger" has become. At one extreme, it is the most derogatory term whites can use in reference to black people. On the other, it is a casual term of endearment, particularly between African Americans. In between lies an expanse of conflict and misunderstanding. In 1993, a white basketball coach at Central Michigan University asked his black players if he could say the word as they did—to mean toughness and determination on the court. They agreed. But he was still suspended after being overheard saying it. When he unsuccessfully filed suit on grounds of freedom of speech, some of the black players offered themselves as witnesses in his defence.

Recently a publishing company, Merriam Webster, was threatened with a review of its business structures and hiring practices by the NAACP, the oldest civil rights organisation in the country, after it refused to redefine the word. Bill Cosby will not use it at all; fellow comedian Chris Rock has devoted an entire sketch to the use of it. Filmmaker Spike Lee uses it, but objects to Quentin Tarantino's "excessive" use of it.

Controversy surrounding the word is about to deepen with the publication in the United States tomorrow of a new book by the black Harvard academic Randall Kennedy. Throwing a hand grenade into the battle-scarred landscape of America's racial discourse, Kennedy has chosen the title *Nigger*.

While the issue is worthy of intellectual inquiry, the title is shamefully sensationalist and opportunistic and has already caused uproar. "The word is a bit like fire," says Patricia Williams, a black professor at Columbia Law School. "You can warm your hands with the kind of upside-down camaraderie that it gives, or you can burn a cross with it. Seeing it floating abstractly on a bookshelf in a world that is still as polarised as ours makes me cringe."

Kennedy's defence is self-promotion: "I write a book to be read." It is clear how it will benefit him; it is not so obvious how it will help the debate. His desire not only to explore the word, but to exploit it for his own ends is yet another example of the commodification of black culture which enriches the few and impoverishes the many.

Entire industries depend on degrading constructs of black American life, used to sell music, sportswear, fashion, entertainment and satellite stations. Social, cultural and economic deprivation has essentially been branded, marketed and sold to the highest bidder. While usage of the word is commonplace only among African Americans, my experience in Sierra Leone illustrates that the issues it raises are international.

The dilemma is not new. When Carl Van Vechten, the original wigger and honorary white member of the Harlem Renaissance, brought out his book *Nigger Heaven* in 1926, the title was met with fury. A few of his black friends approved, but most pleaded with him to chose another title. Van Vechten insisted he had etymology on his side. "Nigger heaven" was the slang term for the upper gallery of a theatre, where black people were forced to sit in cheap seats—an image that he thought echoed Harlem's position as one of the northernmost sections of Manhattan Island. His defence was irony. But a black America in which most could not vote and many could not find work was in no mood for irony at its own expense. The book was burned from the podium of an anti-lynching rally.

The example is instructive. While Van Vechten understood the words, he misjudged the context. For the word did not drop out of the sky, nor is it uttered in a vacuum. It was born in a culture that was forcibly segregated and racially oppressive. It is because the races remain, by and large, separate that they have maintained their own linguistic traditions; it is because they remain unequal that such a loaded word can retain such contradictory meanings for blacks and whites. In other words, without racism both its offensiveness and its camaraderie would be meaningless.

I claim no consistency in my own view on it. It is not a word I use or am even comfortable around, but I have become immune to it in films and music. Being British may have a great deal to do with that. Nonetheless, I am well aware of the subversive quality of turning oppressive language on its head and using it defiantly. Such is the journey that has transformed former slaves from coloureds to blacks and finally to African Americans and lesbians and gays into queers. Nonetheless, the last noun that Stephen Lawrence heard before he was stabbed to death by racists is not something I wish to claim. The manner in which his case was dealt with shows that the people who think it can be just as vicious as those who say it. That is why it is hard to imagine a situation—outside of a court of law—where it would not be highly problematic for white people to use the word.

So long as racism exists there is no ironic or benign interpretation that cannot be miscontrued. I was in the presence of Germaine Greer last year when she referred to a "nigger in a woodpile." By the time she had tried to render a justification, I was off. There is none. At least, not one that I'm interested in hearing. If white people find this restriction on their vocabulary unreasonable they need only bring forward

the day when racism is eradicated—a day all black people look forward
to—after which they can say what they like. Those who lurk behind the
pillar of freedom of speech in their determination to use it are welcome to the right to be insensitive. But they must accept at least one basic consequence: others have the right to be offended.

Back in the twenties, the African American diplomat and intellectual James Weldon Johnson believed time would be kinder to Van
Vechten than black critics had been. "As the race progresses it will become less and less susceptible to hurts from such causes." Lack of
progress means the hurt is still there.

Don't Blame Uncle Tom

March 30, 2002

This is suicide. For a politically engaged black writer I might as well pen my own obituary. Or at least sentence myself to a life in purdah—for the words will almost certainly be taken down in evidence and used against me at a later date. But we cannot always espouse fashionable causes. So hang it. It is time that someone spoke up for Uncle Tom.

This month sees the 150th anniversary of the publication of *Uncle Tom's Cabin*, and it is time that Uncle Tom was rehabilitated. Not the Uncle Tom of popular insult; not the "neutralised Negro," "non-practising black" or "Reverend Pork Chop" charged with undermining black freedom struggles by ingratiating himself with his white overseers. Not the Tom of racial slur, but the Tom of literary history: the original Tom, husband of Chloe, father of Mose, Peter and Polly and creation of Harriet Beecher Stowe. It is time to save the signifier from the sign. *Uncle Tom's Cabin* is one of those books which is more likely to be cited in anger than to have been read at leisure. So while most people think they "know" Uncle Tom as the Stepin Fetchit of plantation politics, few have actually met the man who lived on the page and whose good name has been so thoroughly traduced.

So let me introduce you. We first see Tom in his cabin in Kentucky where his slave master, Mr. Shelby, is forced to sell two of his slaves to clear his debts. Shelby chooses Tom and Harry, the young son of fellow slave Eliza. Preferring the risk of being caught to the certainty of being split up, Eliza makes a run for it with her child. But Tom, to whom Shelby had promised freedom, refuses to flee.

Later, separated from his wife and family, Tom heads deeper down south in the hands of a slave trader, while Eliza makes it to Canada with her son and husband, who has also fled from another owner, and eventually settles in Liberia.

Tom, meanwhile, is floating on a passenger boat down the Mississippi under the watchful eye of the slave trader when he sees a white girl, Eva, fall overboard and dives in to save her. Eva persuades her father to buy him and Tom becomes the property of Augustine St. Clare, a wealthy planter from Louisiana. St. Clare also offers Tom his freedom but dies suddenly before it is granted. His wife refuses to honour the promise and sells Tom to the vicious Simon Legree. Legree admires Tom's diligence but is frustrated by his refusal to do his bidding. When he orders Tom to whip a fellow slave, Tom refuses and is beaten himself.

When two other slaves go missing, Legree threatens Tom with death unless he tells his master where they are. Tom says he knows but won't say and is fatally thrashed. As he lies, dying, the son of Mr. Shelby arrives with the money to honour his father's promise of freedom in time to see the family's once favourite slave perish at the hands of a brute.

The story was originally run in an anti-slavery newspaper. But when it was released in book form in March 1852, it was an immediate sensation. In the United States alone it sold three hundred thousand copies in a year, and more than two million copies by the end of the decade.

What is now commonly regarded as a sentimentalist, racist text was at the time received as a vicious polemic against slavery in general and against the fugitive slave law in particular. In an America divided at the time between the slave-owning South and the "free states" of the North, the law demanded that Northerners returned slaves who had escaped back into the bondage of the South.

In a nation bitterly split and destined for civil war on this very issue, the book's publication, not to mention its success, provoked a vicious reaction. "*Uncle Tom's Cabin* was the epicenter of a massive cultural phenomenon," writes Richard Yarborough, a California-based academic, in his essay, "Strategies of Black Characterization in Uncle

Tom's Cabin," "the tremors of which still affect the relationship between blacks and whites in the United States." In the nineteenth century, the editor of the *Southern Literary Messenger* instructed his
reviewer: "I would have the review as hot as hellfire, blasting and sear-
ing the reputation of the vile wretch in petticoats who could write
such a volume." Within two years, pro-slavery writers had answered
Uncle Tom's Cabin with at least fifteen novels, similarly polemical in
style but arguing that slaves in the South were better off than free
workers in the North. One of these novels was called *Uncle Robin in
His Cabin in Virginia and Tom Without One in Boston.*

When Abraham Lincoln met Stowe in 1862, one year into the
American Civil War, he greeted her with the words: "So you're the little woman who wrote the book that made this great war." But the
novel's impact was global rather than national. Among those who
hailed it as a masterpiece were Ivan Turgenev, Victor Hugo, Leo Tol-
stoy and George Eliot. The British prime minister, Lord Palmerston,
read it three times and admired it not so much for the story as "for the
statesmanship of it."

It was Lenin's favourite book as a child. "When we try to trace the
origins of Vladimir's political outlook, we often look to what he read
in his late adolescence and early manhood," wrote Robert Service in
his biography of Lenin. "But we need to remember that, before these
Russian and German male authors imprinted themselves upon his
consciousness, an American woman—Harriet Beecher Stowe—had already influenced his young mind." Within the confines of its age then,
Uncle Tom's Cabin was a progressive text, exerting an influence which
few works of literature have done before or since, into the political debate of the time. The problem is that the confines of its age are very
narrow indeed. Written by a white woman principally for other white
people when black people were still regarded as chattel, its failure to
transcend its age is what made it vulnerable to caricature and criticism
at a later date. "Although Stowe unquestionably sympathized with the
slaves," writes Yarborough, "her commitment to challenging the claim
of black inferiority was frequently undermined by her own endorsement of racial sterotypes."

For, in terms of any broader sense of universal humanism or anti-
racism, let alone radicalism, it is deeply problematic. Stowe likes her
"mulattoes" tragic and handsome and her Africans wild and brawny.

The black characters in the book are stock types with only three means to confront their enforced degradation—submission, brutalisation or banishment. "Uncle Tom must be killed; George Harris exiled! Heaven for dead Negroes! Liberia for living mulattoes," an unnamed black writer argued. "Neither can live on the American continent. Death or banishment is our doom." The one thing Stowe could not imagine, even though real-life heroes like slave rebel Nat Turner and underground railroad organiser Harriet Tubman existed to fuel her imagination, was that some might want to stay and fight. "In order to appreciate the sufferings of the Negroes sold south, it must be remembered that all the instinctive affections of that race are peculiarly strong," she writes in the book. "They are not naturally daring and enterprising, but home-loving and affectionate." In another work, she describes black people as "confessedly more simple, docile, childlike and affectionate than other races."

Like most liberals, she believed that support for the downtrodden demanded sympathy rather than solidarity. Like most liberals, she thought that liberation could only be granted by the good grace of the powerful rather than achieved by the will and tenacity of the powerless. In one polemical passage Stowe asserts: "There is one thing that every individual can do [about slavery]; they can see to it that they feel right." To that extent Tom must also be rescued from Stowe as well.

So, if you are looking for a revolutionary role model, someone who remains master of his own destiny in the most humiliating of circumstances, then Uncle Tom is not your man. But then few people are. His sense of duty, even in bondage, depresses. When his wife encourages him to escape with Eliza he tells her: "Mas'r always found me on the spot—he always will. I never have broke trust . . . and I never will." His inability, or unwillingness, to adapt his principles to a greater good, frustrates. Encouraged, by another slave, to murder the vicious Legree while the latter lies in a drunken stupor, Tom says: "No! good never comes of wickedness. I'd sooner chop my right hand off . . . The Lord hasn't called us to wrath. We must suffer, and wait his time."

If ever there was a character to illustrate Marx's most famous quote that "[religion] is the opium of the people," it is Uncle Tom, who would rather wait for freedom in the afterlife than fight for it on earth. But the less famous part of that same quote better sums up Tom's morality and provides the cornerstone for his defence:

"Religion," wrote Marx, "is the sigh of the oppressed creature, the heart of a heartless world and the soul of soulless condition." For when Tom is apparently at his most supine he is, nonetheless, motivated by a desire to remain true to his Christian faith rather than to ingratiate himself with his master.

It is from these deep pools of self-belief and moral absolutes that he manages to preserve his humanism, despite conditions which degrade him daily. It is in this consistency that we find Tom's integrity. It is through it that he is able to assist and defend his fellow slaves and, at times, stand his own ground and still keep himself from loathing whites.

When St. Clare asks him if he would not be better off a slave than a free man, Tom responds with a straight: "No." "Why Tom, you couldn't possibly have earned, by your work, such clothes and such living as I have given you," says St. Clare. "Know's all that Mas'r," says Tom. "But I'd rather have poor clothes, poor house, poor everything and have 'em mine, than have the best, and have 'em any man else's."

Picking cotton alongside a woman whose health is failing, he dumps handfuls that he has picked in her bag. "O, you mustn't! You donno what they'll do to ye," she says. "I can bar it!" said Tom, "better'n you." Shortly afterwards, Legree offers him an easier life if he will whip the woman. "I mean to promote ye, and make a driver of ye; and to-night ye may jest as well begin to get yer hand in. Now, ye jest take this yer gal and flog her."

Tom is punched when he refuses but finally tells Legree. "I'm willin' to work, night and day, and work while there's life and breath in me; but this yer thing I can't feel it right to do . . . t'would be downright cruel . . . if you mean to kill me, kill me; but as to my raising my hand agin anyone here, I never shall,—I'll die first." He isn't killed although he is beaten senseless and has scarcely recovered when Legree finds out two other slaves have fled. He asks Tom to tell him if he knows anything about it and threatens him with death if he refuses.

"I han't got nothing to tell Mas'r," he says. "Do you dare to tell me, ye old black Christian, ye don't know?" asks Legree. "I know, Mas'r, but I can't tell anything. I can die." And die he does.

To discover just how this literary figure of passive resistance becomes a byword for betrayal and subservience, we must look to theatre, film and politics. Stage adaptations removed any remotely radical anti-slave messages and turned it into a minstrel show. "Tom troupes" toured the country and characters sang songs like "I Am but a Little Nigger Gal" and "Happy Are We Darkies So Gay." Tom provided the role for the first black film lead in 1914. Elsewhere, white actors occasionally blacked up. Those performing in film adaptations of the novel included Shirley Temple, Judy Garland, Bill "Bojangles" Robinson, Abbott and Costello—Felix the Cat even played Tom in an animated version.

By the Second World War, Uncle Tom had become a byword for lickspittle subservience in the face of racial oppression. Richard Wright called his collection of short stories about black life in the American South *Uncle Tom's Children*. The protagonist in his most renowned work, *Native Son*, is called Bigger Thomas—an eponymous Northern descendant of Uncle Tom. James Baldwin lambasted the novel: "It was [Stowe's] object to show that the evils of slavery were the inherent evils of a bad system, and not always the fault of those who had become involved in it and were its actual administrators." The oldest and most moderate civil rights organisation in America, the National Association for the Advancement of Colored People, tried to proscribe the book and ban its dramatisations.

The fictitious Tom's actual attributes and flaws soon became incidental. Black America had another use for him in real life. He was to represent the lackey, the moderate, the conciliator and the sell-out. If Stowe had not invented him, African Americans would have had to. True, he might not have been called Tom. It could have been Uncle Ben of long-grain rice fame (Tom's female counterpart is Aunt Jemima, the grand matron of pancake mix). Black radical Malcolm X once said: "Just as the slavemaster in that day used Uncle Tom to keep the field negroes in check, he was the same old slavemaster who today has negroes who are nothing but modern Uncle Toms—twentieth-century Uncle Toms—to keep you and me in check." But the truth is it was the term Uncle Tom itself that was really designed to keep black people in check. As a defensive response to racism, those who use it seek to enforce allegiance and cast out dissent purely on grounds of race.

Black people are not alone in this desire to police their borders in this way. Many cultures that feel on some level embattled will attempt to proscribe behaviour deemed equal to betrayal. That is how Zionist Jews get to brand anti-Zionist Jews "self-haters"—"They're people of

Jewish extraction who've had most of the Jewishness extracted," one academic explained to me recently. Similarly, those not deemed to be sufficiently Irish become "West Brits." Malcolm X was not talking about Uncle Tom the character but Uncle Tom the construct. The Tom of the novel had preferred to die than oversee his fellow slaves. But to Malcolm X, and many others before and since, Uncle Tom was the man preaching reform when others were preaching revolution; the one who advocated peace instead of war; the person who urged others to stay at home instead of taking to the streets; the leader who preached racial equality instead of Black Power.

In short Uncle Tom is whoever you want him to be. Arbitrary in application—who decides who is an Uncle Tom and on what basis?—and prohibitive in nature, it exemplifies the very limits of race-thinking. Even though it is an insult that falls most readily from the lips of self-avowed radicals, it is in fact a reactionary form of psychological and behavioural racial policing within black communities.

Nowhere is this more obvious than in the *American Directory of Certified Uncle Toms*, released earlier this year. The book comes with the subtitle: "Being a Review of the History, Antics and Attitudes of Handkerchief Heads, Aunt Jemimas, Head Negroes in Charge and House Negroes Against the Freedom of the Black Race." It was published by the self-appointed "Council on Black Internal Affairs" which was set up after the Million Man March and cast itself as the supreme arbiter of black authenticity. The council set the lofty target of "[monitoring] the progress of the black race toward its inevitable freedom." The book, wittily written as it is, remains a landmark document in the history of internal race regulation.

It ranks over fifty black leaders, past and present, according to a five-star Uncle Tom rating, with five being the worst. Michael Jackson, who has had plastic surgery which left many of his black features destroyed, gets one star; Bayard Rustin, the gay activist who organised the march on Washington at which King made his "I have a dream speech," gets five; W.E.B. DuBois, a pioneer of Pan-Africanism who died in Ghana publishing an Encyclopedia Africana, is also, according to the authors, a five-star Uncle Tom.

Colin Powell (five stars) becomes "an official, government issue Uncle Tom," Maya Angelou (two stars) is "the much glorified but innocuous Negro emissary of ebony culture," and Oprah Winfrey (four stars) is "the best unambiguously black ambassador of plantation placidity since Hattie McDaniel gushed over Scarlett in *Gone With the Wind*." You do not have to like these people to find these assessments obnoxious. Like the insults "coconut," "Bounty bar" and their American equivalent "Oreo"—all of which mean black on the outside and white on the inside—the racial determinism on which these insults are hinged is in the very worst tradition of identity politics.

The book promises not only constant vigilance—"More will be nominated. More will be exposed. More will be certified"—but also redemption: "Only by refashioning his mind and recasting his role in black affairs can the Uncle Tom declare himself to be a friend of his own black race."

In so doing it presents race not as a starting point from which to understand the world from your own experience, but the sole prism through which the world should be viewed and understood. It emphasises not what you do but who you are. As such it is, effectively, a de-blacking—an attempt to deny racial legitimacy as well as the possibility of genuine debate and disagreement among black people.

If U.S. supreme court justice Clarence Thomas keeps voting against the interests of African Americans then say that. If you think that in the U.K. the *Voice* editor, Mike Best, has contributed to a culture that could lead to more widespread harassment of black youth with his comments over stop and search, then say that too. Blame them for being overly ambitious, rightwing, misled, misguided, bankrupt or washed up. Blame those who back them for being patronising, cynical, opportunistic, manipulative or disingenuous. Call them what you want.

Blame them for what they have done, not who they are. But whatever you do, don't blame Uncle Tom. He has suffered enough.

Louis Farrakhan: Banned but Believable

May 31, 2002

We are on the eleventh floor of the Los Angeles Biltmore Hotel and Marc has never felt so white. Everybody else in the television crew—the director, the cameraman and me—is a black Brit. Everybody else in the room is a member of the Nation of Islam. For them black is not just a description, but a destiny. All roads—political, economic, social, spiritual and sartorial—lead to it. Race defines them.

And right now it is defining Marc too. In a couple of days this Los Angeles–based freelance sound man will be working on a homes and garden show. But today, he is in Minister Louis Farrakhan's suite wondering what to do with the microphone. Ordinarily, in a briefly intrusive, intimate moment, he would clip it on an interviewee's shirt. But this is no ordinary situation.

In his eyeline are the broad chests and bow-ties of Farrakhan's bodyguards. They will take a bullet for their boss; they will not take any nonsense around him. Take a step closer than is necessary towards Farrakhan and they will take a step closer than is comfortable towards you. The night before we had all been thrown out of a banquet dedicated to the first family—Farrakhan's family. An official had asked me to stand in a certain place and I had asked why. We were out on the street before you could say "separate but equal." Now we are in Farrakhan's suite, waiting for him to arrive. One of the minders takes the microphone from Marc and says he will put it on. Then, in walks

Farrakhan, tall, erect, bespectacled. His skin is smooth caramel, his suit only slightly darker and there is little evidence of his seventy years in his face or his gait. The room bristles, not with excitement, but with a mixture of reverence and obsequiousness. Big men suddenly made small in the presence of the largest man they can imagine.

Only when he takes his chair does it become apparent that whoever has taken the microphone from Marc does not know what to do with it. Farrakhan looks up, slightly exasperated but completely composed. "Whose responsibility is this?" he asks. His voice is a velvet purr, his mouth a lustrous smile. Marc tentatively raises his hand.

"Well don't be afraid," says Farrakhan. The former calypso singer who once went by the name of the Charmer. "Come here and put it on. I'm not going to hurt you."

Farrakhan is very believable. In fact, for the leader of an organisation which believes, among other things, that white people were made out of germs by a mad scientist and were originally born with tails, he is unbelievably believable. Others who have interviewed him recall how his charm can dissolve into rage when pressed on certain matters. He has been known to occasionally descend into a babble of conspiracy theories and numerology. "That number nineteen," he told a bemused crowd at the Million Man March in 1995. "When you have a nine you have a womb that is pregnant. And when you have a one standing by the nine it means that there's something secret that has to be unfolded."

But on the day we see him he is more eloquent and articulate than almost any political figure I have met. Remarkably for most people, politicians or otherwise, his speech is not punctuated with ums and errs. He speaks as if to be quoted or possibly in fear of being misquoted. His enunciation is clear, crisp and concise.

In February, when Tony Blair was asked in parliament by one of his own backbenchers to give a brief characterisation of the political philosophy which he espouses and which underlies his policies, he muttered something about the NHS and took his seat looking flummoxed. Ask Farrakhan what the Nation of Islam stands for and he does not miss a beat. "The core principles on which the NOI are found are one, freedom, two, justice and three, equality," he says. "All of this is inherent in Islam. We are Muslims. And we believe that we have been deprived of true freedom, true justice and true equality. So we petition the government of the U.S. since we live here, to give not only us that freedom, but give that freedom to all and justice to all and equity to all. And if we cannot get that within the political, economic and social environment within the United States then we ask to be separated into a state or territory of our own, where we would have a chance to give these rights which we have been denied, to ourselves."

So there it is. About as straightforward an enunciation of black nationalism as you can get from America's leading proponent of the cause. Almost fifty years after the U.S. Supreme Court decision on *Brown v. the Board of Education* outlawed segregation, the Nation of Islam points to the failure of integration and argues that when it comes to a judgment on "separate but equal," if they cannot have the equal, they would rather be separate. It is not a mainstream view, certainly. But in a country where voluntary segregation is both widespread and endemic, it is hardly an extreme view either, particularly among African Americans.

Even rightwing Republicans express astonishment at his ban from Britain, which was repealed last July and then reimposed in April. Not because they like him, but because he has now become such a fixed point on the nation's racial landscape that even to most of his detractors he is no more than a familiar irritant. It has been generally, if begrudgingly, acknowledged that he represents something that needs to be taken account of, even if nobody is quite sure what that force is.

To that extent, both Farrakhan and the Nation of Islam are as American as homecoming or the Super Bowl. His message of self-help and strong community is deeply rooted in America's individualistic, pioneering psyche. "First we try to unite our people, pool our resources, build schools and economic development for ourselves and our people," he says. In a nation where organised religion plays a powerful force he is one among many. "We are trying to link with Muslims all over the world. We have gotten involved in politics because we recognise that there is a gain that we as a people can have if we get involved in politics—not as an ignorant person just throwing a vote away, but using our vote and leveraging our numbers and our money to see what we can extract from a recalcitrant system which has not given us what we feel our sacrifice, our suffering and the blood that we have shed has given us the right to have."

Born from a specific response to American racism during the 1930s and establishing itself primarily as a Northern, urban force during the fifties and sixties, the Nation of Islam now has a strength in the United States that it would be difficult to imagine a similar organisation possessing in any other country.

True there are sympathisers all over the world and followers in Canada, the United Kingdom and even Switzerland, but in nothing like the numbers and with nothing like the presence or influence that they have in America. That is why the ban on Farrakhan coming to Britain has been such a blow. The Nation sees Britain as the gateway to building a base among black, Arab and Asian youth around Europe and thereby gaining an international credibility that has thus far eluded it. Critics also believe that it gives the organisation a chance to revive its fortunes—both financially and politically.

"England is very, very important to the Nation of Islam for several reasons," says Vibert White, a former member of the Nation of Islam and professor at the University of Illinois. "It's a chance for Farrakhan to breathe new life into a movement which has really become stagnant in the last few years."

Farrakhan believes he has been denied access to a crucial audience. "What do I hope to accomplish on coming?" he asks. "To see those who follow me, to give the blacks, the whites, the Muslims, a chance to hear me and judge me for themselves."

Farrakhan believes it is his troubled relationship with the American Jewish community that forms the basis of his ban from the U.K. He dates this back to his support for Jesse Jackson's presidential bid in 1984. African Americans and Jews form two of the Democratic Party's most loyal constituencies. Farrakhan's supporters say that when it looked as though Jackson, by far the most pro-Palestinian contender, might win, the Jewish community got nervous and started to accuse him and his more controversial supporter, Farrakhan. "I think it's because after the Jesse Jackson campaign there was a polemic in dialogue between myself and the Jewish community," explains Farrakhan. "And because that dialogue was not resolved it meant the Jewish community in the U.K. utilised their influence to say that I was not a good person. So from that day to this I have been banned."

There is, of course, another version of events. After Jackson was lambasted for describing New York as "Hymietown"—for which he apologised—Farrakhan claimed that "Israeli hit squads" had been dispatched to kill him. He was briefly courted by the extreme right, who supported his calls for segregation and expressed hatred for Jews. In 1984, he said Israel will "Never have . . . peace, because there can be no peace structured on injustice, lying and deceit and using the name of God to shield your dirty religion under his holy and righteous name." He had, in fact, accused others who he believed strayed from the tenets of their faith of following a dirty religion. "Sheikhs who live in opulence when their people live in squalor are practising a dirty religion," he said. "Christians [who] preach love, but practise hate and tyranny, use God to cover up their corrupt and dirty practices."

He did later apologise for using the phrase about Jews, saying it was "not appropriate" and "it was my mistake." But by now the die had been cast. Even those sympathetic to Farrakhan refer to him "flirting with the outrageous" and doing little to "dismiss the impression" of anti-semitism during the eighties. But most also agree that he has spent the past decade trying to patch these relations up.

He has had some success, notably his overtures to the Jewish vice-presidential candidate Joseph Lieberman during the 2000 election campaign fell on willing ears. But he expresses frustration that other attempts have met with constant rebuff.

"It cannot be resolved without dialogue. But it can be resolved," he says. "I've said to the Jewish community: 'If there's something that I said that is not truthful, then I do not want to be a party to that which is false, so if you can show me where what I said was error then you won't have to ask me to apologise, I will go before the World where I made the error and make the appropriate apology.' But that can't happen without a dialogue."

The fact that he remains a pariah to many, he believes, is due to the potency of the message passed down by the Nation of Islam's founder, the honourable Elijah Mohammed. "I believe that the message of truth from Elijah Mohammed is a threat to the control that many have had over black people and others as well," he says. "So they purposely put a veil over me that he is anti-white, anti-semitic, anti-American, he's anti-gay, he's anti-Christian. So when you put that on me, people of intelligence, rational people say: 'I don't want anything to do with that man.' That is exactly the intention of those in power. But we are gradually breaking those chains and coming out of this prison of media misrepresentation of Louis Farrakhan."

Farrakhan often talks about himself in the third person. Less lyrical in his speech than Jesse Jackson, his contemporary and regular confidant, he is also less evasive—giving answers to questions that are asked rather than set speeches he has pre-prepared. Nevertheless he is not short on rhetorical flourishes of his own, riffing on words or phrases until they become minor refrains. Style reinforcing substance to make the simple sound complex.

"First, raise the black man and woman from a state of economic, political, spiritual, mental, moral and social death," he says, when asked about the theme of his week-long trip to Los Angeles. "But then the whole of humanity is suffering. The whole of humanity is lost. So if that message of Islam can find us and reform us and make us better human beings, that same message is good for Latinos, that same message is good for Native Americans, that same message is good for the whites of America and the whole human family as well."

It is a far cry from the demagoguery you will see from him on stage. The short bursts of lectern-pounding rage that will intersperse his Castro-length, three- or four-hour-long speeches. He once invited a select group of black journalists to his home in Chicago to ask them how he might handle his image better. They told him if he was worried about being misquoted he shouldn't speak for hours at a time. When Farrakhan tells an audience: "I'm gonna finish here," you know there is at least half an hour to go.

But while his tone and time-keeping may still vary greatly, the content of his speeches has, of late, become extraordinarily focused thanks to the events of September 11. After an initial vacillation, during which he went from condemning the attacks and U.S. foreign policy to espousing outrageous conspiracy theories, he settled on a fairly consistent position against the war in Afghanistan. "I think the U.S. government had every right to respond. But that response should have been appropriate to the wickedness perpetrated against the United States," he says.

The war, he believes, is driven by the desire for oil and could have been averted. "In the Holy Koran there is a scripture that says: 'Whenever an unrighteous person brings you news, you should look carefully into it less you should harm a people in ignorance rather than be sorry for what you did.'

"Afghanistan was never on the list of terrorist states, even though the Taliban were there and even though al-Qaida was there and even though Osama bin Laden was there. So Mullah Omar Mohammed asked President Bush: 'Show me this overwhelming evidence which you say you have and I will detain Osama bin Laden and turn him over to the relevant authorities.' And President Bush's response, which I don't think was proper, was: 'I'm not negotiating.' He said he showed this overwhelming evidence to Prime Minister Blair, but he was not going to bomb Prime Minister Blair and the United Kingdom, they were going to bomb Afghanistan, and so the Taliban deserved to know the truth and then see how they would react toward Osama bin Laden. Unfortunately they were not given that chance."

It is at this stage that one realises Farrakhan's unique position. He is America's most prominent Muslim. He also has no stake in the system as it stands. That makes him one of a handful of people in America who can draw a large crowd to denounce the war in almost any major city. There is no office he wishes to run for, no part of the white-dominated power structure with which he is in negotiation. In other words, he can say what he likes. For better, and sometimes for worse.

Halfway through the interview, a nurse comes in with some tablets. Farrakhan is still sick. His health is no personal matter. "Minister Farrakhan is the Nation of Islam," says Arthur J. Magida, the author of *Prophet of Rage: A Life of Louis Farrakhan and His Nation*. "The Nation relies on his charisma, his organizational skills and his image as perhaps the most courageous and defiant black man in the United States. If he is sick the Nation is sick."

This is not a problem unique to the Nation of Islam. Black America has long provided dynamic individuals, but they have rarely bequeathed vibrant or longstanding institutions. The Southern Christian Leadership Conference ceased to be a vital force when Martin Luther King died and the Rainbow Coalition is little more than a platform for Jesse Jackson.

The internal structures of the Nation of Islam resemble a mixture of military and monarchy. No substantive decisions are made without him and yet for an organisation of the Nation's size to function decisions must be made in his absence. And so each layer of the organisation tries to anticipate what the stratum above wants, all the way up the pyramid. Initiative is discouraged; institutionalisation is embedded;

individuality dissolves. Members move in swarms, following the most powerful in the pack. When two senior players meet, it looks like a scene from *Goodfellas*. The leaders shake hands and hug, then their entourages greet each other and for a moment they are all one. Then from this mingle of similarly dressed and identically coiffured humanity, they regroup into their two distinct entities, and head off in separate directions.

The end result is a mixture of officiousness and incompetence. Enduring constant, sour-faced, futile frisking in which one bag is checked twice and another not at all, waiting hours for Nation officials who claim they are only minutes away, watching men with earpieces strut purposefully around in circles, requiring identity tags that do not exist because they have not been issued: all creates the impression of an organisation in which people enjoy the trappings of authority but with neither the power to make it meaningful nor the system to make it workable.

Few would deny that the Nation of Islam and Farrakhan are problematic. His black nationalism and his history of inflammatory, anti-semitic remarks make both the message and the man unsavoury to some. But it is difficult to find anyone in America who seriously thinks his coming to Britain would be a problem either. The one thing that the Nation of Islam has never been associated with is violence towards other groups.

Violence within the organisation, following Malcolm X's departure in the sixties and Elijah Muhammad's death in the mid-seventies, was intense. But there is scant evidence of violence towards Jews, whites or any other group.

"After all, Britain once ruled the entire world," argues Farrakhan. "Britain has nothing to fear from listening to a man and making their own judgment as to whether he is worthy of being listened to or discarded."

Since there is no reason to believe he would be a danger to public order, it is only his ideas that could pose a threat. And if Britain's multicultural society cannot challenge those head on, we can hardly blame Farrakhan for that.

Different Class

November 23, 2002

When Malcolm X went to Jedda in the early 1960s, he was shocked by his reception. Back home he was a pariah—a race-baiter and white hater—who would become even more loathed by the U.S. authorities when he returned to preach not racial segregation but socialism. In Mecca it was a very different story. A senior Sudanese official hugged him and declared, "You champion the American black people!" An Indian official wept, declaring his compassion "for my brothers in your land." In his autobiography, Malcolm X wrote: "The American Negro has no conception of the hundreds of millions of other non-whites' concern for him: he has no conception of their feeling of brotherhood for and with him."

When U.S. Secretary of State Colin Powell addressed the Earth Summit in Johannesburg in September, he was greeted not in a spirit of brotherhood but with a barrage of booing. A year earlier, at the anti-racism summit where Powell had refused to show up and the United States resisted all talk of reparations for slavery, the cartoonist for the South African newspaper *Citizen* ridiculed him: "Coming Uncle Tom?" ask two characters representing participants at the conference. "De Massa in de big house says I ain't," responds a Powell dressed up as a house servant. Given that Powell is one of the most liberal figures in the Bush administration, one might only imagine what views are reserved for his African-American colleague Condoleeza

Rice, the hardline hawk with the president's ear, his chief adviser on international affairs.

There was a time when the rest of the world looked at black America and saw dissidence. They stood on Olympic podiums victorious and rebellious, saluting their national anthem with a clenched fist. In 1960, a year after the Cuban revolution, Fidel Castro left the Shelburne hotel in Manhattan after they demanded that he pay his bill in advance, and headed for the Teresa Hotel in Harlem to a hero's welcome.

But not any more. Thanks to shifts, both subtle and seismic, in class, politics and culture, black America is now presenting a radically different face to the world. Today, they offer the developing world the official policy of one of the most reactionary U.S. administrations in recent times. Where its singers once railed against the affliction of being raised in the ghetto, now they trumpet the aspirations of life among the ghetto-fabulous. Where its sports personalities once reigned in boxing, now they are masters at golf. And whereas they were once hailed in Africa, now they are heckled.

Such observations come in the form of a description, rather than a criticism. Black America's ascent to such positions of power and prominence in areas where they now find themselves blamed for some of the ills that their nation visits on the world is, on one level, a mark of success. Their status as second-class citizens was an emblem for the global oppressed. It was a view that was rooted in politics, but which extended to culture and sport, too. In a 1927 poem, the fledgling Soviet Union's poet laureate, Vladimir Mayakovsky, wrote: "If I were a Negro/I would learn Russian/just because/Lenin spoke it." Years later, nationalists in Northern Ireland adopted civil rights songs as they marched through West Belfast, while Angola's newspaper, *Diario de Buanda*, lamented "the tragedy of Negro life in America" after the Freedom Riders were bombed in Alabama.

But this solidarity stemmed as much from black America's position of weakness as from its culture of resistance. Much of the world identified with them because they, too, were deprived of basic rights. For a brief moment during the 1960s, the demands of black America chimed with those of colonial Africa and Asia—everyone was fighting for the right to vote. Shortly after Kwame Nkrumah was elected the leader of a newly-independent Ghana, he invited black American intellectual W.E.B. DuBois to edit an Encylcopedia Africana and

Paul Robeson to assume the chair of music and drama at Accra university.

But once those rights were won, the paths diverged. Black Americans lived in one of the most powerful nations of the world; Africans and Asians in two of the poorest continents. One of the first institutions to be integrated was the military, thereby sending black Americans to the frontline of incursions across the globe. As the focus shifted from civil rights to economic rights, so a handful of African Americans slowly started to seek to protect their economic interests and align themselves, albeit tentatively, with the right. Equality of opportunities, in short, earned black Americans the chance to be every bit as reactionary and imperialist as their white countrymen.

So long as those rights were honoured in principle but breached in practice, those opportunities were fairly rare. Riots that raged through America's Northern cities during the late 1960s, the rise of the Black Power movement and the assassinations of Martin Luther King and Malcolm X kept the plight of black America firmly in the spotlight. In a world with two superpowers, where allegiances were often based on the principle that, in times of crisis, the enemy of my enemy is my friend, black America had lots of friends because America had plenty of enemies. In postwar Paris, antagonism to U.S. political hegemony found expression in the support for the growing number of black artists in the city: "Opposition to the racism of the United States was reinforced by the political climate of anti-Americanism," writes Tyler Stovall in *Paris, Noir: African-Americans in the City of Light*. "The Parisino Left now regarded Americans as a symbol of ideological consciousness."

Black Americans had, in effect, gained exemption from criticisms of U.S. foreign policy abroad, because they were considered victims of the same repressive regime at home. This was true even for the few who became official representatives of the U.S. abroad. Ralph Bunche, who negotiated a truce between Arabs and Jews in the Middle East in 1947 and later went on to become the United Nations undersecretary for political affairs, became the first black American to be awarded the Nobel Peace Prize. Andrew Young had been America's first black ambassador to the U.N., albeit under a Carter administration that pursued the most liberal foreign policy since the war, before he was forced to resign for holding informal talks with PLO representatives.

An impression created by black American intellectuals and articulated by politicians found its most potent expression in popular culture and sport. There was an organic connection between black artists and performers and the aspirations of African Americans. Their lyrics provided a soundtrack for the politics of the day that resonated beyond North America. Early in 1968, Aretha Franklin appeared on a platform with Martin Luther King. A month after he was murdered, "Think" was released—a love song and a warning to white America: "You better think, think about what you're trying to do to me/Yeah, think let your mind go, let yourself be free/You need me and I need you/Without each other there ain't nothing people can do," and then the rallying cry "Freedom."

In sport, there was Wimbledon tennis champion and human rights activist Arthur Ashe. But largest and loudest of them all, on the world stage, was Muhammad Ali. "We knew Muhammad Ali as a boxer, but more importantly for his political stance," says Zairean musician Malik Bowens in the film *When We Were Kings*. "When we saw that America was at war with a third world country in Vietnam, and one of the children of the U.S. said, 'Me? You want me to fight against Vietcong?' It was extraordinary that in America someone could have taken such a position at that time. He may have lost his title. He may have lost millions of dollars. But that's where he gained the esteem of millions of Africans."

Precisely at what point black America stopped giving this impression to the rest of the world is not clear. Up until the late 1980s, rap groups such as Public Enemy still vowed to Fight the Power, Tracy Chapman was talkin' 'bout a revolution and Gil Scott Heron linked the oppression of blacks in South Africa with their treatment in the U.S. "New York's like Johannesburg, L.A.'s like Johannesburg, Freedom ain't nothing but a word, Let me see your ID." Then, in the early 1990s, Jesse Jackson, still black America's most recognisable face abroad, offered himself as an alternative ambassador to Iraq even as the Pentagon was preparing for war and returned with freed hostages.

Today, one of the most prominent figures on the American music scene is Sean Combs (Puff Daddy, now P. Diddy), proudly declaring, "It's all about the Benjamins." (American inventor and statesman Benjamin Franklin appears on the hundred-dollar bill.) Combs is not so much a music-maker as a brand: you can wear his Sean John line of clothing, or eat his Seafood Pan Roast with the black bourgeoisie at Justins, the restaurant he founded that is named after his son. His role model, he said recently, is not Martin Luther King but Martha Stewart—the Delia Smith of middle America, whose name sells products at an astonishing rate.

At some point, following the passing of civil rights legislation in the mid-1960s, an economic fracturing within black America gradually produced a rupture in relations between black America and the rest of the diaspora. This was by no means a seamless transition. Soul singer James Brown went on a U.S.-sponsored tour of Vietnam in 1968; a year later, the late James Farmer served in the Nixon administration as assistant secretary for health, education and welfare. Throughout the 1960s, baseball supremo Jackie Robinson remained a committed Republican and a fervent supporter of America's role in the cold war.

But so long as those opportunities remained limited, resistance was widespread. So much so that even those who had either opted for or been co-opted by the white-dominated mainstream have felt compelled either to qualify their allegiance to the right through racial assertion or simply to quit altogether.

Shortly after Brown returned from backing the troops in Vietnam, he recorded his anthem "Say It Loud (I'm Black and I'm Proud)"; Farmer left the Nixon administration in disgust; Robinson left the San Francisco Republican convention that nominated Barry Goldwater, the party's most rightwing candidate of the past century, saying, "I had a better understanding of how it must have felt to be a Jew in Hitler's Germany."

The growing differences within black America started to be replicated in the huge disparity of experience between black America and the rest of the diaspora. In 1995, black Americans spent $1.2 billion on hair care, a little more than the GDP of Gambia, the home of the ancestors of *Roots* author Alex Haley.

The combination of more wealth and less consciousness undermined the potential for solidarity with other black people from poorer nations. This has been most vividly expressed culturally. Upon arriving in Zaire for the Rumble in the Jungle, Ali declared that he was "home." In contrast, in 1992, when the dons of global basketball, the

U.S. Dream Team, went to the Olympics in Barcelona, the U.S. Olympic Committee begged Charles Barkley to tone down his comments after he hit an Angolan player. Among other things, Barkley said, "The guy probably hadn't eaten in a few weeks . . . I'll hit a fat guy next time . . . I thought he had a spear."

Underpinning all of this has been a profound sense of patriotism that informs U.S. political culture across the boundaries of race and ethnicity. Martin Luther King, we should not forget, insisted that his dream was "rooted in the American dream." This should come as no surprise. Bar a handful of pilgrims and the Native American Indians, African Americans are the ethnic group with the longest geographical attachment to the U.S. Unlike other racial minorities in the west, they are not relatively recent immigrants. So, in times of national crisis, they rally around their flag in a way that those of Arab descent in France, say, or of Caribbean descent in Britain could not imagine. A *New York Times* poll last year shortly after the terrorist attacks showed that 75 per cent of black Americans approved of the performance of President Bush, while another, by the Pew Research Center for the People and the Press, showed that 68 per cent backed the war against Afghanistan.

The fact that this level is significantly lower than whites—90 per cent and 88 per cent, respectively—shows that race still has a considerable impact on national allegiance. "It's about a contradiction in their own lives," says Keith Woods of the Florida-based Poynter Institute. "About the difference between feeling like Americans and at the same time feeling like America hasn't fully embraced them."

This contradiction has found full expression in a ferocious debate within black America itself. In October, the singer and one-time civil rights activist Harry Belafonte compared Powell to a "house slave." "Colin Powell's permitted to come into the house of the master. When Colin Powell dares to suggest something other than what the master wants to hear, he will be turned back out to pasture." And the online magazine *In These Times* describes Bush's entourage, the most diverse in U.S. history, as "Uncle Tom's Cabinet," saying, "It is a sad, ironic testimony to the current complexities of racial politics in America that African-Americans like Colin Powell and Condoleeza Rice can attain unprecedented career advances in tandem with the sweeping disenfranchisement of thousands of black voters." The most dominant campaign among black activists on the left, over the past few years, has been for reparations for slavery—a movement that has sought to cement links with the developing world and with Africa in particular.

So the shift from internationalism to insularity within black America has never been straightforward—and, far from being complete, remains very much contested. In common with all Americans, the events of September 11 are forcing black America to reassess its relationship with the world. But there can be little doubt which way the pendulum is swinging, or of the impression that is being given globally. In the words of a South African columnist shortly after September 11, "Even aggrieved minorities are Americans first. For as much as [they] like to uphold the roots of [their] ancestors and look to Africa as a point of origin, the US is [their] home. At this moment, [they] probably want those terrorists 'smoked out of their holes' as Bush threatened. That makes [them] as American as [their] president."

A Supreme Showdown

June 21, 2003

As a teenager, Jennifer Gratz's mind was focused and her heart set. With good grades and an impressive range of extracurricular activities on her CV, she was determined to go to the University of Michigan in the nearby town of Ann Arbor. Michigan has one of the best reputations of any publicly funded university in the United States, and Gratz grew up in Southgate, a working-class suburb of Detroit. Her father was a retired police sergeant, her mother a secretary. Neither had finished college.

But Gratz, who was seventeen at the time, plugged away. She finished 13th in a class of 298, and was the vice president of her student council and Southgate's homecoming queen. "Jennifer did everything we asked her to do, and more," her former assistant principal, Ron Dittmer, told the *Washington Post*. "I wouldn't ask any more of my own daughter."

So intent was Gratz on her goal, and so certain was she that she would achieve it, that she did not apply to any other universities. So when a thin letter bearing her rejection arrived, she was devastated. On opening it, she cried, turned to her father and asked, "Dad, can we sue?" Gratz believed she had been turned down because she was white. The University of Michigan uses a points system when selecting graduates, and applicants from underrepresented racial minorities are automatically awarded extra points.

On April 1 this year, Gratz, now twenty-six and a software trainer for a vending machine company in California, had her day in the highest court in the land. Surrounded by demonstrators in an atmosphere one lawyer described as "electric," the U.S. Supreme Court heard arguments for and against the claim that Michigan had acted unconstitutionally when considering her application.

By the end of this month, when the Supreme Court announces its verdict, Gratz's personal disappointment will have a judicial legacy, with potentially enormous consequences for the whole country. Before she even opened the letter, it already had a political context. It was 1995 when Gratz was rejected—the year O.J. Simpson was found innocent and hundreds of thousands of black men marched on Washington with separatist leader Louis Farrakhan at their head. In a nation that has had many years fraught with racial tension, this one stood out.

On Capitol Hill, the pollsters had identified a new voting bloc as the primary constituency of the rightwing Republican Revolution that had swept to power in the House the year before. They called it the angry white male. And there was nothing that made them angrier than affirmative action—efforts to improve the employment or educational opportunities of racial minorities and women.

"Why did 62 per cent of white males vote Republican in 1994?" asked Bob Dole, the Republican presidential candidate in 1996. "I think it's because sometimes the best qualified person does not get the job, because he or she may be one color. I'm beginning to believe that may not be the way it should be in America."

Unbeknown to Gratz, one white man was particularly annoyed with affirmative action. Carl Cohen, a philosophy professor at the University of Michigan, read an article claiming that the acceptance rate among black students at the most prestigious universities was higher than among whites. Cohen filed a request to see his university's admissions policy and discovered the racial weighting in the points system. When local Republicans found out, they called a conservative Washington-based law firm, the Center for Individual Rights (CIR), and asked it to take up the case. The CIR put out an appeal for plaintiffs and Gratz—along with another unsuccessful undergraduate applicant, Patrick Hamacher, and a failed law school hopeful, Barbara Grutter—came forward.

Although the law school does not use the points system, it still counts race as a factor in admissions. Its case is technically separate, but since it touches on the same issues at the same university, the Court agreed to hear them both together. The plaintiffs say that, by taking race into account, the university violated their Fourteenth Amendment rights to "equal protection of the laws." Now the Supreme Court is poised to rule on whether race can ever be used as a factor in university admissions.

But the ramifications of its decision will go way beyond the campus at Ann Arbor or the field of education. "If you're right," said Justice Ruth Ginsburg, addressing Gratz's lawyer at the April hearing, "this case is much larger than 'public universities.' It's all colleges and universities, and it's the entire realm of employment." At present, the great majority of universities and corporations operate affirmative action. Even in individual states where affirmative action has been effectively outlawed, colleges have still found ways to ensure diversity.

This case is potentially every bit as momentous as *Brown v. the Board of Education,* the Supreme Court ruling that less than fifty years ago declared "separate but equal" facilities for different races to be illegal. What started then as a case about schooling in the small town of Topeka, Kansas, provided the political impetus and legal framework for the civil rights movement. Just a year later would come the Montgomery bus boycott and the birth of a new era of anti-racist activism. "The law got rid of segregation and the law can bring it back," said one Michigan administrator who did not wish to be named.

It is a mark of the contentiousness of the current case that it has produced one of the few public splits within President George Bush's administration. In January, the White House filed papers with the Supreme Court supporting Gratz and accusing the university of operating a "quota system." Bush also spoke out against college admissions policies that "unfairly reward or penalise prospective students solely on their race."

A week later, Colin Powell, who as secretary of state is the highest ranking black American in the country, openly disagreed: "I am a strong proponent of affirmative action," he said. "I believe race should be a factor [in college admissions]. I thought the University of Michigan had a strong case." The other senior black member of Bush's team, Condoleezza Rice, also crafted a nuanced response. Rice, who openly acknowledges that she was a beneficiary of affirmative action when she went to Stanford University, said she believed that race can and should be a factor in admissions policies, but continued to back the president.

It is a sign of the breadth of concern over the case that the university has submitted a record number of supporting statements, or amicus briefs, not only from other universities but from military leaders and the corporate world as well. Eight years after Gratz's rejection, she and her co-plaintiffs are poised to make racial and legal history. The president is supporting her. And an incongruous collection of household names—including Gulf War leader Norman Schwarzkopf, civil rights champion Jesse Jackson, Nike and IBM—are against her.

In spring, the University of Michigan's campus is a verdant, splendid place—a patchwork of impressive gothic architecture and modern buildings, all woven together with coffee shops, bars and bookstores. To describe it as a university town would be misleading. The university does not describe the town; it is the town. The median age of Ann Arbor is less than thirty.

It is little wonder that Gratz—who was subsequently turned down by Notre Dame University, and eventually went to the Dearborn campus of Michigan, near where she lived—was so keen to come here. The university, which was founded in 1817 with the motto "An uncommon education for the common man," is ranked first in the country for its teaching of management, environmental health, undergraduate research, human resources, African American history, social work, anthropology, archaeology and U.S. politics. Among its flagship departments, its law school comes seventh, its business school, thirteenth, and its medical research work, eighth.

In 2002, 25,081 students applied for just 5,186 places. Whichever way you cut it, around twenty thousand people are going to be disappointed. The question for the university is not whether or not it takes applicants who are qualified, but which qualified applicants it wants to take. "It's an issue of math," says Julie Peterson, a spokesperson for the university. "There is no way that all of the students qualified to come here are going to come here. No matter what system you use, there are going to be some students who feel, 'That's not fair.' "

Herein lies the central problem with Gratz's allegation that she was rejected because she is white. The number of African American,

Native American and Hispanic students who apply to the university is very small, so they have only a negligible effect on the odds of white students being accepted. Take 1995, the year Gratz was turned down: minorities made up just 11 per cent of the applicants. Even if all of them had been rejected, the percentage of white students accepted would have risen only from 25 to 30 per cent.

The truth, says the university, is that Gratz would not have got in, anyway—not because she is white or because she was not smart, but because, given the stiff competition, she was simply not smart enough. "People don't get in for a lot of reasons," says Peterson. "It's a myth to say, 'But for that minority student, I would have got in.' It's mathematically ridiculous. Race is a very emotional subject in our country. People have very strong feelings about it, and they are not always grounded in fact."

The system that Michigan uses to filter the unwieldy flood of hopefuls is a mixture of the complex and the crude. It awards a maximum of 150 points, with applicants needing at least 100 to be considered. The university allots 110 of these points purely on the basis of academic achievement. The remaining forty (the absolute maximum, regardless of your circumstances) come under the heading "Other factors." Here, you can get five points for both personal achievement and leadership/service; four if your parents or step-parents went to the university; and three for the quality of the compulsory essay explaining why you want to go there. An applicant from the state of Michigan automatically gets ten points; one from an underrepresented county within Michigan gets another six; and an applicant from another underrepresented state gets two.

The plaintiffs have challenged none of these. But in the bottom right-hand corner, under the subheading "Miscellaneous," stands the nub of the controversy in black and white. Here, the university awards five points if you are a man who wants to go into nursing, and twenty points, at the provost's discretion, if you are at socioeconomic disadvantage, a scholarship athlete or from an underrepresented racial or ethnic group. The latter alone is the target of the plaintiff's ire. No one can score more than twenty in this section. So a poor, black, male basketball supremo who wants to go into nursing would score only twenty, as would a wealthy, white tennis champion.

The university does not claim it is ideal. "The bottom line about all this is there's no perfect admissions process in the world," says Marvin Krislov, vice president and general counsel of the university. "What you're trying to do is capture a lot of different factors, and from those factors you try to get a competitive environment where there's a mix. There's an ideal of learning from each other."

Whatever its shortcomings, it is not, as the Bush administration claims, a quota system. Over the past four years, the percentage of underrepresented minorities accepted as undergraduates at Michigan has swung between 12 per cent and 17 per cent. The number of such students at the law school ranges from forty-four to seventy-three, and currently stands at 12 per cent of the total—one thing that can be said for the points system is that it is transparent. Academic ability remains the primary ingredient of a mix in which race is just one element. The result, they say, is a better education on campus and more constructive citizens in the outside world.

The university does not simply believe this, it says it can prove it. Among the supporting research submitted to the Supreme Court to back up its case was a report by psychology professor Patricia Gurin, the interim dean of the college of literature, science and the arts in Ann Arbor. Analysing surveys of more than ten thousand students of all races from around two hundred colleges and universities, Gurin concluded that university provides a unique opportunity to confront segregation during early adulthood, when people are at their most questioning.

The study showed that white students who attended more diverse colleges were more likely to show academic motivation and growth in learning, and placed a greater value on academic skills five years after they left university than those who did not. They were also more likely to have a racially diverse group of friends, live in a diverse area and work in a diverse environment. While there were similar if less marked results for minorities, African American and Hispanic students in diverse colleges were also more likely to participate in community service when they left.

Studying at a diverse campus holds two main benefits, claims Gurin: students learn better while they are there and they become more constructive citizens when they leave. "Diversity of all forms in the student body—including racial diversity—is crucially important in helping students become conscious learners and critical thinkers, and

in preparing them for participation in a pluralistic, diverse society."
John Payton, a Washington lawyer representing the university before
the Supreme Court, said: "Their education is much more than the classroom. It's in the dorm, it's in the dining halls, it's in the coffee houses.
It's in the daytime, it's in the night-time. It's all the time."

Wander around the Ann Arbor campus and you will see plenty of
students of different races. Ask them if the university is diverse and
they will say yes. Ask if they have friends of different races and they
say yes. But ask if it is usual for people to mix outside their racial group
after class and they pause. "No," says one Latino student who did not
wish to be named, but who seems to reflect the common view. "People
usually stick to their own, where they feel more comfortable."

Evidence of this voluntary segregation is everywhere. On the
Greek letters of the African American and Hispanic fraternities that
students wear on their jackets; at the Association of Black Profession-
als, Administrators, Faculty and Staff's annual meeting; on the Martin
Luther King poster advertising the black law students' alliance in the
law school.

The university does not deny the extent of voluntary segregation
on campus—given that 92 per cent of white students and 53 per cent
of African-American students enrolled grow up in racially separate
communities, it says that the problem is partly inherited. Through
various in-house programmes, it also tries to engineer greater integration on campus.

"A lot has been made of this self-segregation argument, and it is
something we worry about," says Krislov. "If people are of a particular
religion or ethnicity, I don't think it's problematic that they self-
identify. But we want to create an environment where there are
enough minority students that the chances of meaningful interaction
between majority and minority students improve. We think we're doing pretty well at that, but we could do better."

Which begs the question: "How many is 'enough'?" The university's answer is that it cannot be defined by a number, but can be described by a single phrase—"critical mass." This lies at the heart of its
rationale for race-conscious admissions. For while a "colour-blind"
approach would make little difference to the odds for white applicants, it would have a huge effect on those of blacks, Hispanics and
Native Americans. "Because of the small pool size, if we had a system

where you just didn't count race at all, we would see a dramatic decline in racial minorities to about 4 per cent," says Peterson. This would leave the university with a "tokenistic" minority presence that would be incapable of making any impact. It was because the university decided that tokenism was not good enough that it decided to take race into account. So while it is false to claim that Gratz was rejected because she is white, it would be true to say that she probably would have been accepted if she were black.

Little wonder, then, that "critical mass" lies at the heart of the plaintiffs' contention. "We believe the socioeconomic stuff is just a show," says Curt Levey of the CIR. "What makes race different is that they're not trying to achieve a critical mass in anything else." The issue became a sticking point at the Supreme Court hearing as the conservative judge Justice Antonin Scalia attempted to portray critical mass as little more than a disguised quota.

"Is 2 per cent a critical mass?" he asked

"I don't think so, your honour," responded Maureen Mahoney on behalf of the university law school.

"OK, 4 per cent?"

"No, your honour."

"You have to pick some number, don't you? Like 8, is 8 per cent?"

"Now . . . your honour."

"Now does it stop being a quota because it's somewhere between eight and twelve, but it is a quota if it's ten? Once you use the term critical mass, you're in quota land."

On June 4, 1965, U.S. president Lyndon B. Johnson delivered the graduation speech at the historically black university of Howard, in Washington, D.C. "You do not wipe away the scars of centuries by saying: 'Now you are free to go where you want, do as you desire and choose the leaders you please,'" he said. "You do not take a person who for years has been hobbled by chains and liberate him, bring him up to the starting line of a race and then say, 'You are free to compete with all the others,' and still justly believe that you have been completely fair."

Given America's propensity to lecture the world on democracy, it is easy to forget just how recently the concept took hold there. Any African American over the age of thirty-nine was born without legal assurance of the right to vote; anyone over the age of forty-nine was born in a country where the separation of the races was legal. It is easy

to forget that the year Nelson Mandela was sentenced to life impris-
onment for opposing apartheid in South Africa, Martin Luther King
was awarded the Nobel Peace Prize for doing the selfsame thing in
America.

"No African came in freedom to the shores of the new world,"
wrote the nineteenth-century French intellectual Alexis de Tocqueville in his landmark book *Democracy in America.* "The Negro
transmits to his descendants at birth the external mark of his ig-
nominy. The law can abolish servitude, but only God can obliterate its
traces."

Anyone needing to jog her memory and find those traces need only
take a forty-minute drive from the leafy quadrangles of Ann Arbor
campus to the bombed-out concrete shell they call downtown Detroit.
Following the race riots of 1967, whites fled the city centre and took
their resources with them, leaving the city the second most segregated
metropolitan area in the country and one of the poorest. The Motor
City that built the cars and made the music that shaped America's
postwar culture and economy is going nowhere.

America was built on discrimination. From the theft of the land
from the Native Americans to the theft of labour during slavery;
from *Uncle Tom's Cabin* in the nineteenth century to the shacks that
house migrant Mexicans in the twenty-first. But it was also built on
an ideal, that "all men were created equal" and free in their "pursuit
of life, liberty and happiness." It is a principle that continues to attract millions of immigrants to the country and inspire the citizens
within it.

These two competing traditions are what make America what it is
today. Without the discrimination, it would not be so powerful,
wealthy or racially and ethnically balkanised. Without the ideal, it
would not be so dynamic, hopeful, confident and culturally vibrant.

It is from this tension—between the prejudice and the promise—
that affirmative action emerged. It is not a new thing. On January 16,
1865, in the dying days of the American Civil War, General Sherman
ordered that "respectable Negroes" be awarded forty acres and a mule.
In March of that year came the Freedmen's Bureau bill, establishing a
government department to supervise the relief and educational activities of freed slaves and refugees. As long as it has existed, it has been a
subject of considerable tension between the legislature, the judiciary

and popular political pressure. Assistance first granted was often later revoked as attempts to address the iniquities of the past came up against the entrenched and unenlightened self-interest rooted in the inequities of the present.

President John F. Kennedy first invoked the term "affirmative action" in Executive Order 10925, after he observed that too few blacks were employed by defence contractors. Four years later, President Johnson demanded that federal contractors take affirmative action to provide equal opportunity. The first president to attach goals and timetables and add women into the equation was none other than Richard Nixon in 1969.

From its inception, there have been those who have attempted to pluck affirmative action from its historical context and claim that it is unfair. But for all the attacks on it, the principle of affirmative action remains surprisingly popular. In a poll released last month by the non-partisan Pew Research Center, 63 per cent of Americans said they supported affirmative action programmes to overcome past discrimination, while 60 per cent thought programmes to increase black and minority students on college campuses were a good idea. A significantly lower percentage said such programmes were fair, but the fact that they supported them anyway suggests that they none the less believed them to be necessary.

Faced with such scepticism, opponents of affirmative action have shifted from portraying it as a programme to overpromote unqualified minorities to employing a more subtle rhetoric borrowed from the civil rights movement no less. White people, they insist, are now the victims of discrimination. The plaintiffs in the University of Michigan case say the admissions procedures are in violation of their rights under the Fourteenth Amendment—ratified in 1868 to ensure equal protection before the law with the original purpose of protecting the rights of freed slaves.

All else being equal, they would have a point. Regardless of the small numbers, the fact is that a handful of white students do not get into the University of Michigan because of something over which they have no control—the colour of their skin. The trouble is, all else is not equal and never has been. President Bush himself provides a salient example. He was admitted to one of the nation's premier universities, Yale, with a C average (where normally A grades are expected) solely

on the grounds that he was a legacy—his father went there. It was not
a racial preference. But it was an unearned advantage that robbed
someone else of a place.

According to the U.S. census, the median household income is
$46,305 for whites, $33,565 for Hispanics, $32,116 for Native Ameri-
cans and $29,470 for African Americans. The poverty rate is 7.7 per
cent for whites, 22.8 per cent for Hispanics, 23.6 per cent for blacks
and 24.5 per cent for Native Americans. A report by the U.S. Federal
Reserve earlier this year indicates that those gaps are widening.

To demand "fairness" in principle in a university admissions procedure, while denying the impact of the unfairness that exists in practice,
is simply not tenable. Universities discriminate between races because
America has discriminated against them. "The reason we need special
treatment is because we had special mistreatment," said Al Sharpton,
the Democratic presidential hopeful, on the steps of the Supreme
Court before the hearing. "It was against the law for us to go to
school. It was against the law for us to read and write. We're not asking the court for favors. We're asking the court to make right what it
made wrong."

It is no accident that this debate has most often been filtered
through issues relating to education. "Going to college is a very big
deal in this country," says Krislov. "It's viewed as the gateway to opportunity." The current dispute is no exception. The University of
Michigan's case is premised on the *Bakke* decision of 1978, when the
Supreme Court declared the admissions policy of the University of
California's medical school unconstitutional because it set aside a fixed
quota of places for minorities. A majority of the court nonetheless
maintained that race could be taken into consideration as one of many
factors in an admissions procedure, so long as the process is "narrowly
tailored" (not too crude) and there is a "compelling interest."

Since then, universities have been free to regard diversity as a
"compelling interest." The CIR's legal challenge fundamentally disputes this. Among the several attempts to whittle away at affirmative
action through the courts, this is by far the boldest to date. Both sides
agree that the points system and the law school procedures are sec-
ondary matters. The big prize will be what the court decides on
whether diversity can ever be a "compelling interest."

"*Bakke* has become part of the national landscape," says Krislov. "It says there are certain ways you can and cannot achieve diversity. [This case] is going to define those methods, at least for a generation or two. The *Bakke* decision was not welcomed by civil rights institutions. At best, they considered it a half-loaf, and now they want to take that half."

April 1 was a bad day to challenge affirmative action. As the U.S. troops made their most significant advance on Baghdad to date, an African American brigadier general, Vince Brooks, announced that a white woman, Jessica Lynch, had been rescued in Iraq by special forces.

Whatever its record abroad, at home the U.S. military is widely regarded as the most successful illustration of affirmative action there is. The U.S. army was integrated by the time of the Korean war, meaning that black and white Americans could carry guns together before they could eat burgers together or sit next to each other on the bus.

Several prominent retired military officials, including three joint chiefs of staff, two former defence secretaries and several four-star generals, submitted a brief supporting the university's entrance procedures. Best known among them was "Stormin' " Norman Schwarzkopf, who led the U.S. military during the Gulf War in 1991.

"In the 1960s and 1970s, while integration increased the percentage of African Americans in the enlisted ranks, the percentage of minority officers remained extremely low, and perceptions of discrimination were pervasive," argued the brief. "Today, there is no race-neutral alternative that will fulfill the military's and the nation's compelling need for a diverse officer corps of the highest quality to serve the country."

From the thousands of pages of amicus briefs before them, the judges focused on just thirty from the military. Before Solicitor General Theodore Olson had made his first point on behalf of the Bush administration, Justice John Paul Stevens interrupted him, demanding his opinion on the military leaders' brief. "I'm not sure," were Olson's first words, before Stevens cut him off again.

"The timing was remarkable," said Carter Phillips, a Washington-based attorney who wrote the brief. "The context of us being at war, in a multicultural environment, with a whole series of concerns about diversity. I don't think you can discount Norman Schwarzkopf." The CIR, meanwhile, is keen to play down their impact, but acknowledges that the military briefs played a role. "I don't think legally it was a problem," says Levey. "But from a PR view, it didn't help that we were in the middle of a war."

To an extent, the university had made its own luck. Its strategy had been to cohere a wide range of voices both within and without academia in support of its case. "We realized the only way to win on this was to unite higher ed and bring in mainstream America," said Lee Bollinger—former president of the University of Michigan and a defendant in the lawsuits, and now president of Columbia University—in the *New York Times*.

"We were very pleased by the support—it clearly made a difference," says Krislov, referring to the amicus briefs. "Support from other universities and civil rights groups you could expect, but the military and the corporations were our two most surprising allies. It said to the court, 'Everyone is telling us that diversity is important.'"

And so, in the biggest of big tents, the university had the alma maters of every Supreme Court judge and several Fortune 500 companies—including Microsoft, American Express, BP and Coca-Cola—behind it. The companies argued that racial and ethnic diversity in colleges and universities is vital to their ability to maintain a diverse workforce and to "continued success in the global marketplace."

Alongside the corporate and military coalition briefs filed inside the courtroom were the civil rights activists on the outside. More than sixty busloads of protesters came from Detroit alone. One placard read, "Affirmative Action: Hey, It got Bush Into Yale." Meanwhile, the Rev. Jesse Jackson was rousing black and Hispanic student protesters: "There are more blacks in prison than in college. Young America, fight back," he said.

The hearing lasted one hour and fifty-eight minutes, with Grutter versus the law school heard first, followed by Gratz and Hamacher against the undergraduate programme. There are nine judges on the Supreme Court, but for the purposes of those presenting, only one really mattered: Sandra Day O'Connor. Nominated by Ronald Reagan as the first female member of the court, O'Connor has proved a more moderate conservative than many at first anticipated. Moreover, she tends to take the court's few waverers with her. As she votes, usually, so votes the court. When the case started, all eyes were on O'Connor. It was she who started the questioning of the plaintiff's lawyer, Kirk Kolbo. "You have some precedents out there that you have to come to grips with," she said. "Because the court obviously has upheld the use of race in making selections or choices in certain contexts."

It was a line of questioning with which the university was more than happy, especially when O'Connor then challenged Kolbo on when he thought race might be considered: "You are speaking in absolutes and it isn't quite that. I think we have given recognition to the use of race in a variety of settings."

But she had some tough questions for the university, too. "In all programs which this court has upheld in [affirmative action], there's been a fixed time period within which it would operate. You could see an end to it. There is none in this, is there? How do we deal with that aspect?" she asked.

Reflecting on the question in his Ann Arbor office, Krislov says, "The simple answer is, we don't know. Things are improving, but we're not there yet. This whole issue starts with the fact that there's a history of segregation and discrimination in this country. If race ever ceases to be a salient factor in American life, then it will be less important as an educational goal. But if you look at what is happening in this country, then I don't think it's going to happen in my lifetime. I wouldn't hold my breath in my children's lifetime."

I Have a Dream

August 21, 2003

Like all great oratory, its brilliance was in its simplicity. Like all great political speeches, it understood its audience. And like all great performances, it owed as much to its delivery as its content. But what made this performance stand out was that it was both timely in its message and timeless in its appeal.

Forty years on, Martin Luther King's "I Have a Dream" is still a great speech. Still pertinent, even though many of its immediate demands have been met. Still relevant, beyond America's borders and the racial context that it addressed. So universal in its humanism that it spoke to Catholics in Northern Ireland during the sixties, black South Africans in the townships during the seventies and eighties and to the Roma in Eastern Europe today.

Yet, if President John F. Kennedy had had his way, it would never have been delivered. And if King had been left to his own devices it would probably never have been remembered.

It was June 22, 1963, when Kennedy met with the nation's civil rights leaders. Just one month before, segregationists in Birmingham, Alabama, had turned hoses and dogs on black teenagers. Only a few days later the president went to Germany where he slammed Soviet repression at the Berlin Wall, calling for freedom abroad that he could not secure for black people at home. The state of America's racial politics had reached the stage of domestic crisis and international embarrassment.

Plans for a march on Washington for jobs and freedom on August 28, organised by the black union leader A. Philip Randolph, were already under way. Kennedy was preparing a civil rights bill that would antagonise white southerners in his own party who were opposed to integration. "I may lose the next election because of this," he told them. "I don't care."

The truth is that he cared very deeply. He asked them to call the march off. "We want success in Congress," said Kennedy. "Not just a big show at the Capitol." Randolph refused. "The Negroes are already in the streets," he told Kennedy.

King, who deferred in age and experience to Randolph, did not speak until the end of the meeting. "It may seem ill-timed," he said. "Frankly, I have never engaged in a direct-action movement that did not seem ill-timed." The march went ahead. By the time Kennedy came back from Europe he had decided that he would try to co-opt what he could not cancel. He declared his support for the march, hailing it as a "peaceful assembly for the redress of grievances."

"Peaceful" was the operative word. The prospect of large numbers of black protesters descending on Washington, D.C., terrified the white political elite, even though the city itself was overwhelmingly black. *Life* magazine described the capital as suffering "its worst case of invasion jitters since the first battle of Bull Run." The Pentagon put nineteen thousand troops on standby in the suburbs; hospitals postponed elective surgery.

From the quarter of a million who turned up police recorded only four arrests—all white people. It was a balmy day—84 degrees, clear skies and a light breeze, and there were some familiar faces in the crowd. Sidney Poitier, Charlton Heston, Lena Horne and Sammy Davis Jr. were there. Marlon Brando carried an electric cattle prod in his hands to symbolise police brutality. King was the day's final speaker and everything in his speech from the cadence of his delivery to the lyrical repetition of its most vital refrains ("We have come," "I have a dream," "Let freedom ring") drew on the religious traditions of black American politics that merge the pulpit with the podium. It was a basic message made beautiful by his mastery of metaphor. Words to him were like stone to a skilled sculptor: raw material that he apparently effortlessly and deftly chiselled away to mould, shape and define something of aesthetic as well as practical value.

By most accounts it was not his greatest speech. Indeed, he had actually started to wind it up without its signature passage when the singer Mahalia Jackson, who stood nearby, encouraged him to go on. When he began to tell the crowd: "Go back to Mississippi, go back to Alabama," she urged him: "Tell them about your dream Martin. Tell them about the dream."

With encouragement from the audience King went on to draw upon a version of a speech he had made many times before (he had delivered it to insurance executives in Detroit only a week before), which centred on his dream of a society in which race was no longer a boundary to individual opportunity and collective strength.

But on the steps of the Lincoln Memorial, with the eyes and the ears of the world upon him, the substance of the words rose to the symbolism of the occasion. In a nation apprehensive about its global status in a decade that would see its attempts to assert its military and political hegemony rebuffed, the speech was a precision strike. Starting with Lincoln and ending with "a dream rooted in the American dream," it challenged segregation but left almost everything else that white Americans held dear intact.

Not surprisingly blacks and whites understood both the speech and the march differently. Eighteen days later, four black girls, changing into their choir robes after Sunday School class, were killed during the firebombing of a church in Birmingham, Alabama.

A *Newsweek* poll shortly afterwards showed that 3 per cent of African-Americans and 74 per cent of whites believed that "Negroes were moving too fast." Given the underlying conditions of racial inequality that prompted the march, it is also not surprising that many of those differences still exist.

For many white Americans the passage of civil rights legislation two years later drew a line under the civil rights era. Since there were now no legal barriers to black participation, some chose to ignore the economic, social and political barriers that remained. Not only would they resist demands to address the legacy of segregation and slavery through affirmative action, they would do so with King's own words, insisting that candidates for university and work be "judged not on the color of their skin but the content of their character."

But King had stated clearly that "1963 is not an end but a beginning." In an interview just a week before his death in 1968, he outlined the priorities that would make the dream a reality. "In the past in the civil rights movement, we have been dealing with segregation and all of its humiliation," he said. "I think it is absolutely necessary now to deal massively and militantly with the economic problem. The grave problem facing us is the problem of economic deprivation, with the syndrome of bad housing and poor education and improper health facilities all surrounding this basic problem."

His call for "sons of former slaves and sons of former slave owners sitting down together at the table of brotherhood," was sincere, but not the whole story. Integration had won African Americans the opportunity to eat in any restaurant. Only equality could ensure that they would be able to pay the bill.

Integration for them was not an end in itself but the means towards what has proved the far more elusive goal of equality. In King's words they "came to the nation's capital to cash a check . . . that will give [them] the riches of freedom and the security of justice."

They are still waiting for America to honour it.

Racism Rebooted

July 11, 2005
The Nation

For Buford Posey, a white man raised in Philadelphia, Mississippi, the Second World War had a civilizing influence. "When I was coming up in Mississippi I never knew it was against the law to kill a black man," he says. "I learned that when I went in the Army. I was seventeen years old. When they told me, I thought they were joking."

For several decades Posey's assumption about the relative value of black life was effectively borne out by the state's judiciary. Among others, the murders of fourteen-year-old Chicagoan Emmett Till, in Money in 1955; the state's NAACP chairman Medgar Evers, in Jackson in 1963; the three young civil rights workers—James Chaney (twenty-one), Andrew Goodman (twenty) and Michael Schwerner (twenty-four)—in Philadelphia in 1964; and civil rights supporter Vernon Dahmer, in Hattiesburg in 1966 all went unpunished.

But recently history has been catching up with the Magnolia State. Over the past decade state authorities have been picking up aging white men one by one and parading them down history's perp walk of shame, complete with orange jumpsuits and handcuffs.

Mississippi is by no means alone in this. Since 1989 twenty-three murders have been re-examined in the South, resulting in twenty-seven arrests, twenty-one convictions (now twenty-two), two acquittals and one mistrial, according to Mark Potok of the Intelligence Project, a branch of the Southern Poverty Law Center, based in

Montgomery, Alabama. But given that Mississippi was home to some of the most notorious race crimes during segregation, it stands to reason that it would be home to many of the most high-profile cases. In 1990, sixty-nine-year-old Byron de la Beckwith was indicted for the murder of Evers, who was shot dead on his doorstep; four years later Beckwith was convicted. In 1997, the case of Dahmer, who died when his house was firebombed by the Klan, was reopened. In 1998, the Klan's Imperial Wizard, Sam Bowers, was convicted of the murder. And earlier this year, Edgar Ray Killen was formally charged with the murders of Chaney, Goodman and Schwerner. His trial ended on June 21 with a jury verdict of manslaughter.

These developments should, of course, be welcomed. Beyond the importance of the prosecutions to the families of those who died and the communities in which the murders took place, they have a broader symbolic significance. They show that the struggle for justice, while long and arduous, can bear fruit in the most barren soil. They also show that these men, along with the scores of others who perished in the same cause, did not die in vain.

But while symbols are important, they should not be mistaken for substance. In June the Senate issued an apology for its failure to enact an anti-lynching law. Its chief GOP sponsor was Virginia senator George Allen, who referred to the legislative inaction as a "stain on the history of the United States Senate." Allen, who used to display a Confederate flag at his home and a noose in his law office, scored an F on the NAACP's report card in the last session of Congress. Both Mississippi senators, Thad Cochran and Trent Lott, refused to co-sponsor the resolution.

So while the crimes that occurred during segregation were rarely systematic—the individuals who carried them out and the manner in which they carried them out were far too crude for that—they were systemic. They were born from a system of segregation that worked to preserve white privilege in the face of a concerted progressive onslaught—a system in which the white community had to collude in order for it to function. While the scale and nature of those privileges may have changed, the privileges themselves still exist. You can see them in the racial disparities in health, employment and poverty; you can watch their physical incarnation in the segregated academies to which so many whites send their children; and you can observe them on death row, where so many black parents see their children being sent.

The work that Chaney, Goodman and Schwerner aimed to do—break the hold of white supremacy—has yet to be completed. Those who hope it never will be would like to use these trials to draw a line under the past and move on, shifting the burden of racist history from the institutional to the individual and travelling light, without the baggage of its legacy. So long as the likes of Killen and Beckwith are held up as the poster boys of that time and place, the mission to rebrand the South as the region that conquered not just racism but history will succeed—distorting our understanding both of what happened then and also what is happening now.

Schwerner's widow, Rita Schwerner Bender, hailed the verdict as "a day of great importance to all of us." But, she added, "Preacher Killen didn't act in a vacuum. The State of Mississippi was complicit in these crimes and all the crimes that occurred, and that has to be opened up."

This in no way diminishes the importance of insuring that those responsible for these crimes are brought to justice, argues Carolyn Goodman, the eighty-nine-year-old mother of Andrew. "[Killen] is a symbol. This is not just about one man. It's a symbol of what this country stands for. Whether it is a country of laws or something else, Bush or no Bush."

But the notion that these crimes had broad approval at almost every level of white Southern society does suggest that there is more to racism in the South than these murders and more to these murders than these trials. "The question is what do these symbols mean," says Charles Payne, the Sally Dalton Professor of History, African American Studies and Sociology at Duke University. The trials are convenient for those who wish to claim that racism was practised only by the poor and ended with segregation, says Payne. "Some people will say this is the face of racism. So racism becomes a historically congealed phenomenon. It is understood as just being the expression of hateful, poor white people who live in the South."

The details of what took place on June 21, 1964, have long been known. Some in Philadelphia believe Killen's actions that night have been, too. The three young men, who had joined the Mississippi Freedom Summer, a civil rights initiative to register black voters in the state, went missing after they had gone to investigate the burning of a black church nearby. That afternoon Deputy Sheriff Cecil Price stopped their car near Philadelphia and took them in, ostensibly on a speeding violation. Price, who has since died, used the time while the activists were in custody to alert local Klan members. When they were released later that night the posse of Klansmen, said to have been organized by Killen, followed them, murdered them and buried them in a nearby earthen dam.

That night, says Posey, who had gotten to know Schwerner and publicly supported the activists, he got a phone call: "They said, 'We took care of three of your friends tonight. You're next,' and hung up. Well, I thought it was Edgar Ray Killen, but you can't see over a telephone." He left town shortly afterward. "Hell, the Klan was boasting about it," he recalls. "If you didn't know who committed the murders, you were either blind or hard of hearing."

In 1967, eighteen men were prosecuted in federal court on conspiracy charges relating to the case; seven were convicted but none served longer than six years. Among those who walked free without a day behind bars was Killen, the beneficiary of a hung jury, thanks to one juror who could not bring herself to convict a preacher.

Since most of this was known or suspected at the time of the murders, there has been no particular legal breakthrough that prompted investigators to revisit the case. "It wasn't like there was any one thing that happened that said, 'Here's the magic bullet,'" Neshoba County district attorney Mark Duncan told the *Arkansas Democrat-Gazette* in January, shortly after Killen was arrested. "It really was that we had gotten to the end. There was nothing left to do." Family members and civil rights activists were prompted to step up the pressure after Dahmer's murderer, Bowers, said in an interview with a state archivist in 1999 that "the main instigator" of the Philadelphia killings had walked free from the courtroom. Those familiar with the case say that at least seven others who were involved in the murders are still alive but not standing trial.

Philadelphia is a small town of seventy-three hundred that is just over half white, just under half black and the rest Choctaw Indian. It sits ninety-eight miles northeast of Jackson and sixty northwest of Meridian, but is actually on the road to nowhere. Ronald Reagan chose the town for his first major campaign speech in the 1980 presidential campaign—appealing to racist Confederate nostalgia with a call for states' rights. Philadelphia's grim racial history put it on the map. But the faded shop fronts and low income levels (one in four families lives in poverty) suggest its grim economic present could just as soon wipe it off again.

Discussing the situation in the days before the trial began, a few people, like Barney Shephard, spoke up for Killen and said that the Mississippi Freedom Summer was a federally backed incursion masterminded by President John F. Kennedy. "The guy has been a good neighbor to me," he said of Killen. "He's eighty years old. And now to bring this up, after forty years, is beyond me." Few were as candid or as conspiratorial as Shephard. The rest of the town seemed to have settled on the notion that justice should be done. But they differed, crucially, on what justice actually means and what it could achieve. And like much else in the town, from where you live to where you worship, these differences fall almost exclusively along racial lines.

Over at Peggy's, a soul food restaurant cum living room just off the town's main square, you sit where you can, serve yourself when you're ready and leave your money in a basket on your way out. Here the trial had gone from being a decades-long taboo to a frequent subject of debate. "For twenty or thirty years nobody really talked about it, and then boom," said Anne, twenty-four, a white waitress at Peggy's. "Now everybody talks about it." Anne grew up in Union, just fifteen miles away, but says she knew nothing about the murders until eight or nine months ago, when she saw the film *Mississippi Burning*, which is loosely based on the failed investigation into the murders. "It just about tore my heart out. If he did it, he deserves to be punished, that's only right . . . But I don't think they should have brought it back up. It is going to cause more problems in town. A lot has changed since then. You didn't see blacks and whites mingle then. You do now. This is a new generation. This could cause more problems."

Hope Jones, a twenty-five-year-old African American teacher at the local school, is part of the same generation but could not disagree more. "We just want to see justice done," she said. "If he's innocent, fine, but we want whoever did it. This could turn ugly . . . It could be a racial thing, but it's not. White people should want justice done also."

Along with the few local whites like Posey who have long campaigned for prosecutions in the case, several others have come around in recent years. Sitting under a huge picture of Ronald and

Nancy Reagan's visit to the Neshoba County Fair in the 1980s, Jim
Prince, editor of the *Neshoba Democrat*, explained that he used to be
against reopening the case but gradually came to see that the town
could not move on without some resolution. Philadelphia would
benefit, he said, because the trial would be the "outcome of doing the
right thing. There would be some vindication, some redemption,
some soul-cleansing. It will be the atonement, really, for this old sin.
We have only got the legal system to go by. That's all we've got."
And if there cannot be redemption, then Prince hopes there can at
least be remuneration. "It's a captivating story," he says. "The dark
of night, the Ku Klux Klan, you know, it's got all the elements for
great drama, but it's a true story and it's a sad story . . . I tell people if
they can't be behind the call for justice because it's the right thing to
do—and that's first and foremost—then they need to do it 'cause it's
good for business."

For some in town, making money may be the first and only reason.
At the Philadelphia Chamber of Commerce you can find a glossy
pamphlet titled "Neshoba County, African-American Heritage Driving Tour: Roots of Struggle, Rewards of Sacrifice." Inside you are
invited to join "a journey toward freedom," complete with a map detailing where the three young men were murdered and buried. Such
civil rights tourism would be a difficult sell as long as the perpetrators
were still on the streets and everybody knew who they were. So
Killen's trial was part of the town's business plan—a bid to capitalize
on its ugly past in order to make money, at least in part, by showing
how it has improved.

The desire of many Southerners for a makeover is understandable,
as is their irritation at the North's continued attempts to caricature
them. The smug and superior manner in which the rest of the country
has embalmed the region in the 1960s, so as to better patronize it, has
echoes of Europeans on an anti-American binge. Like the Europeans,
Northerners have a point—but without sufficient humility and self-
awareness of their own shortcomings, that point can soon implode under the weight of its own arrogance. According to a census report
from 2002, the top five residentially segregated metropolitan areas in
the United States are Milwaukee, Detroit, Cleveland, St. Louis and
Newark. According to the Kaiser Family Foundation, you will find
higher rates of black poverty in Wisconsin, Illinois and West Virginia

than in Mississippi. And of the senators who refused to co-sponsor the anti-lynch-law apology, more than half were not from the South.

Mississippi shares the South's desire for change, and indeed has changed considerably. Two huge casinos run by Choctaw Indians are now among the largest employers in the Philadelphia area. You can see black and white youngsters interacting casually at school, and a few black people have moved into white areas. But these changes have come about not because most white Southerners wanted them to but because many black people and a handful of whites forced them to. "I'm happy to see everybody joining forces to make sure that we get this done now," says Eva Tisdale, fifty-five, a native Mississippian who came to Philadelphia to participate in the Freedom Summer and stayed. Tisdale believes it is the business case, not the moral case, that has won over many of the whites who now back resolution of the legal case. "We organized marches and we marched and there were no white people marching—not from Philadelphia. So I know the reason we came together is not the same reason for all of us."

For if a lot has changed in Mississippi, an awful lot has also stayed the same. In a state where African Americans constitute 36 per cent of the population, they make up about 75 per cent of prisoners. In a state that is already poor, black people are poorer still: according to the latest census, Mississippi has the fifth-lowest median income in the United States; the per capita income of black Mississippians is 51 per cent that of their white counterparts. If there are tougher places to be black than Mississippi it is because those places are so bad, not because Mississippi is so good. The problem is not that some whites are trying to rebrand the South but that they are now peddling false goods. "There's a kind of civic religion in asserting that the past is the past and we should put all these problems behind us," says Payne. "Some people are using the progress that has been made to wipe out any sense of the past, as though they have conquered the past. The extent to which these convictions can get people to think critically about how privilege is shaped is the extent to which they strike me as being real and useful." Some would rather not acknowledge that racial privilege exists at all. "Race is not an issue now for younger people," says Prince. "Today, if you're willing to work hard and be honest, then you're able to succeed. There is equal opportunity in Philadelphia."

If Prince is right, then the poverty, low levels of educational achievement, unemployment and high prison rates among blacks not just in Philadelphia but elsewhere in the state and the country can be explained only by black people's genetic inability or inherent unwillingness to seize those opportunities. And so it is that even as these trials seek to cure one symptom, the racist infection mutates into an even more hardy strain. Killen may end up behind bars, but the logic and the system that produced him and made him infamous still remains free.

Only Helicopters Disturb the Chilling Calm

September 5, 2005

As their provisions ran low and the flood water outside their apartment building remained stubbornly still and stagnant, Ron Bell and Linda Smith saw the helicopters flying overhead all week but wondered if anyone would ever come to get them.

"They could see us and we could see them but they kept going for other people who I reckon were more desperate," Ms. Smith said.

So she and Mr. Bell sat over several feet of putrid foamy water and hoped for the best.

"The local convenience store had been looted so we could go in there and get quite a lot of canned goods and water. We knew we would live for a certain amount of time. But we also knew that we would run out eventually if nobody came."

Finally, six days after Hurricane Katrina turned their world upside down, a boat carrying the National Guard arrived to rescue them and their next door neighbours, Carl Boot and Arlise Pickham.

"We had a radio so we had an idea of what was going on. We were just hoping someone would come and find us. We had maybe a day's more food left and then we were going to have to figure something else out."

Yesterday they were sitting outside the New Orleans convention centre. By the end of last week the venue had become a flashpoint for rage and discontent as thousands of angry people, desperate for help, gathered in hope of being evacuated. As a reminder of their frustration a handwritten sign still sits outside, stating "Bush come over here in hell. This is the shelter in hell."

Yesterday afternoon there were fewer than a hundred people outside the centre, as buses and planes ferried refugees out of the city.

Meanwhile, a steady trickle of residents who had been hunkered down for almost a week started to emerge, looking for a way out of the devastated city. On Saturday the Federal Emergency Management Agency rescued 580 people from flooded homes.

The buzz of helicopters over the deserted urban wasteland lent the city a chilling calm. Stray dogs yapped at the feet of National Guardsmen and a man played his guitar to an audience of one on Canal Street.

But while the streets were mainly empty, the city is anything but. More survivors are expected to surface as word spreads that the shelters have been cleared, the looting halted and the city is under control as the National Guard step up their search and rescue operation.

But the anger remains. "People had to go out to the streets to loot just so we could have food to eat," said Melamio Farin, outside the convention centre. "Why has it all been done so badly? It's all political. The rich get richer and the poor get poorer."

Over at the Superdome, Naem Hassan and his wife sat with their trolley full of their belongings—two elderly people surrounded by several guardsmen. They had been waiting for four hours. Even though the roof had been blown off their house and the city had imploded into mayhem, for the whole of last week they had followed a routine. Each morning they would come out and make their way to the shelters.

"We kept coming to the places they said we should come to every morning but we could never get out," said Mr. Hassan.

Every night they would sleep in their roofless house in fear of looters. On Saturday they ran out of food. And yesterday, when they arrived at the Superdome they were the only ones there.

The Hassans want to head for Atlanta where their children live. But few if any evacuees have any idea where they will end up.

"Where am I going?" Mr. Farin said. "I'm going wherever . . . I've got relatives in San Diego but who knows."

Mr. Bell added: "I don't know where they'll take us. But it's got to be better than here so I don't care."

But others vowed to return. "We hope to come back when it's straightened out," said Roy Wilson as he wandered down Canal Street. "My family live in Mississippi so I guess we'll go there for now."

Back at the Superdome, Mr. Hassan chatted playfully with the National Guardsman. "Don't pat it," he said to the soldier as he idly tapped his pump-action shotgun. "It ain't going nowhere."

But the Hassans are. Shortly afterwards a guardsman told them to get ready. "Take what you can carry," he said, pointing to the trolley with all their worldly possessions. "Everything else just leave."

Left to Sink or Swim

September 5, 2005

"Stuff happens," said the U.S. defence secretary, Donald Rumsfeld, when called to respond to the looting taking place in Baghdad after the American invasion. "But in terms of what's going on in that country, it is a fundamental misunderstanding to see those images over and over and over again of some boy walking out with a vase and say, 'Oh, my goodness, you didn't have a plan' . . . It's untidy, and freedom's untidy, and free people are free to make mistakes and commit crimes and do bad things. They're also free to live their lives and do wonderful things, and that's what's going to happen here."

The official response to the looting in New Orleans last week was, however, quite different. The images were not of "newly liberated Iraqis" making away with precious artefacts, but desperate African Americans in a devastated urban area, most of whom are making off with nappies, bottled water and food.

So these are not scenes of freedom at work but anarchy to be suppressed. "These troops are battle-tested. They have M-16s and are locked and loaded," said the Democratic governor of Louisiana, Kathleen Blanco. "These troops know how to shoot and kill, and I expect they will."

Events on the Gulf Coast following Hurricane Katrina have been a metaphor for race in the United States. The predominantly black population of New Orleans, along with a sizeable number of poor whites, was left to sink or swim. The bulging banks of the Mississippi momentarily washed away the racial divisions that appeared so permanent, not in a common cause but a common condition—poverty.

Under-resourced and without support, those who remained afloat had to hustle to survive. The ad-hoc means they created to defend and govern themselves under such extreme adversity were, inevitably, dysfunctional. Their plight was not understood as part of a broader societal crisis but misunderstood as a problem apart from that crisis. Eviscerated from context, they could then be branded as a lawless, amoral and indigent bunch of people who can't get it together because they are in the grip of pathology.

Katrina did not create this racist image of African Americans—it has simply laid bare its ahistorical bigotry, and in so doing exposed the lie of equal opportunity in the U.S. A basic understanding of human nature suggests everyone in New Orleans wanted to survive and escape. A basic understanding of American economics and history shows that, despite all the rhetoric, wealth—not hard work or personal sacrifice—is the most decisive factor in who succeeds.

In that sense, Katrina has been a disaster for the poor for the same reason that President Bush's Social Security proposals and economic policies have been. It was the result of small government—an inadequate, privatised response to a massive public problem—the very reason why African Americans reject such an agenda so comprehensively at every election.

"No one would have checked on a lot of the black people in these parishes while the sun shined," Mayor Milton Tutwiler of Winstonville, Mississippi, told the *New York Times*. "So am I surprised that no one has come to help us now? No."

The fact that the vast majority of those who remained in town were black was not an accident. Katrina did not go out of its way to affect black people. It destroyed almost everything in its path. But the poor were disproportionately affected because they were least able to escape its path and to endure its wrath. They are more likely to have bad housing and less likely to have cars. Many had to work until the last moment and few have the money to pay for a hotel out of town.

Nature does not discriminate, but people do. For reasons that are particularly resonant in the South, where this year African Americans celebrated the fortieth anniversary of legislation protecting their right to vote, black people are disproportionately represented among the poor. Two-thirds of New Orleans is African American, a quarter of whom live in poverty.

In the Lower Ninth Ward area, which was inundated by the flood-waters, more than 98 per cent of the residents are black and more than a third live in poverty. In other words, their race and their class are so closely intertwined that to try to understand either separately is tanta-mount to misunderstanding both entirely.

"Negro poverty is not white poverty," explained President Lyndon Johnson in a speech to Howard University in 1965. "Many of its causes and many of its cures are the same. But there are differences—deep, corrosive, obstinate differences, radiating painful roots into the community and into the family and the nature of the individual. These differences are not racial differences. They are solely and sim-ply the consequence of ancient brutality, past injustice and present prejudice. They are anguishing to observe. For the Negro they are a constant reminder of oppression."

Daily scenes of thousands of African Americans being told to be patient even as they died; their children wailing as they stood stranded and dehydrated on highways; their old perishing as they festered in filthy homes full of feces; their dead left to rot in the street—it was a reminder too many for some.

By Friday night, rapper Kanye West had finally had enough. On a live NBC television special to raise funds for the victims, he lashed out. "I've tried to turn away from the TV because it's too hard to watch," he said. "Bush doesn't care about black people. It's been five days [waiting for help] because most of the people are black. America is set up to help the poor, the black people, the less well-off, as slow as possible."

While West's comments expressed a blatant truth for all with eyes to see, to some they were more outrageous than watching thousands of people dying live on television from neglect in the wealthiest country in the world. NBC made it clear he had stepped off the reservation. "Kanye West departed from the scripted comments that were pre-pared for him, and his opinions in no way represent the views of the networks. It would be most unfortunate if the efforts of the artists who participated tonight and the generosity of millions of Americans who are helping those in need are overshadowed by one person's opinion."

The fact that this person's opinion, shared by so many, explains why those in need need so much help is, it seems, irrelevant. Perhaps NBC executives should have read that black radical magazine *Time* last week, where West graces the cover. The title? "Why You Can't Ignore Kanye: More GQ than Gangsta, Kanye West Is Challenging the Way Rap Thinks About Race and Class."

Good Old Boys, Bad Old Days

October 31, 2005

Murphy and Johnny sit on a bench at the bus stop where Rosa Parks started her now famous journey and shoot the breeze over a carton of Popeye's fried chicken. Murphy is white; Johnny is black. Both are in their sixties. "Back in the day we couldn't have sat here like this or we would have gotten ourselves killed," says Johnny. "He'd have his bench and I'd have mine."

Reminiscing about the bad old days, Murphy recalls the segregated cinemas. "You had to sit on the balcony and we had to sit downstairs," he reminds Johnny. "I always wanted to sit in the balcony because I thought you could see better. But I didn't want to bring trouble on my folks, so I never tried it."

From the portable photo albums that are their wallets, Murphy flips open a picture of his black wife and Johnny flashes a shot of his mixed-race grandson. Murphy is not in touch with his parents any more. "We stopped talking when I got engaged," he says. "I didn't know my mama was a closet redneck. I said, 'What about all the black people you knew when Dad was in the army?' She said: 'Son, we just did what we had to do.' I felt like I'd been living a lie."

As Rosa Parks came back to lie in honour in her home town on Saturday, following her death aged ninety-two last Monday, thousands turned out to view her body and acknowledge her contribution to the racial transformation of the nation.

Her coffin was due to be flown to Washington last night, where she will be the first woman to lie in honour at the Capitol Rotunda—a tribute usually reserved for presidents, soldiers and prominent politicians. George Bush was expected to pay his respects. Then she will be flown to Detroit, where she spent the latter part of her life, for burial on Wednesday.

In the cradle of the Confederacy, a weekend of church services and other commemorations evoked not just the woman and her actions but the times that made them necessary.

Ivery Giles, now eighty, was on the bus with Ms. Parks that day on December 1, 1955, when the forty-two-year-old seamstress refused to give up her seat to a white man. She had finished her shift making salads at Greens store. "I was tired and just wanted to sit down without moving so I went straight to the back." Ms. Parks got on shortly afterwards and made history. "The bus driver got a little angry but I wasn't worried," she says after seeing Ms. Parks for the last time at St. Paul African Methodist Episcopal church. "I can't say I ever thought Rosa Parks would do that, but you never know what people will do when they're moved."

Lloyd Howard was a fourteen-year-old shoe-shine boy working round the corner. "It was a tense time. Word went around the next day that she'd been arrested and that there would be some kind of action. But there was no saying what white people might do back then and they ruled by fear."

The subsequent boycott of the city buses lasted almost thirteen months. Davis Jordan, sixty-eight, used to drive the ninety miles from Birmingham most days to help ferry people. "I was eighteen, so to me it was fun," he says. "The police used to stop us all the time. But when I got here I used to have all these pretty girls in my car. I didn't know if we were going to win but I was hoping."

Sitting outside Ms. Parks's old apartment, Floyd McCary, sixty-eight, remembers bowing to threats from his boss on the day Martin Luther King led a protest in town. "My bossman said, 'You can go out and march behind those niggers if you want to, but you won't have a job to come back to.' "

A short drive down Rosa Parks Avenue, where Ms. Parks lived when she made her stand, is all it takes to see that racial inequality and segregation are still endemic. Forty per cent of African Americans in

Alabama live below the poverty line—three times more than whites. The city is 48 per cent white, but at least 90 per cent of those who went to see Ms. Parks's body were black. However, Montgomery has a black police chief and some believe will soon have a black mayor.

"Progress has been made," says state representative Alvin Holmes. "But we're still fighting for equality. Racism and segregation is no longer de jure, but it is still de facto. Whites still don't want to live near blacks. The schools are resegregating because housing is still segregated. The fight's not over." The Reverend Al Dixon says: "It's the same game with a different name. We now know that you can be free and broke. We can check into any hotel we want. But we can't pay the bill."

Ms. Parks ended her life penniless in Detroit, with a church helping her pay her rent until her landlord stopped charging her. Those who spoke at the Dexter Avenue Baptist Church on Friday spoke of her resolve and humility. Self-effacing and politically committed into her old age, she was on the receiving committee to meet Nelson Mandela in 1990 in Detroit. She expressed embarrassment that she had come, repeating: "He won't know me." When Mr. Mandela glimpsed her he chanted, "Ro-sa Parks, Ro-sa Parks, Ro-sa Parks" and then the two aged activists fell into each other's arms and rocked backwards and forwards.

Part III

POLITICS

Challenging the Big Buck

April 16, 2001

As George Bush plays chicken with the Chinese and fast and loose with the environment, it is time for the left to play truth or consequence with Ralph Nader. The Green Party presidential candidate stood against the two main parties, arguing that there was no difference between them and that America needed an alternative. America ended up with what looks like being the most rightwing president since before the war.

Bush didn't win the election; he won a court case. But, with the slenderest of endorsements, he promises to inflict severe damage. In Congress, many Republicans are beginning to think he is beyond the pale. Even Uncle Sam's faithful poodle, the British government, is yapping at his heels. Some in the cabinet are calling on Tony Blair to put the special relationship "into deep freeze." John Prescott flies to New York today to try to persuade Bush to change his mind about scrapping the Kyoto agreement on controlling greenhouse gases.

So first, some truth. There is a difference between Bush and his Democratic challenger, Al Gore. For Nader to have claimed otherwise during his campaign was disingenuous and opportunistic. We do not know what Gore would have done by this stage had he won, but we can be quite sure it would not have been this.

His first decision as president would not have been to deny aid to non-governmental organisations that support abortion overseas through surgery, counselling or lobbying. Nor would Gore have put forward a budget planning to eliminate $309 million in grants to help public housing authorities get rid of drug dealers or a programme to preserve wetlands so that he could give trillions to the wealthy. And least of all would he have turned his back on the Kyoto Accord.

Now, for a consequence. If Nader had not stood, then Gore would be president. This is as close to a political fact as a statistic dares to be. True, polls showed that one-third of those who voted for Nader would otherwise not have voted at all. But it is also true that more than half of Nader's supporters would have voted for Gore, delivering him majorities in both Florida and New Hampshire and winning him the electoral college.

For the left not to acknowledge this is spineless. If it wants to be taken seriously it must first take itself seriously. Nader stood to make a difference and he succeeded. In politics, as in life, a sign of maturity is accepting responsibility for your actions.

Moreover, only once those points have been conceded is it possible to mount a credible defence of Nader's candidacy. Because Nader not only had a right to stand but was right to stand. The problem with George Bush is not that he is a vicious rightwing ideologue—the man can barely tie his shoelaces—it is that he is the paid representative of corporate America.

It is no good challenging Bush without challenging the system that produced him—a system in which big money, not ideas, selects the candidates and then backs both sides to make sure it picks the winner. Since Gore and the Democrats were not only complicit in that system but abused it to their own ends while in office, they were incapable of taking on that task even if they had wanted to. It took an outsider. Nader alone provided a meaningful choice in what is rapidly becoming a multimillion-dollar, corporate-sponsored charade masquerading as democracy.

Nader was right not because there was no difference between the two main parties but because there was insufficient difference. The Democrats' pitch to potential Nader supporters was: "At least we're not Republicans." The 2.7 million people who voted for Nader felt they wanted more from democracy than that.

Democrats love to blame Nader for Bush. Their logic is sloppy. Democrats deny a myriad of other far more compelling or equally tenuous factors that put Bush in the White House. They ignore the fact that, after two terms in office, they could not win Clinton's or Gore's home states. They deny that the situation was so close in Florida that any candidate who stood, including the Natural Law Party, could reasonably claim to have made the decisive difference.

One could as well blame Theresa LePore, the election supervisor who botched the ballot papers, or Katherine Harris, the Republican secretary of state in Florida who obstructed the recounts. In such a tight race, Nader was *a* factor, not *the* factor. Under such circumstances, to fixate on him as the principal reason for Gore's defeat is perverse.

The charge also reveals astonishing political arrogance. It suggests that the Democrats have a right to the left vote regardless of what they say and do. Clinton can withdraw welfare benefits from the poor, promote a free-trade agreement (NAFTA) that sells jobs to the lowest wages and weakest unions in the continent, broker global trade deals that hammer the poor or starve Iraqi children and still expect liberals to turn out for his successor.

Democrats scream betrayal without realising that before there is betrayal there must first be friendship and trust. They demand loyalty, but show none in return. Having spent a decade distancing themselves from the left, they express shock that the left might choose to respect that distance and go it alone.

Nonetheless, the question of whether a principled stand against big money is best served by the practical outcome of a Bush presidency remains pertinent. The answer may change as his term progresses. For the time being, on balance, it was. For evidence look no further than Kyoto. Bush's decision to renege on the treaty is a vicious attack on the environment. But Clinton's record was not much better. He signed up to Kyoto, but he did not honour it. The United States, by far the world's largest polluter, promised to cut carbon-dioxide emissions by 7 per cent from 1990 levels by 2012. Instead, emissions rose by more than 10 per cent on 1990 levels by 2000.

It was thanks to Clinton's administration that last year's climate talks in the Hague collapsed. The problem was not only that he could not get the legislation through a Republican Congress, it was that he dared not take on the might of the oil and gas companies. They gave Republican candidates $10 million last year; but they gave Democrats, including Gore, $4 million. Bush may be in hock to them, but Clinton was in awe of them.

But much also depends on what Nader does now. The corporate domination of American politics cannot be undermined once every four years at election time or on television-panel discussions and the lecture circuit. The truth is that it will take not just a party but a movement, joining together the disparate voices of labour unions, tree huggers and pressure groups that made themselves heard at Seattle, to make complete sense of his candidacy. Having made a difference at the polls, he must now make a difference in civil society. Only then will it be clear that the consequence of Nader's candidacy was not to derail the Democrats but to restore democracy.

Left Over?

February 11, 2003

You can tell a lot about what is on a nation's mind from what is on its bookshelves. And in America that makes for sobering news. The top five non-fiction titles on the *New York Times* bestsellers list at the end of last month were: 1) *Bush at War*; 2) *The Right Man* (Bush's former speechwriter relives his first year in the White House); 3) *Portrait of a Killer* (Patricia Cornwell on Jack the Ripper); 4) *The Savage Nation* (a rightwing radio talk show host saves America from "the liberal assault on our borders, language and culture"); and 5) *Leadership*, by former Republican New York mayor, Rudolph Giuliani.

Michael Moore's *Stupid White Men* makes a brave and impressive showing at number seven, but otherwise the literary profile seems to mirror the country's political course. With Republicans in control of the White House and both houses of Congress, America appears to be in a belligerent, rightwing mood. And while most of the world might complain about the Bush administration or, at most, seek to contain its excesses, only Americans can get rid of it.

Which raises the question: whatever happened to the left in America? What became of the political culture that stopped the Vietnam War, brought about civil rights and very nearly made Jesse Jackson the Democratic presidential candidate? Where are the popular, progressive forces that could challenge the Bush administration from within? Ask leftwingers this—people who have devoted their life to progressive causes—and most of them will laugh. "The left is not a word you mention in polite company here," said one. "We talk about the right, but we never talk about the left."

The difference is more than linguistic. While the left in Europe does not represent a fixed point—Roy Hattersley, for example, finds himself on the left now, but he didn't fifteen years ago—it is more or less a known quantity. The assortment of social democrats, greens, trade unionists, communists and Trotskyists share a tradition and broad aims, even if they often spend more time arguing with each other than the right.

"The concept 'American left' is subject to quite a range of interpretations," says Noam Chomsky. "Take the solidarity movements in the eighties, which broke new ground in the history of European imperialism, when thousands of Americans not only protested but went to live with the victims of the U.S. terrorist wars, both to help and to offer some protection against the terrorist forces run from Washington. Was that 'left'? The roots were mostly Main Street, Iowa.

"Today I spoke to a group of union organisers and leaders. Are they 'left'? They certainly are open to a far-reaching critique of state capitalist institutions, though I suppose a lot of them are 'Reagan Democrats.' It's a complicated country."

Just how different America can be was evident from the placards at the most recent anti-war demonstration. Compared with similar British marches, it was more religious—"God Loves People Against the War," "Peace Is Jewish"—and more patriotic—"Love My Country, Hate My Government," "Peace Is the American Way." It was also far less union-oriented—there were very few banners from trade unions—and without any discernible input from mainstream politics.

"Democrats are subject to the same thing Republicans are—big money," says Katha Pollitt, a columnist for the *Nation*. "What we think of as the left is really a collection of single or dual issues that network with each other but there really isn't a home for them. There are people doing good work in their community but they're not really hooking into the electoral process."

There are the students against sweatshops, the environmentalists, feminists, anti-racists, union organisers and pacifists: the collection of groups that have found themselves incredibly effective beyond their own field on the few occasions when they have been able to work together, as in Seattle a few years ago.

But whatever you want to call it, and wherever its home is, contrary to popular belief on both sides of the Atlantic, the American left does exist. True, there were few people flocking to the banner calling on people to "Break with Democrats [and] Build a Workers' Party to Fight for Socialist Revolution" at the anti-war demonstration in Washington earlier in January. But there were several thousand others marching with placards saying everything from "Drop Bush not Bombs" to "Regime Change Starts at Home."

On their own they would have reflected little more than a sizeable but, nonetheless, unrepresentative and discontented rump. Dominant among the march organisers, although not the demonstrators themselves, were members of Workers World, a Marxist group which, among other things, has expressed support for Slobodan Milosevic and the regimes in Iraq and North Korea. The Not In Our Name statement condemning war has attracted thousands of signatures, including those of Susan Sarandon, Gloria Steinem, Gore Vidal, Alice Walker and Kurt Vonnegut. But key figures within it are members of the Revolutionary Communist party. The *New York Daily News* mocked them as "a coalition of superannuated Maoists, anarchists, Saddamites, Starbucks-resisters and anti-imperialists."

But all the evidence suggests that while the left may be small and elements of its leadership may be extreme, its general message is beginning to resonate well beyond its own borders. "The left is never popular as such, but the issues it raises can be popular," argues activist and historian Howard Zinn. This has been most striking in recent times on attitudes towards the war. "What was really encouraging about these last demonstrations wasn't just their size but who was on them," says Pollitt. "They came from a very broad section of the country. There were lots of homemade signs and people from as far away as Fargo, North Dakota."

All the polls suggest a steady increase in opposition to war if the United States acts without U.N. approval, and support for giving the weapons inspectors more time. A Republican business group recently paid for a full-page advertisement in the *Wall Street Journal*, warning Bush: "The world wants Saddam Hussein disarmed. But you must find a better way to do it." Seventy-two city councils, including Philadelphia, Austin, Chicago, Baltimore and Cleveland have passed anti-war resolutions. And while comparisons with Vietnam remain valid, they must also be contextualised. "Some of us were in the street about the Vietnam war in 1961," says Grace Paley, one of the founders of the Greenwich Village Peace Center in 1961. "But there were no big demonstrations for four years. This is moving much faster, but so is Bush."

Chomsky agrees. "Today, in dramatic contrast to the sixties, there is large-scale, committed and principled popular protest all over the U.S. before the war has been officially launched," he says. "That reflects a steady increase over these years in unwillingness to tolerate aggression and atrocities."

And while this has been most striking over issues relating to the war, it is being seen in other issues, too. Membership of the country's best known civil liberties advocates, the American Civil Liberties Union, has surged 20 per cent since September 11. Membership of the environmentalist group, the Sierra Club, has risen by 16 per cent since 2000, primarily in response to the threat Bush poses to the environment, a spokesman suggested. Bush's approval ratings are coming down to where they were when he first took over. "On nearly all the key issues—health care, education, Social Security—the Democrats still have an advantage," says Carroll Doherty, the editorial director of the non-partisan polling institute, the Pew Research Center. "In a completely ambiguous way, the left represents American values right now," says Jennifer Baumgardner, a writer and activist.

Anecdotal evidence suggests this is more than just wishful thinking. In Peoria, Illinois, long a signifier for the mood of Middle America in much the same way as the man on the Clapham omnibus was in England, the local newspaper's website has run more letters that are sceptical about the war than in favour of it. "We all know that Saddam is scum and causes much suffering. He's less of a danger right now than is the United States. Define terrorism," writes Paul Snodgrass in one of them. Following a lecture tour to promote his book last summer, Michael Moore said he felt he was addressing mainstream America. "I look out at the auditorium or gymnasium and I don't see the tree-huggers and the granola-heads. I see Mr. and Mrs. Middle America who voted for George W. Bush, who just lost $60,000 because their

401(k) [private retirement plan] is gone," he said. "They believed in the American Dream as it was designed by the Bushes and Wall Street, and they woke up to realise that it was just that, a dream."

On Flatbush and Seventh Avenue in Brooklyn on a cold week night, Jay holds up his handmade poster, declaring: "Bush Is Lying." There are around ten people at this anti-war vigil, carrying billboards and posters. Cars occasionally hoot in support. Jay says he has had no abuse. "If you're doing an article about the left in America, you'd better hurry up before we're all gone," he jokes. But across town, at the city technology college, around two hundred activists have gathered on the same night to protest against plans to close token booths in subway stations and put up fares by fifty cents. If anything, the focus for many Americans at this time of international turmoil is more local than ever. Individual states, which have to run balanced budgets, are facing the most severe fiscal crisis since the war and are either hiking taxes, cutting services or increasing prices, and often a mixture of all three.

And while people are angry, the Democrats have not emerged as a natural beneficiary of their frustration. Despite war doubts and rising unemployment, Bush remains popular. More than half approve of his work in the past few weeks, 76 per cent regard him as a strong and decisive leader, and 83 per cent believe he is ready to make hard decisions. "People who disapprove of him on the economy still admire him personally," explains Doherty. And if support for the war is soft, then opposition to it is no less so. Slightly more than half (52 per cent) say they would still support U.S. military action, even if the weapons inspectors do not find evidence that Iraq has chemical, biological or nuclear weapons.

This mood, of course, has a lot to do with September 11 which, much more than in Britain, made an already hostile political landscape virtually uninhabitable for the left. When Susan Sontag suggested that "cowardly" was not an appropriate word to describe the perpetrators of the World Trade Center attack, there were calls for her to be stripped of her citizenship. On September 12, Alan Madison of the Sierra Club sent a memo to its local organisations asking them to hold off on demonstrations and advertising. "In those days you had to resonate with the population. You had to communicate in a way that would be in keeping with the times. No one was thinking about environmental issues at that time," he said.

"There was this sense that a lot of things can't be said that should be said. It was terrible," says Pollitt. "Flag-waving became the secular religion. Even *Dissent* magazine was asking whether there is any such thing as 'a decent left.' Patriotism is always available to attack the left about."

Complaints that the media was, at worst, openly partisan in favour of Bush and, at best, cowed into withholding criticism against his administration—and therefore refused to cover demonstrations and other leftwing activities—are too widespread just to be dismissed as the sour grapes of conspiracy theorists. One of the nation's most respected television anchormen, Dan Rather, said that the patriotic fervour that swept the country after September 11 prevented the media asking difficult questions. "It is an obscene comparison . . . but you know there was a time in South Africa that people would put flaming tyres around people's necks if they dissented," said Rather. "And in some ways the fear is that you will be necklaced here, you will have a flaming tyre of lack of patriotism put around your neck."

But as time goes on it becomes increasingly untenable to pin the left's relative weaknesses on September 11. Not because it does not remain a factor, but because for any political force to remain relevant it must adapt to the situations it finds itself in any given time. "The terrorism agenda does affect things," says Doherty. "But increasingly it is not dominating the overall agenda."

In any case, the left's problems did not start on September 11. Half a century after McCarthyism, it is still struggling to gain a foothold in mainstream political culture. "It wasn't that big on September 10," says Pollitt, who believes a shift to the left in America would demand a fundamental shift in the way American politics operates. "Moving to the left would demand more than what politics is about in this country, which is putting campaign ads on television."

Bush's victory in November 2000 had left many demoralised, says Zinn. "Certainly, a lethargy had set in . . . a hollowing out of enthusiasm and accusations that [Ralph] Nader was responsible for the election of Bush," he says. Rows over the extent Green candidate Nader's decision to stand in such a close race handed victory to Bush will, it seems, continue to obsess the left long after the hanging chads of Florida are forgotten.

On a cold night in Times Square, the Missile Dick Chicks—a political satire on the chart-topping, all-American Dixie Chicks, who sang the national anthem at the Super Bowl last month—are well into their routine. Three women, each with a red, white and blue wig and model missiles strapped to their waists like vibrators, are singing, to the tune of the Supreme's "Stop in the Name of Love": "Shop, in the name of war / You need a whole lot more / Don't think it over." A mostly bewildered audience includes a sprinkling of appreciative voices for their innovative protest. Behind them, a neon ticker tape quotes Powell saying the U.S. will work with the U.N. if it can and act with "a coalition of the willing" if it has to, and that the Dow has fallen again.

While the left has managed to slow down the right, it is a long way from being in a position where it can set the agenda.

"The Democratic party has no foreign policy," commentator George Packer wrote in the latest edition of the leftwing magazine *Mother Jones*. "It hasn't since Vietnam. Their failure to stand up to the Bush juggernaut is more symptom than cause. They can't stand up because they have nowhere to stand, no alternate vision of what purpose America's enormous power in the world should serve."

Earlier this month it emerged that Democrats were so desperate to popularise their message that they formed a group, Democracy Radio Inc., overseen by a former Democratic Congressional staffer, Tom Athens, to go on the lookout for liberal populists to take on the rightwing shockjocks and Fox News Channel presenters who dominate the airwaves.

"We're going to go out and identify talent and help them to create programming and actually connect them with local stations," Athens said. "We want to plant a thousand seeds and see how many flowers actually arise."

Few held out much hope. "Most liberal talk shows are so, you know, milquetoast, who would want to listen to them?" said Harry Thomason, the Hollywood producer who is close to Bill Clinton. "Conservatives are all fire and brimstone."

The large number of Democrats who have declared themselves for the presidency suggests that Bush remains vulnerable. But few inspire great enthusiasm, either because they have no chance or because it is felt they will make little difference.

It is a testament to the left's strength that from the bleakest of sce-
narios they have created a space within which they are not just exist-
ing, but expanding. It is a sign of their weakness that they are
expanding from such a small base that they are able to influence public opinion but not lead it. "There is an opening, but it's going to need
some ideas to take advantage of it," says Doherty. "That's the big piece
of the puzzle."

Born in the Eye of the FBI

June 7, 2003

On the evening of June 19, 1953, Robert Meeropol was sent out to play while his parents were being executed. He was six years old, and while he had only a vague idea of what was happening, he knew that whatever was going on did not bode well for his future. "We were watching a ball game at a friend's house when this newsflash crawled across the bottom of the screen," says Meeropol, "but I didn't know what it said." His brother Michael, however, who was ten, knew only too well what it meant and what was about to happen: "That's it, good-bye, goodbye," he said.

With the whole drama unfolding on the cusp of his infant consciousness, Robert's experience was more impressionistic. "I didn't know what was going on, but I must have sensed the essence of Michael's reaction," says Meeropol, now fifty-six, who was adopted by Abel and Anne Meeropol, friends of his parents, after the execution. "The only way to get away from it was to be sent outside to play ball. It was never difficult to get me to go outside and play ball, or to get adults to distract me, because I wanted to be distracted. I wanted to get away from whatever was causing the trouble. When it got too dark, they called us in. They sent me to bed and I went to sleep. I wanted to avoid the situation."

What was baffling for a young child was all too clear for much of the adult world. Robert's parents, Ethel and Julius Rosenberg, were sentenced to death after they were found guilty of conspiring to pass secrets on the atomic bomb to the Soviet Union. They were communists in postwar America—a time and a place where such a political affiliation could lose you your liberty, livelihood and, in the Rosenbergs' case, your life.

By the early 1950s, Senator Joseph McCarthy's crusade was in full swing. Communism, he argued, represented "a great conspiracy, on a scale so immense and an infamy so black as to dwarf any previous venture in the history of men." In 1950, the McCarran Act—also known as the Internal Security Act—was passed, forcing communist organisations to register with the federal government. Meanwhile, some of America's most prominent writers and performers, including Arthur Miller, Orson Welles, Langston Hughes, Lillian Hellman and Dashiell Hammett (not to mention hundreds of others), were called before the House Un-American Activities Committee. Those who appeared were ordered to explain and often renounce their views, and to name other communists or risk being blacklisted.

Fifty years on, the Rosenbergs' trial and execution remains the most potent emblem of this gruesome period in U.S. history. Jean-Paul Sartre described the execution as "a legal lynching that has covered a whole nation in blood." "When two innocents are sentenced to death, it is the whole world's business," he added.

And the world duly made the Rosenbergs their business. Before their execution, American embassies across the globe were flooded with petitions and letters; one protester was killed in the crush at a "Liberez les Rosenbergs" rally in the Place de la Concorde, Paris. The liberal consensus at the time was that they were both completely innocent. Investigations and revelations since the end of the cold war have revealed that Julius Rosenberg probably did pass secrets to the Soviet Union, although nothing remotely as serious as those relating to the atomic bomb. Meanwhile, Ethel was almost certainly innocent— sentenced to death on the accusation that she typed the spying notes, but in truth because she refused to testify against her husband.

Her brother, David Greenglass, whose testimony played a major role in sending her to the chair, has since admitted that he lied. He said that he gave false testimony because he feared that his own wife might be charged, and that he was encouraged by the prosecution to lie. "I don't know who typed it, frankly, and to this day I can't remember that the typing took place," said Greenglass, who was sentenced to fifteen years and released from prison in 1960 for his part in the so-called "spy ring."

If the Rosenbergs' deaths were symbolic of America's political intolerance, the fate of Robert Meeropol, and that of his older brother, illustrated the precariousness of the lives of children whose parents were members of the Communist Party. Most were too politically immature to grasp fully either the stance or the risks their parents were taking as a result of their political convictions. But most, even at Meeropol's tender age, were emotionally aware enough to comprehend that the fabric that bound together their families was under constant threat. And in an era where everything their parents touched turned to red, they, too, found themselves the objects of state scrutiny and political vilification.

"Ethel and Julius were at the very centre of my terror," said the late Miriam Zahler, whose mother was a Communist Party member and shop steward in Michigan. "What I knew was that they were innocent, they were facing death and they had two children. I wondered who was taking care of Michael and Robby." When Zahler asked her mother why the Rosenbergs were imprisoned, she told her daughter it was for passing out leaflets. "I concluded that if the Rosenbergs were in jail because they passed out leaflets, my mother, who also passed out leaflets, might be arrested, too."

Ros Baxandall's father had worked for the communist international movement, the Comintern, at its headquarters in Vienna between 1932 and 1936. She was thirteen when the Rosenbergs were executed, and took the day off school to protest against the execution in New York's Union Square. "Obviously, I didn't think they should be executed, but I thought they were guilty because my parents would have done the same thing. They really did think the Soviet Union was wonderful."

They called them "red diaper babies": children raised in the American Communist Party.

The term red diaper baby was originally an insult, aimed at the Communist Party's internal aristocracy, which ensured that those with parents in the party would find themselves promoted rapidly through the party ranks during the 1920s. But during the mid-1960s, the phrase was reclaimed after the rightwing John Birch Society published the names of red diaper babies at the Berkeley campus. It was supposed to stigmatise them, but ended up having the opposite effect. "The effort at intimidation backfired," wrote Judy Kaplan and Linn Shapiro in their book, *Red Diapers: Growing Up in the Communist Left.* "Students found each other through the list, which helped their organising efforts immeasurably."

Although not all red diaper babies would grow up to be as radical as their parents, most have found that their particular experience as children during that peculiar time in politics has left them with a shared heritage. "Every story is complicated by the fact that it is both a story about a left culture and completely personal," says Linda Gordon, sixty-three, whose father was a trade unionist and party member. "While we all do have that common experience, everything is filtered through individual personalities."

Gordon says that the experience made her "a fearful person"; Baxandall says that it gave her "an ambivalent attitude toward fear." Like Meeropol, both Gordon and Baxandall's parents were Jewish; Gordon grew up observing most Jewish rituals, while Baxandall's parents were hostile to religion. Whatever their differences, Gordon, now a history professor at New York University, concludes, "No matter what your politics or personality, I think all red diaper babies have in common this notion that people have the power to make things happen and people have a responsibility to make things happen." She and Baxandall were both active in the women's movement. They first met at a Black Panther demonstration in Connecticut.

Nina Hartley, the daughter and granddaughter of communists, and one of America's best known porn stars, describes herself as a "third-generation feminist" and a secular Jew. While her parents, it's said, eventually became Zen Buddhist priests, she has been a vocal advocate of the empowering force of sex and an avowed leftist. "I'm proud of my heritage's intellectual history and its empathy with the persecuted," she has said. "Politically, I'm leftwing. I want everyone to have a job, everyone to have food, clothing, shelter and education. Utopia might be communist but in the meantime we have to have socialism."

Another red diaper baby, Carl Bernstein—the *Washington Post* reporter who along with Bob Woodward broke the Watergate scandal—rebelled against his father's atheism as a child. He describes in his memoir how he insisted on being bar mitzvahed. "You don't want me to be Jewish," he recalls telling his parents. "This has to do with your politics. And it's not right. And you don't really believe in freedom. It's communism . . ." When eventually he got his way, the FBI were across the street taking down car licence numbers during the bar mitzvah ceremony. Subsequently, the family hastily left their home near Washington, D.C., for a week, while subpoenas were being handed out for a hearing of the House Committee on Un-American Activities to investigate the Rosenberg Defence Committee.

Paradoxically, some of the red diaper babies went through much of their lives unaware precisely what their parents' political allegiance actually was. Ros Baxandall, chair of American Studies at the State University of New York, didn't find out that her father was in the party until he was on his death bed. "During our adolescence, no one mentioned the word 'communism,'" she says. "We didn't realise until the 1960s that our dad had been in the party. Our mother still denies knowing that her husband was a red."

Gordon says she cannot remember being told, but seemed to have always known, from right back when her grandfather would argue politics with her father in Yiddish. This was partly a sign of the times. Their parents may have been communists, but they nonetheless lived in an era when children were supposed to be seen and not heard, let alone talked to. "They had so many problems of their own they didn't know what to do," says Baxandall. "They were of a different generation, which generally didn't believe in being straight with kids."

This combination of being politically subversive and domestically conventional could have devastating effects on children. Gordon remembers a time when a woman she had never seen before turned up at her house. "This woman appeared in my bedroom. I didn't really register who she was at first, but I gradually realised that the police were after her, and that really underlay my anxiety about the police coming to get my parents, and then, one day, she was gone. That had a terrible effect on me."

Their parents' politics also had some specific influences on how they were raised. "They were very weird about certain things," recalls Baxandall. "The only time I was really hit was when I told on my sister and my father called me a stool pigeon and a rat. So they had these overreactions to things that others didn't."

But their parents' failure to inform them of what they were doing also revealed a culture of fear that had engulfed the party at that time. Panicked by McCarthyism, the Communist Party leadership believed America was on the verge of fascism during the early 1950s and ordered many of its members into hiding. Soon, around a third of its active membership was underground or abroad. "Party offices were closed down, mass work cut back and membership consciously allowed to drop off," recalls Harry Haywood in his book, *Black Bolshevik*. When he went to ask what he could do to help the party, he was told, "Aw, just go out and lose yourself."

This cautiousness would remain with their parents for most of their lives. "I never heard Anne say, 'When we were in the party,' " says Meeropol, who now runs the Rosenberg Fund for Children, a charity that assists children of progressive activists. "But as Abel got older, he did—and when he did he always dropped his voice to a whisper." Anne and Abel (who wrote the words of "Strange Fruit," the song made famous by Billie Holiday) left the party around the time they adopted Robert and Michael. Robert believes they did so because the courts might have frowned upon communists adopting the boys.

In such an atmosphere, to tell your children that you were an active member of the party was to make both yourself and them vulnerable. What they did not know, they could neither divulge inadvertently nor have beaten out of them by the police. "My parents wouldn't explain things," says Gordon. "Partly they just didn't, and partly they thought they were protecting me by not explaining."

The FBI kept red diaper babies, as well as their parents, under close surveillance, often stalking them when they knew their parents would not be around. "My parents said to ignore them and not to talk to them," says Baxandall. "But I used to throw Tampax at them when they would be there sitting outside our house."

When the FBI finally released some of its files under the Freedom of Information Act, many red diaper babies would find reports going back into their childhood. "Mine goes way back to a letter I wrote to the school newspaper about some lynching in the South," says Baxandall. "I had no recollection that I wrote this letter, but it was in my file. They spent a lot of time documenting things that were very easy to document. I had a very old Volkswagen car that I sold. They had a record of this. They would document the movies I went to. But, later on, I swam in front of the nuclear submarines in a protest and they didn't have anything like that in my file. Nothing meaningful or political." Parents were not necessarily as keen as their children to see what the state had on them. "I wanted him [her father] to send for his file and he wouldn't," says Gordon. "I don't want to go into that," he told her.

Making sense of this world—in which your family was constantly threatened although you did not know precisely why, or by whom—made for a disorienting childhood. "I knew they were different," says Baxandall. "I knew they read different publications. They had African American friends, there were always people staying at our house who were hiding. I was given children's books that no one else was given. But they had so many secrets. Once, I must have been about six, I said to my parents, 'How come all your friends are in jail or divorced?' My dad said: 'We're proud of those in jail.'"

Only in retrospect did it become apparent to her that others realised they were different, too. "It turns out that my friends knew my parents were very left," says Baxandall. "[My father] would quarrel with every textbook I ever had. I'd bring these things up about the French Revolution and my teacher would say, 'Let's have your father come, rather than you quoting your father.' I remember a friend of mine saying, 'Don't your parents ever talk about money?' Even though I tried to fit in, I was still more political than most people. In my high school yearbook, it says I would most likely marry 'Eric the Red.'" The overall effect on many red diaper babies was to leave them feeling embattled and alien from America as a whole.

"A dark cloud of generalized anxiety hovered at the edge of my consciousness," writes Meeropol of his childhood in his recent book, *An Execution in the Family*. "A sense that something about my family was terribly wrong and that my circumstances might get even worse. Most of the time, when I ignored or forgot about the upheavals of my life, I felt reasonably safe. But 'we' (whoever that was) were under attack from whatever was out there and I wanted to keep a low profile, beneath the notice of my enemies."

While the "enemies" presented themselves clearly enough, identifying quite who the "we" constituted was more subtle—particularly with so little help from their parents. "One way of identifying people was through the music," says Meeropol. "If people were into folk music, like, say, Pete Seeger, that might be a sign they were on the left. I would ask kids on the street what paper their parents read. There was a tendency for communist children not to be interested in consumption quite as much and not to wear such fancy clothes."

So, if their parents' membership in the Communist Party left them with one foot outside the broader American society, it gave them one foot in another smaller but tighter knit leftwing culture. This was particularly true of New York, where 40 per cent of the party members lived at one time. "There were some neighbourhoods in New York where the Communist Party was quite strong enough that there were many kids, and it was not by any means always deviant," says Gordon.

Baxandall recalls, "Every weekend we'd go to visit people and we'd have these brunches. My parents and their friends would talk and the children would all go off, and I knew these children were much more like me. They came from similar situations. There was such a feeling of community that took away that sense of alienation. I mourn that loss, rather than any vision my parents might have had."

For Meeropol, attending leftwing summer camps was the only time he felt truly comfortable. "Then you were all of a sudden in a majority. That played a very important role, because we could talk about all of this stuff and we could be friends with them and we didn't have to keep secrets—or at least as many secrets. I could see what it would be like to be functional in that community, rather than always be outside of the community."

But, for most of the time, when they were not in this secluded environment, the sense of political isolation could have serious psychological effects. These were most pronounced with Meeropol, who not only lost his parents but was also anxious to preserve some sense of anonymity after he changed his name to Meeropol. For much of his childhood and youth, he feared being outed and having to relive his parents' ordeal. "I passed throughout high school, disguised as a mild-mannered liberal," he said, referring to the way in which some very light-skinned African-Americans would "pass" for white during the segregation era and beyond. "That's exactly what I did. When I went to the law firm, I passed. When I wanted to do an urban anthropology project and joined a business organisation and cut my hair, I passed. I seemed to have this fascination for passing."

But passing took a toll on his personal life, and his inability to open up almost prematurely ended his relationship with Elli, while he was at university; she would later become his wife. "There was this core of who I was that I couldn't talk to anybody about, so I wanted to keep things on a superficial level, because if they started going in a direction that was more intimate and more personal, they might get somewhere I couldn't go. It wasn't conscious. I just couldn't go there."

While Meeropol's experience was acute, it was by no means unique. "Lots of people in the women's movement were red diaper babies, but we never said anything to each other about it," says Baxandall. "We didn't know that we had that in common until later. There's a terrific self-censorship."

The American Communist Party emerged from a split in the American Socialist Party shortly after the Russian Revolution in 1919, and dutifully tied its programme and policies to those of the Soviet Union. Its membership, like much of the American working class at the time, was drawn from those who were born abroad. While it was never very large, for a brief moment during the Great Depression of the 1930s the party was fairly influential.

"At a time of widespread hopelessness and despair, the party's cadres were doing something," writes Ellen Schrecker, a historian of the McCarthy era. "They mobilized unemployed workers and marched them to local city halls to demand relief. They organized neighborhood groups to prevent homelessness by carrying the furniture of evicted tenants back into their apartments . . . They saved nine black teenagers, from Scottsboro, Alabama, from execution on trumped-up charges. Communists, it seemed, were everywhere . . . or at least in most of the big struggles of the early 1930s."

Between 1936 and 1938, the party doubled its membership, to just over eighty thousand, while the Sunday edition of its newspaper, *Daily Worker*, had a circulation of one hundred thousand. The party and its members would feature in great works of American literature such as Ralph Ellison's *Invisible Man* and *Native Son* by Richard Wright, who was a member. "As long as we did not make too much noise about it," said Earl Browder, the party's leader during the 1930s, "we became almost respectable. Never quite respectable. Almost."

But as war broke out in Europe, the party's numbers started to dwindle. The Soviet Union's ambivalent attitude towards Nazism—first

opposing it, then accommodating it, finally doing battle with it—
forced zigzags on the party line that lost supporters worldwide. With
the end of the war, America's political class defined the Soviet Union
and all of those who supported it as its principal enemy and started the
witch-hunts that would later make the McCarthyite era so notorious.
When Soviet premier Khrushchev denounced Stalin's crimes in 1956,
the American party became a rump.

Those raised in the party during the postwar period would reach
adulthood in an entirely different political era. With Vietnam, black
power, feminism and the rise of identity politics, the agenda of the
"New Left" held far more relevance to many red diaper babies than
the rigid ideology that defined their parents' radicalism. Few of them
sought to join the party. "As a teenager, I certainly would have described myself as a communist, but I would never have thought of
joining the party," says Meeropol. "It never really crossed my mind.
Then, by the time I got to college, I had the feeling that there was
something stuffy about it. The party was a conservative element on
the left."

This caused some political tension between the generations. Baxandall recalls that her father was not impressed by the campaigning
methods adopted by the New Left. "My father was so upset about the
gulags, but he thought the New Left was wrong. He didn't like the ag-
itprop. He didn't go on marches. He thought I was too critical of the
Soviet Union."

For all the differences between them and their parents, one thing
they did inherit was a honed awareness of the fragility of U.S.
democracy—an insight that informs their impressions of recent developments in the nation's political culture following September 11.
"America is on a political course that is alarmingly similar to the Mc-
Carthy period," says Meeropol. "The prime motivating factor for the
average American, according to what the media and the polls tell us, is
fear. In the McCarthy period, we reacted to fear by believing that our
way of life was going to be destroyed by the international communist
conspiracy that was going to get us. Today, the entire Bush administration policy is founded on fear.

"If you were to go to the USA Patriot Act, [an act approved by
Congress and President Bush in October 2001, "enhancing" domestic
security and surveillance procedures] and plug in the word communist

where the word 'terrorist' appears, you would have an act that looks very much like the McCarran Act." What's changed, says, Meeropol, is that whereas McCarthyism victimised people for what they believed, the current repression places them under scrutiny simply for who they are. "We can't point to an organised political entity that can be attacked in the same way that the Communist party could be attacked so we just round up people who are South Asian or Middle Eastern. The difference is that instead of attacking activists, people are being attacked because of their status. So a lot of people being detained today just happen to be the wrong religion or the wrong colour or the wrong nationality."

Baxandall believes that, while the threats to civil rights are analogous, the political landscape is different in ways that are both more and less promising. "We had a name for it back then. We called it McCarthyism. We had an analysis of it and a much more political voice. Now there's no organisation and no political voice, and that's a big problem. But back then, our numbers were so puny; now, it's not as left, but it's more mass. A lot of people feel that there's something wrong all over the United States. It's just that, so far, it hasn't come together."

If it does come together and the administration continues on its present path (two big, but not unlikely, ifs), Meeropol believes that history could well be on course to repeat itself: "This administration has put in place the mechanism to create a whole new generation of red diaper babies."

Gay Is the New Black

June 16, 2003

"The difference between being black and being gay," said one gay activist, "is that you don't have to come down at breakfast one morning and break it to your parents: 'Mom, Dad, I'm black.'" In American politics at present it also means that if you're black, you are less likely to be the subject of overt abuse from Republicans. And if you are, then you can at least usually expect them to be punished for it.

The same can not be said for lesbians and gay men. Six months after senator Trent Lott was forced to resign after suggesting that America would have been a better place if a segregationist had won the presidency in the forties, his colleagues appear free to spout homophobia at will and whim.

Most recent was the decision by the U.S. Justice Department—where Attorney General John Ashcroft holds prayer meetings every morning—to ban its employees from holding a lesbian and gay pride event (this is gay pride month). Such was the furore that by the end of last week the decision had been partly reversed—the event can go ahead but this time without government funding. More shocking was Pennsylvania senator Rick Santorum—number three in the nation's upper chamber—who in April ranked homosexuality alongside polygamy, incest, adultery and bestiality.

After some initial dithering, to gauge the public mood, Lott was dumped. After similar prevarication, Santorum was defended. "[He] took a very courageous and moral position based upon principles and his world view," said Tom DeLay, the house majority leader.

Republican strategist, Rich Galen, summed up the contradiction thus: "In America in 2003, you can't say bad things about African Americans, but you can still say bad things about gays. That's where we are."

That is is not quite true. Racism in America's public discourse is certainly more subtle than homophobia, but no less pervasive. Whenever politicians refer to welfare, crime, inner-city deprivation, teenage pregnancy or affirmative action—which is often—they are talking about race, and rarely in terms supportive of minorities.

While racism has been employed to galvanise the white Republican base in past elections—most notably by president George Bush's father in 1988 and Newt Gingrich in 1994—homophobia may yet become the rallying cry for the next one. When it comes to finding a signifier for the indulgent excesses of liberal Democrats and the Republicans' no-nonsense adherence to the values of middle America, gay is the new black.

"Candidate Bush said in the second [presidential] debate that he felt marriage was a sacred covenant, limited to a man and a woman," said Kenneth Connor, president of the rightwing Family Research Council. "That was not a huge issue in 2000. Mark it down. It will be a big, big issue in 2004."

This is not President Bush's wish. He would rather the whole issue just went away. Since he came to office he has appointed an openly gay ambassador and AIDS tsar. But all his judicial appointments so far have been hostile to gay rights, and his refusal to reprimand Santorum indicates that he is all too willing to tolerate intolerance in his ranks.

For Bush this is not a matter of moral principle but political calculation. He has made enough of an impact on restricting abortion rights to keep the faithful happy and provide a lightning rod for Democrats and women's groups. He does not need any more enemies. As the standard-bearer of compassionate conservatism he has no wish to be seen as isolating a relatively small group for special opprobrium—unless of course they are Arab immigrants, in which case he can hide behind national security. The order to allow the Justice Department's gay pride event to go ahead after all is widely believed to have come from the White House.

Moreover, the ramifications of scapegoating lesbians and gays would go way beyond the actual gay voters—who according to the gay advocacy group, the Human Rights Campaign, make up just 5 per cent of the electorate. A Republican Party that is mean to a few is widely regarded as having the potential to be mean to the many. The issue of sexual orientation may not be as explosive a touchstone as race, but a homophobic campaign would attract few new voters and repel many—particularly among moderates, women and the young. The issue of gay marriage is incredibly divisive. Polls show that while most Americans (51 per cent) are against it, more than a third—a large proportion of whom are women—support it.

The response to last weekend's lingering televised kiss between Marc Shaiman and Scott Wittman, two gay winners of the Tony awards, also suggests political culture is lagging way behind popular culture. "I love this man," said Shaiman. "We're not allowed to get married in this world. . . . But I'd like to declare, in front of all these people, I love you and I'd like to live with you the rest of my life." The audience cheered. Of the 8 million viewers there were just ten phone calls and sixty-eight emails containing negative feedback.

Despite this, some of Bush's most fervent and active supporters are still keen to bring the issue to the fore. Conservative Christians, who used to exert pressure from outside, now form an influential base within the party. Today they exercise either "strong" or "moderate" influence in forty-four Republican state committees, compared with thirty-one in 1994, according to a study in the Washington magazine *Campaigns and Elections.* The man who used to run the Christian Co-alition, Ralph Reed, is now the head of the Georgia Republican Party.

The conservative right have been increasingly irritated with what they regard as Bush's ambivalent attitude towards gay rights. After Marc Racicot, the Republican national chairman, met with the HRC, Connor asked whether he was fit to run Bush's campaign, claiming he was "out of touch with Bush's most loyal and committed voters."

Whether the evangelical right can deliver on their threats is an-other matter. As fundamentalists, compromise does not come easily to conservative Christians—particularly on social issues. But with Bush enjoying more than 90 per cent approval ratings among Republicans, the president could call their bluff. He knows they won't vote Demo-crat, though he fears they might stay at home.

And even if Bush could persuade his own side to bury the subject, the courts could resurrect it. A Supreme Court ruling on a law in Texas which criminalises sexual practices between same-sex couples that are lawful when performed by heterosexuals is expected any day now. The Massachusetts supreme court should rule on the legality of same-sex marriages by mid-July.

The most that conservatives can hope from either judgment is a confirmation of the status quo. More likely, however, is that one or both will extend the rights of lesbians and gay men, sending the Christian right into a frenzy and demanding that Bush make a stand. Under pressure from his own side he would be forced to show us where the conservatism ends and compassion really starts.

God Help America

August 25, 2003

Montgomery, Alabama, is no stranger to stand-offs. The gold star embedded into the marble at the front of the state capitol marks the spot where Jefferson Davis stamped his foot and declared an independent Confederacy and where former governor George Wallace promised "segregation now, segregation tomorrow, segregation forever." From that very point you can make out the bus stop where Rosa Parks took her seat and the church where Martin Luther King made his stand, launching the bus boycott that sparked a decade of civil rights protest.

Stand on the star today and you can witness the city's latest confrontation as the Alabama supreme court house plays host to prayer circles and television trucks in a showdown between the state's most senior judge and the country's highest court.

This particular dispute is cast in stone. Two-and-a-half tonnes of granite, displaying the Ten Commandments, which was placed in the rotunda of the courthouse two years ago by Alabama's chief justice, Roy Moore. The U.S. Supreme Court told him to remove the monument, which violates the separation of church and state. Moore refused, saying that Christianity forms the bedrock of the American constitution and his conscience.

Since the deadline passed at midnight on Wednesday, Christian activists have descended on the town from all over the country, keeping a twenty-four-hour watch to make sure the monument is not moved and establishing phone trees to rally the faithful if it is. Many have T-shirts with slogans every bit as intolerant as the South's reputation. "Homosexuality Is a Sin, Islam Is a Lie, Abortion Is Murder," says one. (It is difficult to imagine how many more people you could offend on one piece of summerwear.)

They appear as dotty as they do devout and determined. "What you're watching is that the socialist, communist elements are attempting to push out God from the public domain," Gene Chapman, a minister from Dallas, told the *Montgomery Advertiser*. Those subversive elements include the national rightwing Christian Coalition and the seven Southern, Republican judges.

On Thursday afternoon, Moore vowed his undying opposition to the removal of the commandments; by Friday he had been suspended and his lawyers announced he was prepared to relent. Yesterday, the monument was still there and the crowds of believers kept coming, determined to martyr themselves before a lost cause.

It would be easy to deride the defenders of the monument or to dismiss the whole charade as the latest illustration of the scale of degradation in America's political culture. However, Britons would do well to remove the mote in their own eye before resorting to ridicule. The only reason America can have these disputes is that it has a constitution that separates church and state (which we don't).

For, while the spectacle is certainly ridiculous, its symbolism is significant. The United States is at one and the same time one of the most fiercely secular and aggressively religious countries in the western world. The nation's two most sacred texts are the Constitution and the Bible. And when those who interpret them disagree, the consequent confusion resonates way beyond Montgomery.

This is a country where eleven states, including Alabama, refuse to give government money to students who major in theology because it would violate the constitution, and where nativity plays are not allowed in primary schools. It is also a country where, a Harris poll showed, 94 per cent of adults believe in God, 86 per cent believe in miracles, 89 per cent believe in heaven, and 73 per cent believe in the devil and hell.

These two competing tendencies produce some striking contradictions. The Supreme Court and both houses of Congress all invoke God's blessing before they start work. But a circuit court has decreed that children should not use the words "under God" when they pledge allegiance to the flag at the start of school.

So while there is a constitutional, albeit contested, barrier between church and state, there is almost no distinction between church and politics. Indeed, when it comes to elections, religion is the primary galvanising force and the church the central mobilising vehicle.

This is one of the few truths that transcends both race and class. White evangelicals and black Protestants are the two groups most likely to say that their religion shapes their votes at least occasionally, according to a survey by the non-partisan Pew Research Center. Since these two constituencies form the cornerstone of both major parties, it would be impossible for either to win an election without them and inconceivable that they could do so without the support of the church.

But the influence of religion goes beyond domestic politics or social issues such as abortion and gay rights to crucial areas of foreign policy. Another Pew poll revealed that 48 per cent of Americans think the U.S. has had special protection from God for most of its history. Moreover, 44 per cent believe that God gave the land that is now Israel to the Jewish people, while 36 per cent think that "the state of Israel is a fulfilment of the biblical prophecy about the second coming of Jesus."

At this point America's internal contradictions become an issue on the world stage: the nation that poses as the guardian of global secularity is itself dominated by strong fundamentalist instincts. There are two problems with this. The first is that, as became clear in Montgomery last week, there is no arguing with faith. Fundamentalists deal with absolutes. Their eternal certainties make them formidable campaigners and awful negotiators—it is difficult to cut a bargain with divine truth. The second is that America's religiosity is not something it shares with even its few western allies, let alone the many countries that oppose its current path. Yet another poll shows that among countries where people believe religion to be very important, America's views are closer to Pakistan's and Nigeria's than to France's or Germany's.

These differences go all the way to the top and explain much of the reason why the tone, style, language and content of America's foreign policy has been so out of kilter with the rest of the developed world, particularly since September 11. For these fundamentalist tendencies in U.S. diplomacy have rarely been stronger in the White House than they are today. Since George Bush gave up Jack Daniels for Jesus Christ, he has counted Jesus as his favourite philosopher. The first thing he reads in the morning is not a briefing paper but a book of mini-sermons. When it came to casting the morality play for the war on terror he went straight to the Bible and came out with evil. "He reached right into the psalms for that word," said his former speech writer, David Frum.

Bush speaks in the name of the founding fathers but believes he is doing the work of the holy father. He cannot do both and condemn fundamentalism. But if he feels he must try, he might start with the sixth commandment: "Thou shalt not kill."

Behind the Bigotry in Middletown, a Stronger, More Positive Community

September 11, 2003

Pat Helms, a member of the civil rights group, the American Civil Liberties Union, won't talk politics at her bridge club anymore. Faiz Rahman, a Muslim lecturer, leaves himself an hour extra for the inevitable security checks when he takes a flight. James Dalton, a Vietnam veteran, won't visit France. Bill Gonsell, the director of Emergency Management, switches on the Fox News Channel as soon as he wakes up.

In myriad subtle ways the daily lives of the residents of Muncie, Indiana, have changed a lot since September 11, 2001. This seventy thousand-strong town of many churches and increasingly little industry gained fame in the twenties as the subject of academic survey of the American heartlands called Middletown. Since then sociologists and pollsters have returned periodically to gauge the mood of Middle America. Geographically, it's slightly more than six hundred miles from the recently renovated storefronts of its main street to the hollowed pit of Manhattan's ground zero. Culturally, it is like a different country.

"Most people in Muncie look at what happened in Washington and New York and think, that's a long way away," said Muncie mayor, Dan Canaan. "Those are things that might happen in the big city but not here."

On a national level the last two years have left some obvious scars. Three-quarters of Americans now see the world as a more dangerous place than it was ten years ago, compared to 53 per cent just before the terrorist attacks, according to a Pew Research poll. A similar number believe that occasional acts of terrorism will be part of life in the future.

But in towns like Muncie, you can see only the occasional evidence of these new concerns. Most schools in the town have closed all their entrances bar one. The county building has a guard and a metal detector while the water treatment plant has a guard and concrete barrier. "Nobody thinks for a minute that Osama bin Laden is going to attack Muncie," said Mr. Gonsell. "But terrorists might attack Chicago or Indianapolis and the fallout from that would affect us."

More evident are the popular public responses to those concerns. Behind the bar at the American Legion there is a red, white and blue neon sign declaring United We Stand. In the foyer of the city hall a large poster covered in American flags drawn by third-graders gives: "A salute to Muncie's heroes." On it the eight-year-olds have written messages to the soldiers saying: "Make us have peace" and "Thank you for going to war."

Muncie played host to many of the setpiece events that took place elsewhere in the country. Two restaurants changed the name of French fries to freedom fries; there were pro- and anti-war demonstrations, both of which attracted about seventy-five people; the sign for the local mosque was destroyed; on national prayer day the Reverend William Keller, a local preacher who has presided over the event for the last ten years, refused to share the pulpit with Muslims, Jews or members of any other religion.

But if some of these episodes revealed an ugly streak, the town's response to them showed an even greater atmosphere of tolerance—a core of local human decency in globally ugly times. After the incident at the mosque, Mr. Rahman held a barbecue which attracted more than two hundred neighbours. When the library hosted a session on understanding Islam there was standing room only. Even Mr. Dalton is convinced that if he sat down with a Frenchman over a beer they would agree on more than they disagreed. Reverend Keller's stance prompted an alternative interfaith service that received twice the number that his did, even though it rained. "The things he said didn't surprise me," said Mr. Rahman. "But the way people reacted did."

For a few people the changes have demanded significant alterations in their working lives. Mr. Gonsell spends half an hour a day reading the *New York Times* and *Washington Post* to keep abreast with international news. In August 2001 he was pilloried in the local press for wasting taxpayers' money when he took the mayor and other key city employees to Mount Weather in Virginia for anti-terrorism training. That wouldn't happen now. "September 11 made my life more difficult because I have much greater workload," he said. "But it has also made it easier because people are far more receptive to training."

At the public library, staff shred records of who has been using the computers and purge the files recording which books have been taken out and returned each day. Under the Patriot Act they are obliged to hand what information they have over to the Homeland Security Department if requested. Getting rid of them is the easiest way to avoid breaching confidentiality. "You don't have intellectual freedom if you have Big Brother breathing down your neck, looking at what you're reading and researching," said Ginny Nilles, the libraries director.

More pervasive than the changes in routine are the small alterations in human relations. Like most, Mr. Dalton now "takes a lot more notice of Middle Easterners." But there is not just suspicion of "the other" but also each other. Ms. Helms is careful with whom she shares her liberal criticisms. "I have got to a point where I'm very reluctant to make nasty remarks about the Bush administration with people I don't know. I like playing bridge so I just don't mention politics when I'm there because I don't know what the reaction will be."

But there have been similarly unpredictable responses from the other side. Mr. Dalton said he has had arguments with his workmates on the railroad, many of whom were against the war in Iraq. "I don't think they know what they're talking about," he said. "There's a lot in this country ain't perfect but I don't think anybody has a better system than we do."

"The day when you would go out of your way to make a political statement are gone," said Joseph Losco, chairman of the town's Ball State University political science department. "I don't know if it's gone for ever but it's gone for now."

But in many ways September 11 did not so much change people's behaviour here as exaggerate certain aspects of it. In a straw poll of students in a European politics class at the university, five out of seven said they had displayed a flag following the attacks. But three of those were doing so already.

Ms. Helms's friend and fellow traveller in the American Civil Liberties Union, Mr. Carson Bennett, said their views never did go down well in Muncie. "But before they just thought you were wrongheaded. Now they question your patriotism."

Bangladeshi-born Mr. Rahman, one of around two hundred Muslims in the town, was no stranger to anti-Muslim discrimination on September 11. When he saw the second plane fly into the World Trade Center he called his wife to tell her not to let his two children play outside.

The attacks made that vulnerability more intense. "The problem is they can put you in jail first and then ask why." When he joined a Muslim delegation to see his local congressman, Mike Pence, the politician put them on notice: "If there is another major event like 9/11 then you guys are in trouble."

Mr. Rahman's response has not been to withdraw but to further engage in Muncie society. He is more likely to talk to his neighbours and colleagues now so they know who he is and what he believes in and they no longer have to fear the unknown. "September 11 made us concentrate on our lives in this country and get more involved in things like schools, hospitals and libraries," he said. "That's one of the positive things to come out of it."

Muncie may be small but it is not hermetically sealed. Last week the local public radio station started broadcasting BBC reports (albeit between three and five in the morning) and three of the seven students said they now looked at foreign news sources and had travelled abroad.

True, according to Mr. Losco, many of his students have never even been to Chicago, four hours drive away. But working class residents here have long been aware of the powerful impact the rest of the world can have on them since globalisation sent much of its industry to Mexico, leaving the university and the hospital as the town's two largest employers. "Having been through that economically there's a sense here that politically we're not going to lose our place in the world too. Because the world's a scary place."

On the Bus with the Freedom Riders

October 3, 2003

The Greyhound bus carrying immigrant workers on their Freedom Ride nudges its way down Philadelphia's Avenue of the Arts like the Tower of Babel on wheels. Two West Africans are teaching each other ballads in French, a Guatemalan and Mexican argue in Spanish, while a Bangladeshi and an Angolan discuss globalisation in English.

But as they turn the corner on their way to a rally at St. Thomas Aquinas Church in a rundown area of South Philadelphia, they break out into a lingua franca of freedom songs and rousing chants. Waving banners, they make their way through a tunnel of applause from residents, religious leaders, trade unionists and civil rights activists as two black women hand them yellow carnations.

But for these passengers the destination is not as important as the journey itself.

The Freedom Riders are a caravan of 18 buses from 10 cities stopping in 103 cities to campaign for greater rights for immigrant workers. They are converging on Washington, D.C., and then will finish their journey at a rally tomorrow in New York. High on their list of demands are legalising the status of undocumented immigrants, extending family visas and improving employment protection.

Based on the original Freedom Ride of 1961, when a racially mixed group of civil rights campaigners travelled through the Southern

states to challenge segregation, each bus stops to speak to workers and
attend rallies in immigrant areas.

If the route of this bus is circuitous, the manner in which many of
its passengers made it to the United States has been no less so.

Lorenzo Aldana left Guatemala where he was foreman on a building site in 1986. His father sold part of his farm to pay $1,000 to a
trafficker who left him stranded in Mexico.

Mr. Aldana worked in the town of Mexicale for a year to save
money to complete the journey.

"I didn't want to go back to Guatemala," he says. "I am the oldest
son and I had to get to America to support my family."

He trekked eight hours overnight with thirty others, including
three women and six children and made it to California where he got a
job picking fruit. Working long hours for less than the minimum
wage, he was unable to protest for fear that he would be reported to
the authorities.

Seventeen years later he pays taxes but still cannot vote.

"I'm here because I want those people in California to know that
they are not alone," he says through an interpreter. "I want legalisation
so that I can have a better life."

Illegal immigrants in the U.S. often pay taxes and live freely for
years. But clampdowns since September 11, 2001, have made leading a
quiet life more difficult.

With around 8 million illegal immigrants in the country, the American workforce—particularly in agriculture, hotels and cleaning—
depends on people such as Mr. Aldana almost as much as his family
depend on him.

"America is either dependent on, or flourishes because of, illegal
immigrant workers," says Dan Clawson, a sociology professor and author of *The Next Upsurge: Labor and the New Social Movements*.

"The country could still function without them but it would function very differently because so much hinges on an economy run on
low wages and no benefits."

While the nationalities and journeys of the protagonists may differ,
the themes they bring with them are similar. They have travelled thousands of miles from some of the poorest places to the richest country
in the world. But they still remain on the margins, even if in the U.S.
they are geographically closer to wealth.

Each one has a tale of economic migration that has separated families; many have swapped skilled low-paid professional work in the developing world for unskilled and relatively higher-paid menial jobs in America.

Luz Medina went from being an elementary school teacher in Colombia to a janitor and cook in Boston so she could send money to her sick mother and two daughters at home.

Ana Amaral from Angola says she lost her job as an international telephone operator in Brazil after an American company bought the firm and fired five thousand people. She became a cleaner in the U.S. to support her mother and children in Brazil.

"It's globalisation," she says. "The Americans came to my country and so now I am here."

Some people on the bus, like Ms. Amaral, Ms. Medina and Mr. Aldana, are illegal immigrants. Others, like Nazda Alam from Bangladesh, or Melvin from Barbados, are legal. "Someone paved the way for me so I will need to pave the way for someone else," Melvin says.

And some are Americans keen to show solidarity.

"Standing up for other people's dignity and civil rights is the same as standing up for your own," says Elmer Stanley, who was raised in Virginia during the civil rights era.

Illegal immigrants taking part in the protest are taking the greatest risk. All protesters wear a tag around their necks saying they are taking part in a peaceful protest, and wish to remain silent. It offers the number of a lawyer. Just outside El Paso in Texas, two buses were stopped by U.S. border patrol agents at a checkpoint, even though they had not left the country.

The original Freedom Riders of the 1960s were met with violent hostility from segregationists in Alabama who beat them with metal bars and firebombed their buses. Freedom Riders today have also encountered opposition to their campaign.

In some cities a handful of anti-immigration protesters have turned up. A group called Stop the Invasion met them in Durham, North Carolina, to demand the deportation of the undocumented riders.

"What they are really demanding is a free ride," says David Ray from the Federation for American Immigration Reform. "Free from respecting our immigration laws and free from the obligations to respect fair and legal immigration."

But when they rolled in to the small town of Reading, Pennsylvania, and Philadelphia, the only tattooed white men there were trade unionists to support them.

"The exploitation of undocumented workers drags down the general standard of living of all workers," says Bill Heenan, the business manager of the Local 471 union that represents workers in three counties. "But that's not their fault. My mother's family was from Ireland and worked in the garment industry and my father's family was from Lithuania and worked in the coal mines and even though they were legal they went through a similar thing."

Confronted with the question of why she doesn't go home if she doesn't like it, Ms. Amaral smiles. "First of all I can't go back because people are dependent on me for money. But secondly why should I?" she asks, gesturing to the people on the bus. "We made this place."

Beyond the Ballot Box

January 12, 2004

At Tom's Restaurant in New Hampton, a small town in Iowa, a young, asthmatic staffer for Howard Dean's campaign slides to the floor clutching her inhaler. She wears her dedication on her sweatshirt. Under the slogan "C4C" (Commit for Change) come the words: "Blog, write, donate, organize, volunteer." Recently she has been doing most of these—or encouraging others to do them—around the clock in an effort to secure Dean the Democratic Party's nomination for president. Earlier she admitted, with a mixture of weariness and pride, that she has not slept for two days. Now, while Dean is pressing flesh ahead of next week's caucus, she is panting for breath.

Fortunately, there is a doctor in the house. Dean was a physician before he went into politics—after a quick diagnosis he sends her to the hospital before heading to the next campaign stop. But reinforcements are already on the way. At a Dean Meet Up in Brooklyn, organised through the Internet, two strangers—Paul Fitzgerald and Kaiser Sandwipi—discuss how they are going to travel the more than one thousand miles to Iowa next weekend to help campaign. They'll be part of the Perfect Storm—an influx of 3,500 volunteers to blanket the state ahead of the election to back Dean. Others at the meet up, most of whom have never been actively involved in politics before, are penning letters to registered Democrats in South Carolina, explaining why they are backing Dean and appealing for others to do the same.

Dean's bid for the Democratic nomination is more than just an electoral campaign. It has all the attributes of a movement—a bottom-up surge of likeminded, motivated people who have discovered they all have something in common and are now mobilising in order to act on it. Around the country strangers are meeting in towns and cities in their tens and twenties, donating money in $10 and $20 bills and coming away with not just posters and badges but to-do lists. "Participation in politics is increasingly based on the checkbook, as money replaces time," argued Robert Putnam in *Bowling Alone*. Dean has managed to get people giving time and money.

Most are young (under thirty-five), college educated and white (a problem for Dean as he heads South next month where blacks comprise 50 per cent of the primary base). For most, the war in Iraq—which Dean opposes—was a symptom of what was wrong rather than the cause for the joining up. To dismiss them as angry is to miss the point. It is the translation of that anger into hope and empowerment that is relevant. "It's about an idea that our country can be much better and I wanted to do my part," says Nathan Gonzalez, twenty-four, who came from California to volunteer in Iowa.

While Dean clearly benefits from all of this, he did not create it and at this point does not really control it. When his campaign manager suggested building a base of supporters through blogs, Dean asked: "What's a blog?" Nobody vets the letters volunteers send to fellow Democrats; the meet ups are rarely chaired by staffers. "When I called head office to ask if I could do certain activities they said: 'You can do whatever you want,' " said Marystarr Hope, who organised the Brooklyn meet up. It is not democratic (these activists have no say in Dean's platform), but it is chaotic and pluralistic enough that it could become so quite quickly.

Nonetheless, the fact that Dean has become the focal point for this energy matters. His winning the nomination would be roughly the equivalent of Ken Livingstone taking over the Labour Party. Not that Dean has the same politics as Livingstone. But, broadly speaking, they stand a similar distance to the left of their party establishments and—recent reconciliations notwithstanding—are equally loathed by their party bosses.

Dean is not the most leftwing candidate in the race by any standard. He is pro-gun, pro–death penalty and a fiscal conservative. But he is the most leftwing candidate to prove sufficiently attractive to sufficient numbers of people to be pivotal in the process. However, in order to run against George Bush he must first run against the Democratic Party leadership. And in order to win that battle he has had to galvanise and energise entirely new constituencies that were either dormant or nonexistent. As such, his insurgent candidacy marks the first electoral awakening of the growing ranks of the disaffected and disenfranchised—a group not confined to America but spread over most of the western world. Over the past decade, they have protested, petitioned or just grumbled in each other's company. But the one thing they have not managed, until now, is to make a decisive difference at the ballot box. Instead, they have chosen between voting for parties they no longer believe in, or parties they know cannot win, or just not voting at all.

In the Dean campaign we are gaining a glimpse of the organisational methods that could bond the disparate and disenchanted at a local and a national level, whether in Germany against Schröder's economic reforms or in Britain against Blair's foreign policy and tuition fees. It does not answer the question as to whether activists should stay in those parties, form new ones or join others. But it does indicate how, wherever they end up, they might mobilise large numbers of people effectively at the polls.

Whether this can be translated into electoral success within the Democratic Party, let alone in the presidential elections, is a moot point. It's an uphill task, although given how steep a climb Dean has endured so far, anything is possible. But what happens to Dean, at this point, is less significant than what happens to the movement. In these early stages, it is vulnerable regardless. If he wins, it risks becoming coopted; if he loses, it risks being disbanded.

We have been here before. During Jesse Jackson's campaigns in 1984 and 1988 the Rainbow Coalition made a huge impact. He didn't win. But, as a result of his campaign, America saw the largest increase in black mayors since the civil rights movement, and black voter registration increased by over 30 per cent in two years. But because the coalition remained an extension of Jackson's electoral ego, when he lost it eventually foundered. "The difference between Christian and Rainbow coalitions is that the Christian Coalition actually exists," says one of Jackson's former aides. "He squandered the possibility to build an organisation or structure."

With a week to go before the caucus, Dean activists can be forgiven for not looking beyond his immediate electoral prospects. But, whether the next president is George Bush, Wesley Clark or Dean, their most valuable asset is not their candidate but the awakened awareness of their potential, as progressive citizens and voters, to make a difference. In the words of the late African American poet and activist June Jordan, they have learned—and are now teaching the rest of us—that "we are the ones we've been waiting for."

Spirit of the Dean Machine

February 18, 2004

If there is one thing more spectacular than the rise of Howard Dean, it has been his fall. On the early evening of January 19, shortly before Iowa caucus-goers assembled to pick the man they wanted to challenge President George Bush, he was poised to turn Democratic party politics inside out.

Railing against the party establishment, he had more money, endorsements and high polling figures than anybody else.

By the end of the evening, he was a third place loser with a scream only a therapist could love. Six weeks and seventeen contests without a win later, he looks a bit like an embarrassing uncle, hanging around the nibbles waiting to be told that the party is over and it's time to go home. Barring some Lazarus-like recovery in Wisconsin, by the time you read this he may have already been escorted out.

But, just as there was a huge amount that the left around the world could learn about his ascent, there are also valuable lessons in his demise that go beyond the United States. For in almost every party—from New Labour to Gerhard Schröder's SDP—there is potential for a Howard Dean to emerge and challenge their party hierarchies. True, if they are interested in enhancing their own career prospects the former Vermont governor is a poor role model. But if they are keen to improve their party's election prospects and set the agenda, he has broken and reset the mould.

Dean's rise showed it was possible to mount a credible electoral challenge from the left even in a country at war, where dissent has been marginalised by both the political and media establishments. Unlike the other two leftwing candidates—Dennis Kucinich and the Reverend Al Sharpton—Dean's candidacy was not symbolic but substantial. He stood in order to win—and for a while it looked as though he might. The fact that he didn't has bitterly disappointed some. The fact that he was in the running shocked even more.

His defeat indicates that even when the challenge does not succeed at the polls, it can, nonetheless, have a crucial effect on the entire political culture and enhance the electoral prospects of the centre-left as a whole. For as soon as Dean's candidacy proved viable it shifted the centre of political gravity considerably to the left, prompting a far more strident tone among all the candidates. By snatching the initiative away from the right, his candidacy made John Kerry look moderate and Bush look extreme.

By changing the terms of the debate, Dean forced all the candidates to address the kind of questions Democratic voters were asking and for which president Bush had no answers. By the time the polls opened, it was Kerry and Dick Gephardt who had to clarify why they supported the war, rather than Dean explaining why he opposed it.

In so doing, they were forced to address a section of their membership that the Democratic Party, like New Labour, have held in contempt for the past decade—that awkward bunch who offer their support conditionally because they regard an election not just as a chance to change faces, but also policies and direction.

In his defeat, Dean revealed that this constituency does not make up anything like a majority. But through his contention he has proved that, when mobilised, it is a sizeable minority that cannot be ignored. Between them, Dean, Kucinich and Sharpton have attracted, on average, just over one-fifth of the votes cast—a figure that held steady in marginal states the Democrats must win in November.

As a result, the Democratic Party is now in far better shape to defeat Bush in November. In a contest where there will be few votes to be harvested at the centre, Dean has energised their base, contributing to record turnouts in most of the primaries and caucuses, and has highlighted Bush's weaknesses.

To pass all this off as a victory would be ridiculous. Having shaped the landscape, Dean found that others were better equipped to build successful campaigns on it. His tone was too edgy, his message too blunt, his spouse too absent for too long. Whatever the different human ingredients that voters look for in a potential president and whatever we may think of them, Dean clearly had too few, and those he did have he used poorly.

So for the significant number of Democrats, particularly, but by no means exclusively, the young, who had invested a huge amount of physical and emotional energy in him, his broader achievements offer little solace.

Their devastation is both understandable and unfortunate.

Understandable because, for many, this was their first involvement in politics, either ever or for a long time. Losing so heavily was dispiriting. Unfortunate because had they believed their own rhetoric the defeat would not have come as quite so much of a shock. They told every one who would listen that they were going to "take back America." But apparently some thought this task could be achieved at the first attempt and that America—corporate, military, fundamentalist—would come quietly. Having berated the media for being biased they were shocked when they were misrepresented.

Whether the energy Dean has unleashed has a lasting effect or not will depend on the great unknown—what the nascent movement that gathered around him will do without him. Those who got involved only so that they could elect Dean will be disillusioned, because their work stops here and does not resonate beyond U.S. shores. Those who joined up so that they could make a difference should be delighted, because theirs has only just begun and holds a lesson for all of us.

A Hierarchy of Suffering

September 20, 2004

The tale of how I became a Nazi and my Nazi harasser became a Jew is as intriguing as it is instructive. Last November I wrote a column about a racist e-mail sent to me by an employee of an insurance company and my frustrations over the manner in which my grievance was handled. The man in question (a white, South African supporter of the British National Party who complained of "undesirables flooding into Britain") was subsequently fired. His dismissal was not as a result of my column but because my original complaint had alerted the company to a previously unreported pattern of racist behaviour on his part.

Of the numerous responses from the public I received, most were supportive but many were more abusive than the original message. One stood out. Incensed that something as "trivial" as racist abuse could lead to a man losing his job, one reader compared me to the person who betrayed Anne Frank. And so, through contorted metaphor and contemptuous logic, the harasser became the victim and the harassed was transformed into the perpetrator.

Victimhood is a powerful, yet contradictory, force. Powerful because, once claimed, it can provide the moral basis for redress, retaliation and even revenge in order to right any given wrong—real or imagined. The defence of everything from the death penalty to affirmative action, Serbian nationalism to equality legislation, are all underpinned, to some degree, by the notion of victimhood. Contradictory because, in order to harness that power, one must first admit weakness. Victims, by their very nature, have less power than their persecutors: victimhood is a passive state—the result of bad things happening to people who are unable to prevent it.

In the past, the right has exploited this tension to render victimhood a dirty word—a label synonymous with whingers, whiners, failures and fantasists. Revealing no empathy with the powerless nor any grasp of historical context, they wilfully ignore the potential for victimhood to morph into resistance, preferring instead to lampoon it as a loser's charter.

"The left had become little more than a meeting place for balkanised groups of discontents, all bent on extracting their quota of public shame and their slice of the entitlement pie," wrote columnist Norah Vincent three years ago. "All of them blaming their personal failures on their race, their sex, their sexual orientation, their disability, their socioeconomic status and a million other things."

Such arguments were always flawed. But increasingly they are beginning to look downright farcical. For if you are looking for someone making political hay out of victimhood nowadays, look no further than the right. The ones most ready, willing and able to turn the manipulation of pain into an art form have found their home among the world's most powerful.

Read the *Daily Mail* and you would believe that Britain is under threat from the most impoverished and vulnerable people in the land. Asylum seekers, immigrants, "welfare cheats" and single mothers are bringing the nation to its knees. While the country is going to the dogs, the Christians are, apparently, heading for the lions. "We, as a people, and the government, must make strenuous efforts to promote and defend our culture, and especially the place of Christianity in it and the rights to self-expression by Christians," wrote Simon Heffer earlier this year.

Across the Atlantic, the right's new role as victims is even more prevalent and pronounced. Straight relationships are threatened by the prospect of gay marriage, white workers are threatened by affirmative action, American workers are threatened by third world labourers, America is threatened by everybody.

At times, this means the powerful appropriating the icons, tropes and rhetoric of the powerless in their entirety, to hilarious—if disturbing—effect. Last year Roy Moore, the former Republican chief justice of Alabama, led a failed bid to keep a monument of the Ten Commandments in his courthouse. Standing before a group of supporters, some of whom were waving Confederate flags, emblem of the slave-holding South, he said: "If the 'rule of law' means to do everything a judge tells you to do, we would still have slavery in this country." Wearing T-shirts proclaiming "Islam Is a Lie, Homosexuality Is a Sin, Abortion Is Murder," they then sang "We Shall Overcome."

In these cases, victimhood serves merely as a pretext for a backlash to reassert, extend or expand the dominance of the powerful. If these people are victims of anything, it is of the threat to their entitlement and privilege.

In others, however, genuine suffering acts as a precursor to genuine vindictiveness. The threat of suicide bombings in Israel serves as the rationale for building the wall to protect Israelis from terrorist attack. In the current intifada, the Israelis have lost more citizens than during the Six-Day War—no one should belittle their pain. Palestinians, on the other hand, have lost about three times as many people due to Israeli military aggression. Who, one wonders, needs protecting from whom—or is some people's pain more valuable than others'?

But nowhere is the abuse of victimhood more blatant than in the U.S. presidential election, where September 11 remains the central plank of the Republicans' strategy for re-election. The fact that their campaign begins with the terror attacks is not only understandable but also, arguably, right—this is the most significant thing to happen in the United States since Bush assumed office.

The trouble is that the campaign's message ends with that day also. September 11 has served not as a starting point from which to better understand the world but as an excuse not to understand it at all. It is a reference point that brooks no argument and needs no logic. No weapons of mass destruction in Iraq? "The next time, the smoking gun could be a mushroom cloud." No United Nations authority? "We will never again wait for permission to defend our country." No link between Saddam and al-Qaida? "They only have to be right once. We have to be right every time."

This is the real link between Iraq and 9/11—the rhetorical dissembling that renders victimhood not a point from which they might identify with and connect to the rest of humanity but a means to turn their back on humanity. They portray America's pain as a result of 9/11 not only as unique in its expression but also superior in its intensity.

When three thousand people died on September 11, *Le Monde* declared: "We are all Americans now." Around twelve thousand civilians have died in Iraq since the beginning of the war, yet one waits in vain for anyone to declare that we have all become Iraqis, or Afghans, let alone Palestinians. This is not a competition. Sadly, there are enough victims to go around. Sadder still, if the U.S. continues on its present path, there will be many more. Demanding a monopoly on the right to feel and to inflict pain simply inverts victimhood's regular contradiction— the Bush administration displays material strength and moral weakness.

In the six weeks before the 2004 presidential election, I drove from Boston (home of John Kerry) to Midland, Texas (once the home of George Bush), stopping in the key swing states on the way. The following four pieces were written during that journey.

"God has a plan. Bush will hold back the evil."

October 9, 2004

Burton Kephart asks me for ten minutes to see if he can save my soul. Opening his Bible to Matthew and Romans he tells me that I was born a sinner, God gave his only son for my sins and if I accepted Jesus into my heart I could be saved.

I ask him what will happen if I don't. "Eternal judgment," he says. "Hell."

Mr. Kephart gave his first-born son, Jonathan, to the American army. In late March the twenty-one-year-old went to Iraq to serve with the 230th Military Police Company. Ten days later he was killed in an ambush in Baghdad.

He was the first person in Venango county, where Oil City nestles on the banks of the Allegheny River, to die in combat since Vietnam. The way his platoon sergeant, Edwin Rossman, tells it, his was a heroic death as he continued to spray insurgents with gunfire even after he had been hit twice in the shoulder during an ambush. "I know at one point when I looked at him, watching as he poured fire into the enemy troops, I knew we had a chance to make it out of there," wrote Mr. Rossman in a letter to the Kepharts.

"If [Jonathan] had not been so relentless we would have suffered heavy casualties."

When the Kepharts heard the news his mother, Donna, went out to buy more yellow ribbons. Then the letters started coming in, from

President Bush to the mayor of Oil City, including one from the com-
mander of the U.S. European command, James L. Jones, conveying
his sadness at the "tragic loss of your son, Scott."

Because of the injuries Jonathan sustained, Burton and Donna were
worried that there would be no open casket. But the army morticians
did a good job. Now his medals and the flag that draped his coffin
stand in a case on the mantlepiece, along with his Military Police band
with its Arabic inscription. He has been recommended for an upgrade
to a silver star.

To understand the impact of Jonathan Kephart's death on those
who knew him, one must first grasp the intensity with which they believe in life after death.

Heaven, for members of the Faith Baptist Church, of which he and
his family were members, is a real place.

"As Christians we know that Jonathan didn't fear death," says Burton, who drives a truck for Lezzer Lumber building materials. "He
was saved and he's now in heaven and we look forward to seeing him
again. You cannot minimise losing a son in this life. But the Lord has
seen fit to take Jonathan to be with him. It was his time."

Religion dominated Jonathan's life. Faith Baptist Church runs a
school and a college next door, both of which Jonathan attended.

Burton sent all of his four children to the church school. Donna
teaches there now, in a room emblazoned with rallying cries to God
and country.

Her primary class learn writing and grammar from a book called
God's Gift of Language. As I leave the class, after they had shown me
the snake they caught that morning and I had told them about England, a small boy called Zeke says a prayer for my travels.

"Public schools are anti-God, anti-Bible and anti-discipline," says
Burton. "We wanted to raise our children in the fear and admiration
of the Lord."

So Jonathan's pastor was his headmaster, most of his friends and
schoolmates were his fellow parishioners and his first employer and
basketball coach, David Foote, is the pastor at the nearby Baptist
temple.

Jonathan was a quiet young man who would transform into a pit
bull on the basketball court. He played point guard, the linchpin of
any basketball team, even though he was smaller than most.

He was a hard worker with a report card full of A's and B's and a 93 per cent grade point average. "He's the kind of kid you'd want your daughter to marry," says Judy Toth, a former neighbour and close family friend. Mr. Foote says: "He loved his country, he loved his parents, he loved his God."

But most were surprised when he enlisted in the army. "I think he wanted that discipline to help him grow up some," says Donna. Burton, who was "born again" after he came back from Vietnam, was not keen on the idea but thought it was Jonathan's decision. "I know what he was going to get into," he says. "I know what war is."

Oil City (population 11,504), formerly known as Oilville, was incorporated in 1863 because of its proximity to Oil Creek. In this part of northwestern Pennsylvania, black gold once flowed freely, making the town a lucrative transport hub for oil making its way down the Allegheny River to be refined in Pittsburgh.

Today its grand Victorian architecture, including an impressive bridge over Petroleum Street, mock a decline which has put one in five residents below the poverty line.

This is where Jonathan spent most of his teenage years. While Pennsylvania went Democrat in 2000 (51 per cent to 46 per cent), Venango county backed the Republicans (56 per cent to 40 per cent). This time the state is leaning towards John Kerry, but only just and only for now. Pollsters say the economy is the single biggest issue, followed by the war in Iraq and the "war on terror."

Among those who knew him, Jonathan's death hasn't changed anybody's views on the war in Iraq. They still support it. In fact if anything, they support it more now than ever. Burton believes that those who oppose it are "un-American."

"It makes me mad, very mad," he says about those who question the war. "Jonathan believed so strongly in what he did in Iraq. I want to see it accomplished because that's what he died for. You'll never convince me that there's no connection between Saddam Hussein and al-Qaida. Never."

What is the connection? "Terrorist activity," says Burton.

They also loathe those who oppose it more than ever. "It changed the way I felt about the press," Mr. Foote says. "If I hear anything negative, I take it personally. I feel that they are saying it about John. It invalidates the sacrifice he made."

And it has reconfirmed their determination to see George Bush re-elected. The Kepharts have a Bush/Cheney sign on their front lawn. Burton believes the country is stalked by evils like homosexuality and abortion, and that the election of the Democratic hopeful will only compound this.

"I fear for this country if Kerry wins," he says. "God has a plan for the ages. Bush will hold back the evil a little bit. He is a God-fearing man. He believes in praying to a God who hears his prayers. He's a leader."

Such single-minded conviction about the war is typical of the political climate, says Michael Hagen, director of public affairs at Temple University in Pennsylvania. "Peoples' reactions to the war in Iraq and terrorism are shaped by their partisanship," he says. "People are interpreting these events very much in terms of their electoral preference."

Moreover, according to the national Annenberg survey, based in the state, 22 per cent of Pennsylvania's electorate are born-again Christians.

The only person I could find who was sceptical about the war or Bush knew Jonathan but was not in his church. "I'm angry about it," says Ms. Toth, the family friend. "It's such a waste. He could have been a great father, he could have been a great mission worker. Now he's dead. And for what? [The war] doesn't seem to have accomplished a whole lot."

But Burton believes that his son's final actions were a form of divine inspiration. "He could not have done what he did in protecting and defending his fellow soldiers without his faith in God," he says.

When we leave a restaurant not far from the Kepharts' house, Burton leaves a pile of scripture with the tip, in the hope that the waitress will read it and find God. Recently, after considerable reflection, he decided to write a tract on Jonathan's life and death. But for now, the one he leaves is entitled "One Heartbeat Away."

Brush-off for New Broom Nader

October 20, 2004

The drive from Detroit to Mason City, Iowa, begins with car plants and ends with cornfields. Turning your back on the Motor City, you pass through the Rust Belt, trace the lower contours of Lake Michigan and, after you've passed Chicago, cruise under the big skies and through open prairie.

The few hours spent in Illinois offer a brief respite from the political advertisements that dominate the airwaves in the swing states. Once in Iowa, they are back, with the soft rock and hardcore evangelism that form the staples across the country.

At the McDonald's in Mason City, Travis is struggling with the till while a customer waits for the change from his Chicken McGrill and double cheeseburger.

Tom Unzicker, a supporter of the independent candidate, Ralph Nader, tries to make Travis's day just that little brighter.

"How would you like to supersize your wages?" he asks, offering Travis a leaflet promising to raise the minimum wage from $5.15 to $10 (£5.56) an hour if Mr. Nader is elected. Travis looks confused and goes back to the register.

After leafleting the mostly elderly customers and a few of Travis's colleagues, but getting little in the way of positive response, Mr. Unzicker gives up and orders a strawberry milkshake. Leaving, he finds one of his leaflets torn up on the counter.

It's been a tough, frustrating and rather unproductive day for Mr. Unzicker, who is working full-time trying to mobilise support for Mr. Nader, the anti-war and anti-corporate crusader, in Iowa and Minnesota. Driving one of the campaign's twenty vans, he is coordinating the efforts in two swing states which the Democrat Al Gore won narrowly in 2000. This time John Kerry and George Bush are on 47 per cent each; Mr. Nader has 1 per cent.

His efforts seem a sorry blend of hapless and hopeless. When he arrived in nearby Clear Lake his only contact there was out. In Mason City the man he was meant to meet was busy. The interview he had planned with the press was cancelled; the one he tried to arrange with another paper could not take place because it had not been planned far enough in advance.

"It's tough," he says. "Much tougher than in 2000. Back then the rallies were big and the support was energetic and enthusiastic. This time people are afraid. They think anything's better than Bush and that things are so bad they have to vote for Kerry. I think if we only have Bush and Kerry to choose from, things are even worse than they think."

Many Democrats still loathe Mr. Nader, accusing him of handing the election to Mr. Bush in 2000 by taking potential votes from Mr. Gore. Their contempt has intensified since he decided to run again and took money from prominent Republicans to do so. In the past year they have tried every possible legal means to keep him off the ballot in each state, advising Democrats not to sign his petitions and challenging the signatures he does get.

Michael Frisby, the communications director of the Stop Nader campaign, says: "The point is not just to keep him from getting on the ballot, but to make him spend money and time in all of these places so he has less money and time to spend getting votes."

Last week Mr. Nader was removed from the ballot in the important swing state of Pennsylvania, many of the signatures he had submitted were judged to be either duplicated or fraudulent. Last night, that decision was upheld by the state supreme court. But he remains in contention in thirty states, including six swing states where polls indicate he has greater support than the thin margin between Mr. Bush and Mr. Kerry.

On Monday he announced a planned ten-state campaign swing before election day, with Iowa and Minnesota on the list.

His campaigners point out that Mr. Bush took far more votes from Democrats in 2000 than Mr. Nader did. They relate tales of intense hostility from Democrats with a mixture of pride and bewilderment.

"I have friends who have said, 'Don't talk to me until after the election,'" Mr. Unzicker says. "One family member asked me not to park the van in front of his house." But his efforts suggest the Nader campaign has more or less collapsed—a leader without an army is caught in an increasingly vicious electoral war.

Calls to state representatives in vital states suggest a moribund list of supporters but no signs of active life. Unlike 2000, when Mr. Nader had the Green Party to campaign for him at the grassroots, he is on his own, backed by just a small band of loyalists including Mr. Unzicker.

"It's not really a movement," says Leighton Christiansen, the Nader coordinator in Iowa City, a small, bustling student town. "It's hard to sustain momentum."

Mr. Christiansen had no definite plans for more campaigning before the election. In 2000 Mr. Nader did well among students, but last week no one could be found to support him at a student debate.

Last month Mr. Nader went to the Iowa City campus and attracted a crowd of 450. "It was a great event," says Mr. Christiansen, a truck driver. "But it didn't really translate into anything."

He hands me a list of possible Nader voters, people who expressed an interest in joining the campaign after the meeting. Beth Straeder, twenty, the only one to return my calls, cast her vote early for Mr. Kerry.

"I liked what he had to say about health care, the war and the minimum wage. Nader is my ideal candidate. But Kerry would not appoint justices to the Supreme Court who would impact on abortion rights, and I decided that was more important to me."

And unlike in 2000, Mr. Bush is now a known quantity.

"A lot of sophisticated leftwing voters made the assumption that Bush would govern as a moderate-to-rightwing conservative," says John Nichols, a columnist for the leftwing magazine the *Nation*. "They underestimated his extremism; they underestimated how much influence people like Dick Cheney and Paul Wolfowitz would have. They didn't understand him then, and wanted to send an important message to the Democrats.

"But they understand him now."

Many of Mr. Nader's most prominent supporters, including the filmmaker Michael Moore, the academic Noam Chomsky and the campaigning journalist Barbara Ehrenreich, have called on him to stand down. His running mate from 2000, Winona LaDuke, is backing Mr. Kerry. At the university in Ames, Iowa, on Sunday, the filmmaker called on students to turn their back on Mr. Nader and support Mr. Kerry. He drew a crowd of seventy-five hundred.

But despite the lack of endorsements and support, Mr. Nader continues to scrape 1 or 2 per cent in the polls.

The presumption these votes would necessarily go to Mr. Kerry is precisely that—a presumption. "I probably wouldn't vote," Mr. Christiansen says, when asked whom he would support if Mr. Nader were not on the ballot. "Both parties represent the same interests, and if we are going to have progressive change we will need to break people from the Democratic Party."

The uncertainty of where the Nader votes would go is reflected in the polls. A USA Today/CNN/Gallup poll suggests that if Mr. Nader were not an option, 52 per cent would vote for Mr. Bush and 44 per cent for Mr. Kerry. But a Zogby poll suggests that 41 per cent of Mr. Nader's votes would go to Mr. Kerry and just 15 per cent to Mr. Bush.

Mr. Nichols believes Mr. Nader's role as a spoiler in this election has been exaggerated. "There is not a single person in America who is going to vote for Nader who desperately wants to get rid of Bush.

"No one at this stage is going to vote for Nader instead of John Kerry. In every election a third-party candidate will get at least 1 or 2 per cent of the vote, and this year Nader's that candidate."

But Charles Cook, a political analyst in Washington, told the *Los Angeles Times*: "Nader could get a half, or a third, or a fifth of the vote he got last time—and be decisive again."

Mr. Christiansen says if he wakes up on November 3 to find Mr. Bush the victor, he won't regret a thing. And if Democrats blame him for a Bush victory, what will he tell them?

"Bring it on," he says. "Bring. It. On."

Braving Springfield's Anti-gay Backlash

October 23, 2004

Cleo Toris leads me on stage to the tune of "I Am a Woman" and clasps my hand to her fake breast. "They tell me you're married," she says. "But are you curious?"

"Curious about what?" I ask. "I'll talk to you later," said Cleo Toris (run the two names together quickly) to the laughter of the mainly gay and lesbian crowd at the Black Tie Affair in Springfield, Missouri.

With a proud crop of manly chest hair poking out of her pink harem outfit, Cleo Toris is no regular drag queen.

But then this is just the biannual turn of raucous stand-up she does for charity.

The rest of the year she is Mark Gideon, a forty-seven-year-old education administrator.

Mr Gideon is the only graduate of the Evangel University, a devout Christian college situated in Springfield (population 151,580), to be crowned Ms. Missouri by the International Gay Rodeo Association. "I got wonderful training at Evangel," he says. "But I was shocked the first time I went into a gay bar and found half my Bible class was in there." There are around seventy-one Springfields (not including the one the Simpsons live in) dotted around thirty-six states and territories of America, from the Virgin Islands of the Caribbean to Vermont in New England. Georgia alone has nine; Virginia has eight.

But the Springfield in Missouri is special. It is the home town of fundamentalist Attorney General John Ashcroft, a man so religious he holds daily Bible study classes in his office and so prudish he ordered the naked breast of a statue in the Justice Department be covered. It is also the headquarters of the Assemblies of God Church—Mr. Ashcroft's church—whose base is locally referred to as the Blue Vatican.

But it is also home to a thriving, resilient and somewhat embattled lesbian and gay community, with five gay bars, a gay theatre, and a community centre. Up in the surrounding Ozark Mountains are several lesbian collectives that nestle alongside hippie communes and militia camps, said to "get on because they leave each other alone." The Black Tie Affair raised money for three lesbian and gay organisations and an AIDS project. "It's changed a lot since I came out in the seventies," says Mr. Gideon. "Back then it was just bars and the park. Now we're better organised."

A year ago the climate looked encouraging. The Supreme Court had recently repealed the sodomy laws, finally making gay lifestyles legal. A few months later Massachusetts became the first state to make same sex marriage legal. Then came the backlash. Missouri passed an amendment to its constitution effectively outlawing gay marriage by a huge margin of 71 per cent to 29 per cent.

President George Bush is vowing to amend the federal constitution to do the same if elected; his challenger, John Kerry, is opposed to gay marriage but argues it should be left to the states. In this election year, gays and lesbians in general and gay marriage in particular have become a central issue. It is the means by which Republicans hope to mobilise their fundamentalist base on election day and the subject Democrats wish would just go away.

In eleven states, including the battlegrounds of Arkansas, Michigan, Ohio and Oregon, the presidential election is twinned with a referendum on amending the constitution to outlaw gay marriage. And polls suggest all of them are likely to pass. "It's just about the perfect wedge issue," says Jeff Wunrow, executive director of the Missouri-based lesbian and gay rights organisation, Promo. "It galvanises Republicans and splits some of the Democratic base."

The day after Missouri's constitutional amendment passed, Melissa Marles was wary when she went into work, where she is "out" to just a few people. "I didn't know what I would hear and I knew I was going to have to stifle my feelings. I thought 'This many people thought it was okay to do that.' I was a little uncomfortable."

When Stephen Adams, a doctor in Springfield, heard the results of the constitutional amendment in Missouri, he was "ready to move." But his partner, Randy Doennig, took heart from the way the gay community stood up to the attack.

"We went door to door campaigning," says Mr. Doennig, president of Promo. "That's the first time we had gone door to door about anything; the first time we were engaged on a local level and we had to talk about gay marriage. They don't take us seriously because we haven't asked them to take us seriously."

Mr. Doennig points out that the vote in the areas where they canvassed was much closer. "Our neighbours and people that we talked to voted for us," he says. "If we all run away and go somewhere else then who changes this place? It just needs a shove."

When you move from Iowa to Missouri you cross the Mason-Dixon line into hybridity; a racial, cultural and historical blur that blends the Midwest with the upper South. This is Mark Twain country—a former slave-owning state that the slave-owners failed to win over during the Civil War. The deeper you journey into it the more languorous the drawl and the more plentiful the churches.

Long before you get to Springfield, Missouri is pronounced "Missurah." In 2000 Mr. Bush won Missouri by 50 per cent to 47 per cent, and this year it was slated as one of the original seventeen key battleground states.

But as the race draws to a close, the campaigns are cutting their losses in areas they think they cannot win and concentrating their resources in those where they have more chance. Mr. Bush, for example, has all but given up on Michigan; and Mr. Kerry has given up in Missouri, where Republicans now hold a six-point lead.

Mr. Kerry's message about jobs and health care and Iraq could not penetrate the touch button "value" issues of abortion, guns and gays in a state where 36 per cent of voters are evangelical Christians.

"I think it's a mistake," says Dave Robertson, a political scientist at the University of Missouri in St. Louis. "I think the election will be close and whoever loses will probably have lost Missouri and regret not doing more to get it."

Back in Springfield, Phil from Chicago heads to the gay bars with an armful of Kerry stickers, determined not to abandon the state just yet. "People are so short-sighted," he says. "They can vote against abortion but there'll still be abortions. They can vote against gays but there'll still be gays."

At the Black Tie Affair, a photographic exhibition illustrates that there has always been a gay community in Springfield, even if the rest of the community was not aware of it. A grainy picture of four men dancing next to an old radio was submitted by a woman who said she knew her "uncle was a little different." Then there is a shot of Rick in his army uniform during the seventies with the caption: "They didn't ask and he didn't tell." And there is a younger Cleo Toris, when she sang with the Mexican Villa Girls.

But the accompanying text shows that when they have put their heads above the parapet there have been mixed results.

In 1989, when Springfield's South West Missouri University put on *The Normal Heart*, a gay-themed play about AIDS by Larry Kramer, one of the men who promoted it had his house burned down. Now the Vandivort Theatre in the centre of town is showing *Bent*, a play about Nazi persecution of homosexuals.

Springfield has no gay pride parade because the town has not outlawed discrimination in the workplace for lesbian and gay men, says Mr. Doennig. "A lot of people are worried about being fired."

But last year the town did see an eight-fold increase in membership to Promo. "We've only been tolerated because we've remained silent," agrees Mr. Adams. "But we just can't be silent anymore."

This Election Is Not a
Vote About Ideas

November 1, 2004

Criticisms of Americans for being insular, while often valid, usually fail to grasp the sheer scale of the place. Texas, the country's second largest state, is the size of Germany, Italy and Denmark combined; its population would fill Switzerland, Portugal and Ireland. Those who accuse Americans of being parochial must first concede that America is a huge parish.

New England, where I started my journey, and West Texas, where I ended it five weeks later, could be in two entirely different nations. Not only had the topography, climate and architecture radically altered, but so had the people and their attitudes towards everything from religion and government to taxes and guns.

In that time the political landscape had changed too. I left the Democratic challenger's home town of Boston with John Kerry fighting to defend his purple hearts and stay in the race as he languished eight points behind Bush in the polls. I left Mr. Bush's home town of Midland with the contest tied and Mr. Bush explaining a looted weapons cache in Iraq.

One of the few things that has remained constant while on the road has been the ubiquity of the stars and stripes. The national flag billows everywhere. It flies from porches, hangs from store fronts and decorates the bumpers of many cars ahead of me. The interstate highway, network television and chain stores aside, the ever-present national flag has been the one constant indicator that I have remained in the same country all along.

But these demonstrations of patriotism offer little or no suggestion of which side of the political divide people are on. You are as likely to find them among Republicans as Democrats. In normal times this strong sense of national identity is the thread that keeps this diverse patchwork of states, cultures and ethnicities together.

But these are no normal times. Indeed, over the last month it has occasionally felt as though these threads may be becoming perilously frayed. For at its heart this election has highlighted the thorny, divisive issue of what that flag stands for. For many, at stake is not just who will run the country, but who owns it and what core values should underpin it.

On the left are those who believe the nation is being transformed by a corporate theocracy. Trekking through the suburbs of Derry, New Hampshire, Pam and Patrick Devaney overcame their shyness to go knocking on doors in search of progressive voters. "I'm not comfortable doing this but it has to be done," said Pam. "Our democracy is at stake. This is the most important election in my lifetime."

"I always thought someone else was out there doing the job for us," said Patrick. "Now I wonder what we were doing when we lived in New Jersey."

On the right are those who fear the encroachment of secular liberalism. "I fear for this country if Kerry wins," said Burton Kephart, from Franklin, Pennsylvania, whose son Jonathan was killed in Iraq. "God has a plan for the ages. Bush will hold back the evil a little bit. He is a God-fearing man. He believes in praying to a God who hears his prayers. He's a leader."

Many Americans of course, lie in between these two extremes. Like the hotel worker in Dearborn, Michigan, weighing her opposition to abortion with her opposition to the war, who was rooting for Mr. Kerry with reservations, they do not fit easily into either camp.

But when the nation goes to the polls today they will only have two camps to choose from and what little common ground there may have been between them has effectively been torched.

Watching the third presidential debate with about forty students in

Iowa City, the Republicans sat on one side and the Democrats on the other. At moments the Republicans would break into cheers or laughter at a phrase or facial expression of one of the two candidates, to the bewilderment of the Democrats. A few minutes later the Democrats would do the same, leaving the Republicans similarly confused.

They were not just watching the candidates on a split screen. They were viewing the entire event as though from a split screen, each side hermetically sealed from the other as though they were witnessing two completely different events in a parallel universe.

On these rare occasions when people are presented with the same raw data, the two camps have managed to fashion conclusions that are not just different but almost entirely contradictory. So rather than partisan arguments adjusting to take account of reality, reality is altered to suit the argument.

So it has been throughout the trip, with both sides rejecting negative polling results as rigged and denouncing the media for being biased in favour of the other side, leaving few basic facts that anyone can agree on.

A recent poll, released by the Program on International Policy Attitudes, showed that the overwhelming majority of Bush supporters still believe that Iraq had ties to al-Qaida or the September 11 terrorist attacks, and had weapons of mass destruction or a programme to develop them. They also believe that the world favours a Bush victory. In each case only a minority of Democrats shared those views.

It follows that from this different understanding of the problems comes entirely polarised conclusions about the solutions.

Rick Sapareto in New Hampshire supports Mr. Bush and the war in Iraq. "I'm very concerned that my boys may end up fighting a war in fifteen years because we failed to take action," he said.

Lisa O'Neill, who lives just a few minutes away, supports Mr. Kerry and opposes the war for almost entirely the same reason. "I have an eleven- and thirteen-year-old who could be drafted if this carries on," she said. When I called them both the day after the first debate each one thought their side had won.

The Democrats that I have met seem much more aware than Republicans that the world will be watching nervously today. Indeed, Republicans seem quite bullish in their indifference. But while the rest of the world has been watching the United States these past few months, the U.S. has not been particularly interested in the rest of the world.

In his classic book, *Democracy in America*, the nineteenth-century French intellectual Alexis de Tocqueville wrote: "All the domestic controversies of the Americans at first appear to a stranger to be incomprehensible or puerile, and he is at a loss whether to pity a people who take such arrant trifles in good earnest or to envy that happiness which enables a community to discuss them."

This is an election about America and its obsessions, old and new, and many of them are indeed incomprehensible. Guns, gays, God, abortion, stem cells, jobs, health care, Social Security and the shortage of the flu vaccine have all been raised at one time or another.

"You'd think with everything else going on in the world they'd have something better to worry about than gays getting married," said Ann Fuhrman, a lesbian living in Springfield, Missouri.

But the United Nations and global warming have not come up once; the Middle East is a big issue for Arab-Americans and Jews everywhere, but nobody else has mentioned it.

So, when they discuss Iraq and the war on terror they do so in terms of the human and financial costs to America. If the occupation were going well you do not get the impression that the invasion of a sovereign country and the lack of weapons of mass destruction would be a major issue.

"I know we're making an attempt to help the Iraqi people," said Yvonne Shostack, in Derry. "But I thought things would be more resolved than they are. People are still getting killed and we're still out there."

But what is most bizarre about this polarisation is that all the emotional energy appears to be concentrated around one pole.

Over the past five weeks I have not met one person who had a passionate word to say about Mr. Kerry one way or the other. Though I don't doubt that some exist, the Democrats I have encountered are primarily motivated by their hatred of Mr. Bush. "If they put up a vacuum cleaner against Bush we'd vote for it and just ask them to change the bag every now and then," quipped Gene Lyons, a columnist for the *Arkansas Democrat-Gazette*.

Republicans are adversely galvanised by their love of Bush. "He stepped up to the plate and showed the world what we can do," said Chris Paxos, at a job centre in Canton, Ohio.

This is not an election about platforms or ideas. It has brought the issue of who owns America and what its values should be into stark relief. But it cannot answer them.

Today will be a referendum on one man—George Bush—and his record. Whoever wins will do so by a narrow margin and inherit a deeply divided nation. But, legal challenges notwithstanding, that will be tomorrow's story. And nobody is looking that far ahead.

If Progressives Can Win in Utah, They Can Win Anywhere

October 3, 2005

Following a concert at the Salt Lake City International Jazz Festival in July, the city's mayor, Rocky Anderson, took some musicians and visiting mayors out for dinner. Some of them had beer; Anderson paid some of the bill.

In a week when John Roberts was confirmed as Supreme Court justice and Tom DeLay, House of Representatives leader, was indicted, this passes for front-page news in Utah. Here, in the home of Mormonism, no city employee is allowed to pay for alcohol with public funds when entertaining. "I truly feel like we're in the middle of a Kafka novel sometimes," says Anderson, who was unaware of the no-alcohol policy and rescinded it on Thursday. "With a little bit of Taliban thrown in."

And then, as if on Kafka's cue, a yellow-naped Amazonian parrot, perched in the corner of his room, let out a squawk. "That's Cardoso," says Anderson, as though introducing one of his most trusted aides. "Don't worry. He won't repeat a word we say in here."

The strangest thing about Anderson is not that he has a parrot in his office, but that he is in office at all. In the state that gave the highest proportion of its votes (72 per cent) to George Bush last year, the mayor of the only major city in Utah is more liberal than most you will find in New York or California.

Anderson, who was re-elected for his second term in 2003, supports gay marriage, opposes the war in Iraq and is a strong environmentalist. He is converting his city's fleet to alternative-fuel vehicles in order to honour his commitment to meet Kyoto's standards on greenhouse emissions by 2012. Two weeks ago he extended benefits to non-married domestic partners of city employees, effectively giving health insurance coverage to gay and cohabiting couples on his payroll. In August, when Bush came to town to bolster support for the Iraq war, Anderson emailed activists calling for "the biggest demonstration this state has ever seen." Two thousand people showed up, making national headlines.

But if Anderson's vision for Salt Lake City is an anomaly in conservative Utah it fits right into the political geography of America. For the mental picture we have of a nation where liberals hug the coasts and northern borders, while Republicans dominate the interior heartlands, is defective. The split of blue states for Democrats and red states for Republicans accurately reflects the votes cast by the electoral college. But the lived reality is more of a blended, purple nation where the division exists not between different states but primarily between the cities and rural areas within them. All of the thirty-two cities in the United States with populations over five hundred thousand voted Democrat in 2004, even though more than half are in Republican states. On the night when anti-gay amendments were passed all over the country, Dallas in Texas elected an openly lesbian, Hispanic Democrat as sheriff.

Indeed the Democrats are essentially an urban party. Without thumping majorities in Chicago, Detroit, Seattle, Milwaukee, Minneapolis and Portland in 2004 they would have lost the states of Illinois, Michigan, Washington, Wisconsin, Minnesota and Oregon—almost a third of the electoral college. It is no mystery why cities lean liberal. Most urban areas are home to the Democrats' most reliable base— African Americans and unionised blue-collar workers. Gays and lesbians tend to flock there to escape isolation and find a critical mass of like minds, while those who move in from out of town are more likely to settle in cities, offering a counterweight to conservative local mores. Salt Lake City (population 181,743) is the only part of Utah where Mormons make up fewer than half the inhabitants.

Navigating this diversity on a daily basis makes bigotry a harder sell—in Europe fascist parties usually perform best in suburbs and smaller satellite towns where people fear diversity but do not live it. Cities also demand the kind of public investment for transport, culture and the environment that sits uneasily with the case for small government.

But cities like Salt Lake offer a few lessons beyond political demography. First, they show that the tendency for coastal liberals to write off as rednecks those who live in "fly-over states" is not just patronising and counterproductive—it is flawed in fact.

Second, they suggest the understanding of the U.S. as a nation riven by a binary divide between Democrats and Republicans is in desperate need of nuance. Not that there isn't some truth to it. But because that truth is limited to the very narrow field of party allegiance rather than the broader sense of how people understand their lives and their politics. Gena Edvalson, a lesbian whose partner Jana is pregnant, says her neighbours in Salt Lake City couldn't be nicer. "They're going to have a baby shower for us," she says. "But that won't stop them from legislating the hell out of us." That is depressing (two-thirds of Utahns voted for a gay marriage ban in November). But it also suggests potential.

Which brings us to the third, and most important, lesson. If those coastal liberals decided to drop in rather than fly over once in a while they might actually learn something. Rather than duck tough issues because of the hostile political environment, progressives here have tried to reframe them in a way that resonates with potential allies. "We don't talk about gay liberation in Utah," says Anderson. "We talk about healthy families and strong communities and say that in the most intimate aspects of our lives the government ought to butt out. You have to stand up even at the risk of losing races—some things are more important than winning a race."

They've lost many battles, but by moulding their message to their principles rather than the other way around, there is still a chance that they might win a war worth fighting. The success of conservatives over the past ten years has not just been a product of big money and a compliant media—they helped but they have always been there. It was fuelled by the very forces that the left most covets—a bottom-up, working-class, grassroots insurgency with a heartfelt belief that they were doing the right thing.

Standing opposite the main federal building Tom King holds a sign saying: "Make Levees not War," along with four others on their weekly Thursday anti-war vigil. "At the beginning people threw open bottles of soda, half-eaten hamburgers and raw eggs at us," he says. But in the fifteen minutes I stood with him only one man shouted: "Get a clue, you bunch of morons," while far more people beeped their horns in support and waved. Last week thousands turned out for an anti-war rally in town.

"We're here in the trenches," says Lorna Vogt, director of Utah Progressive Network. "They should learn from us because the rest of America is becoming more like Utah, not the other way around."

With liberals elsewhere concerned about a theocratic putsch in Washington, Troy Williams, a producer on the local, liberal radio station, points out the short distance between the Mormon headquarters and Utah's state capital. "The separation between church and state here," he says, "is only two blocks."

Bush in Ethical Meltdown, but All Liberals Can Do Is Gloat

October 31, 2005

Liberals called it "Fitzmas." And it was a long time coming. But even though it took almost two years for special prosecutor Patrick Fitzgerald to make it down the chimney, it was worth the wait. Lewis "Scooter" Libby, the chief of staff of Vice President Dick Cheney, faces up to thirty years in prison and a fine of $1.25 million if found guilty of lying over his role in leaking the identity of a covert CIA agent. Meanwhile, the continuing investigation of George Bush's consiglieri, Karl Rove, holds out the possibility of further charges against a more senior White House staff member.

In a week that saw Bush withdraw his Supreme Court nominee, Harriet Miers, and that followed a week in which Tom DeLay, the Republican House leader, was arrested for money laundering and conspiracy, liberals were gorging themselves on a festival of alleged corruption, criminality and incompetence prepared and served by conservatives.

The extent to which these most recent developments have exposed the Bush administration's real agenda and modus operandi should be welcomed. But legal defeats for the right should not be mistaken as political victories for the liberal-left, which has yet to convince anyone that it represents a meaningful alternative.

There is a thin line between what we know to be true and what we can show to be undeniable. Whether it's Rodney King or Abu Ghraib, only with incontrovertible evidence does an assertion shift from a debating point to a reference point. All that separates the misfortunes of Kate Moss from the fortunes of David Cameron is the money shot. We can tolerate the notion that a potential Conservative Party leader has taken cocaine so long as we haven't seen it; we cannot tolerate the fact that a waifish model has taken cocaine because we have.

Fitzgerald's investigation crossed that line, laying out in clear detail the proof for some of the central criticisms the liberal-left has asserted about the Bush administration over the past five years.

First, that the case for the invasion of Iraq was built on a lie. This goes to the heart of the matter. Valerie Plame was a covert CIA agent whose husband, the former ambassador Joseph Wilson, was sent on a CIA-sponsored trip to investigate whether Iraq was seeking to buy uranium from Niger for nuclear weapons. Wilson concluded that this was unlikely, but the claim ended up in Bush's state of the union address anyhow. When it came to Saddam's supposed weapon's cache, the White House was not the victim of flawed intelligence. It was the wilful perpetrator of known falsehood.

Second, that lie could only be sustained by discrediting those who dared to expose it. On July 6, 2003, Wilson accused the Bush administration of exaggerating the case for war in an article in the *New York Times*. Libby sought to trash Wilson's credibility by telling reporters that Plame helped arrange her husband's trip, thus revealing her identity and sparking the investigation. It is a crime knowingly to divulge the identity of an undercover CIA operative.

For the team that stood a candidate whose wealthy connections ensured he never saw combat while rubbishing the actual war record of his opponent, John Kerry, this was business as usual. Two days after Wilson's piece appeared a Pew poll showed that over the previous four months, the number of Americans who believed the military effort in Iraq was going very well had slumped from 61 per cent to 23 per cent; the number of those who thought it was not going well had rocketed from 4 per cent to 21 per cent.

Three months after Bush landed on the *USS Lincoln* emblazoned with its Mission Accomplished banner, both the message and the mission was tanking; it was time to shoot the messengers along with the Iraqis.

Third, the case has revealed the supine character of America's

mainstream media in the run-up to the war. Primarily, it showcased
the sharp practices of *New York Times* reporter Judith Miller. In
Miller's own account of her grand jury testimony, she wrote: "When
the subject turned to Mr. Wilson, Mr. Libby requested that he be
identified only as a 'former Hill staffer' [rather than "senior administration official"]. I agreed to the new ground rules because I knew that
Mr. Libby had once worked on Capitol Hill." I once played centre forward for Cygnet Rovers of Stevenage. But to cite me as "a former
footballer" would, in most instances, be as true as it is misleading.
Miller's uncritical approach amounted to dictation that bolstered the
administration's flimsy case for going to war.

"WMD—I got it totally wrong," she told *Times* reporters recently.
"If your sources are wrong, you are wrong. I did the best job that I
could."

Neither the *Times* in particular nor U.S. journalism in general
should be judged by the standards of one reporter. But while Miller's
reporting style in the run-up to the war was appaling, its content was
not aberrant. Following the terrorist attacks of September 11, the administration circled the wagons around the flag and the media found
itself on the wrong side. Politically embedded at home before they
were military embedded abroad, their fear of appearing unpatriotic
trumped their fear of misinforming the public.

So the investigation has given us one of the clearest indications to
date of how we got to this point. Given the malevolent partisanship of
the Republican Party it is not surprising that many liberals gloat at the
prospect of a full-scale Republican implosion. But such schadenfreude
is premature. The wounds of recent weeks have all been self-inflicted—
the result of a mixture of hubris, malice, greed and ineptitude. There
is no doubt that they have damaged Bush politically. A Washington
Post/ABC poll this weekend shows his approval rating at an all-time
low, with the public believing Bill Clinton ran a more ethical administration after the Monica Lewinsky scandal than Bush does now. Meanwhile, an AP/Ipsos poll released on Saturday shows support for the
war at an all-time low of 37 per cent.

But the Democrats are not faring much better, with only margin-
ally more support than Republicans, according to a poll taken before
the indictments and Miers withdrawal, but after Hurricane Katrina
and DeLay's arrest.

Having supported the war and without coherent proposals for disengaging, they are ill-placed to take advantage of the Republican's current troubles.

Either unable or unwilling to present a clear agenda of how they would do things differently, they have been effectively mute for several months. With no opposition, popular disenchantment with the Bush administration's ethical failings is descending into cynicism.

Indeed, the only group that has really flexed its muscles in recent weeks has been the Christian right, which derailed Mier's nomination to the Supreme Court. Bush is likely to nominate another candidate later this week who will be more to their liking, thereby tipping the balance of the court against abortion and affirmative action. Unless the Democrats develop the wherewithal to challenge them, conservatives will then shape both the law and the politics of the country for a generation. And Fitzmas will be little more than a lingering reminder of what the law can do when politics has failed.

Part IV

CULTURE

Warren Beatty: Rebel with a Cause

January 23, 1999

Warren Beatty is on the phone. His left hand is on the wheel, guiding his sleek, black Mercedes nonchalantly around the twisting roads above Beverley Hills. His right hand is clutching the receiver. We are gliding along the tarmac contours of fame, past the homes of Jack Nicholson and Marlon Brando, past Beatty's old, white-glass house on Mulholland Drive, which collapsed in the 1992 earthquake, and towards the Mediterranean-style white stucco mansion that is the temporary family home.

"I'm doing an interview now but what time will you be going to sleep? Okay, I'll call you later," he says. We approach an automatic gate, pull into his drive and go straight to the dinner table, which is decked in white and shimmering in candlelight. The phone rings again. He hesitates briefly then jumps up. A short silence is followed by an already familiar refrain.

"I'm doing an interview right now, how late can I call? Okay, I'll call later," he says, returns to the table and picks up the conversation where he left it. Within half an hour it would ring again.

Beatty loves the phone. It has jokingly been referred to as his second most legendary appendage. Friends say his head is awash with numbers which he remembers for an extraordinarily long time; Joan Collins, to whom he was briefly engaged in the early sixties, said he would even answer it while they were making love. "If you ask, 'Will

Warren phone you five times in a day,' the answer is yes," says Tom
Sherak, a Fox executive. Beatty's telephone voice is a purr of velvet: he
gives good ear.

"The voice means everything to me. I guess I'd rather see people
than talk to them on the phone but it's the next best thing," he says. "I
enjoy it. My profession is devoted to subtext. I respect text, facts and
so on but I'm really interested in subtext—nuance and inflection.
That's what you get on the phone. That's why I'm not too comfortable
with e-mails. I have people who will do that for me." Beatty is entitled
to be fazed by new technology; he is sixty-one and has earned his
stripes. There is an entire generation of cinema-goers who know he is
famous but don't quite know why. Before men went to the moon,
apartheid imprisoned Nelson Mandela or British troops went to
Northern Ireland, Beatty had tasted fame. He was there before Robert
Redford, Dustin Hoffmann or Harvey Keitel. In the beginning there
was Beatty, and Hollywood said he was good.

"I haven't really dealt with being well-known as if I had an alternative to it. Anybody who becomes a movie star when they're twenty-two
or whatever I was, is going to be eccentric. It's an eccentric situation.
You become rich and famous out of proportion to that which is anticipated. Quite a candy store there," he says.

His friends are famous. If Beatty could get together a dinner party
of those he counts among his pals (bringing a few back to life in the
process) it would be an illustrious line-up, including Russian poet and
writer Yevgeny Yevtushenko, the late writer and essayist James Baldwin,
Rainbow Coalition leader Jesse Jackson, novelist Tom Wolfe and writer
and biographer Alex Haley.

But it is the women who stayed for breakfast who will always attract
more interest. For Beatty is not just famous for being talented, or even
famous for being famous. He is also famous for having slept with the
famous. His past girl friends include Madonna, Diane Keaton, Julie
Christie, Brigitte Bardot, Judy Carne, Joan Collins, Isabelle Adjani
and Michelle Phillips.

But that was then, when Beatty's world was funnelled through the
vortex of his own ego. Nowadays he does not look his age—he could
easily pass for a good-looking fifty—but he does act it. If he enjoys the
tittle-tattle of Tinseltown he must be bilingual, for he is equally

comfortable talking about American politics, Russian literature and cultural history without pretension.

It is difficult to believe that he could have got as far as he has in the film industry—not to mention his love life—without a degree of vanity. Carly Simon may or may not have had him in mind when she wrote the song "You're So Vain," but Beatty certainly has an acute awareness of his own value.

He also understands the fickleness of fame. In the late sixties, he walked into a restaurant in Moscow with Yevtushenko to a flurry of excitement. "I didn't realise I was that popular in Moscow," he said. "You're not. They think you're me," said the poet, whose work was renowned but whose face was unknown to most of his countrymen. "They're saying that must be Yevtushenko." He is also a skilled operator in Hollywood politics. Lord Puttnam, then plain David, the producer of *Chariots of Fire*, which won several Oscars in the same year that Beatty's *Reds* came out, remembers Beatty offering the olive branch after a long-running and well-publicised spat: "We were vying for the same people and materials which, I think, started off as a row about costumes. Then Beatty came up to me at a New Year's Eve party in L.A. two years ago and said, 'Do you remember what our fight was about?' I couldn't and he said he couldn't either. 'Look I've always liked your work, let's drop it,' he said and then he hugged me. I was very touched. It was very generous." For the past six years Beatty has been happily married to actress Annette Bening, forty, and is the father of three young children aged between seven and two—Kathlyn, Ben and Isabel. "I've had more fun than I deserved to have. Now I'm having a different kind of fun," he says. "But I have a new centre of attention. Before, I was number one in my house and then slowly I've gone to number two, then three and then four and each time you go down one you get more and more happy." The fact that his life is slowing down does not seem to bother him. What does upset him is the pace at which the rest of the world is speeding up. He complains that political primaries are over within just a few days; gubernatorial campaigns are reduced to thirty-second television spots; the Internet, which he has never used, is devaluing the currency of information.

"Before, you had to wait two or three weeks before you could find out what was going on with a film, how it was doing and what the critics thought of it. Now it comes out in twenty-five thousand movie theatres throughout the country on the same day. By the end of the weekend it's almost over. It doesn't even matter what the critics say any more." Stop the world, Warren Beatty wants to get off.

The fact that Beatty is prepared to talk about his latest film, *Bulworth*, is significant in itself. For a long time he refused to give interviews even to promote his own movies. "I think it's crazy to take what aspires to be a work of art and loquaciously expand on what you think about it. Ideally you'd like a movie to speak for itself. It's like giving subtitles to one, two or three years of work. But nowadays it's such a mass medium you have to. Especially if you make very few films."

He is ferociously protective, not only of his private life (which is understandable) but of anything he just doesn't want to tell you. "Warren has a theory," says James Toback, a friend of twenty years who has collaborated with Beatty on a number of projects. "Never disclose to anyone what isn't absolutely essential to disclose. There's very little accidental about Warren; if he says something, there's a reason for it." He is also the master of the pregnant pause, sitting there after making a comment, leaving you to believe he is about to say something else but then not delivering a single word.

He likes to research journalists before they see him, getting one of his staff to pull up stories they have done. A few hours into our interview he raised something I had written in a small British leftwing magazine. "I check out the author because it gives me something to focus on," he says. "Otherwise I'm just going to think about myself and that's just boring. This way I can engage. Newspaper interviews are especially difficult because you give an interview and then you have no control over it at all. At least with TV, people can hear your inflection and make up their own mind. With text, you don't know where it's going." Journalists have often taken this personally but the fact is, with Beatty, nothing is straightforward. He is a part of the Hollywood establishment yet enjoys taking a sideswipe at the film industry; a Democrat who has become disillusioned by his own party; a millionaire who has a problem with money. Even as he keeps earning it by the shedful he cannot bear how it degrades the two things outside of his family he holds most dear—film and politics.

"The number one issue in politics is campaign finance, and in movies there is only marketing costs. The quality of communication is

CULTURE   231

going down. You have to know when enough money is enough. It's a
rare quality," he says.

And how does someone with as much money as Beatty check its ne-
farious influence? "I don't know that I do, but I try. I suppose I just try
to keep ahead of it." It's a quality that Senator Jay Billington Bulworth,
the eponymous central character he plays, stumbled upon almost too
late. The film, which Beatty also produced, directed and co-wrote,
starts with him sitting in his Capitol Hill office alone, unshaven and
unhappy, weeping for his lost idealism as he replays his campaign ad,
which calls on white middle-class families to vote for him in order to
protect themselves against the spectre of black crime.

So intense is his self-loathing that he takes a contract out on himself and then flies back to Los Angeles where, with nothing to lose, he
goes on a truth-telling binge and starts to inform everyone, from Hollywood's elite to blacks in the South Central district what he thinks of
them. The consequences are very funny. In a state of excitable and unpredictable insomnia, he starts rapping a diatribe against the political
establishment, falls for Nina, a black woman he meets at a church
meeting, and tries to get the contract cancelled so he can pursue his
love interest.

It is a comic, bold hybrid of political satire and farce, extraordinary
to see on general release from Hollywood, since it has the potential to
offend everyone, from big business to Democrats and from Jews to
blacks. He thanks some of the senior figures in African American literature, both past and present, for giving him the confidence to approach humour in this way.

"Jimmy Baldwin was a great influence on me. He said: 'Don't be
more respectful of blacks than whites, it won't work, no-one will believe it.' I learned a lot from his essay 'The Burden of Representation'
where he explains that you just can't represent everybody. You shouldn't
even try. Likewise Amiri Baraka [formerly Leroi Jones] made me feel
great about my own sense of humour." The leftwing politics in the
film are explicit. At one stage Bulworth even mentions "socialism"—
"In America that's like saying cocksucker," Beatty says with a chuckle.
Elsewhere, contributors at a Hollywood party ask Bulworth's views on
sex and violence in films. "The funny thing is how lousy your stuff is,"
he says. "So many smart people workin' so hard on 'em and spendin'
all that money on 'em. It must be the money . . . turns everything to

crap. Jesus Christ, how much money do you guys really need." Why would Beatty bite the hand of Hollywood, which has fed him so well and for so long? "Bulworth is not Beatty," he says. "This is a senator having a breakdown in the film so he's not going to be at his most sophisticated. He might say, 'Money is turning everything to crap.' I would say the words 'median' and 'mediocre' come from the same core and money is the cause for an awful lot of mediocre activity because the median is very lucrative." So Beatty is Bulworth with better lines. Beatty has not had a breakdown and never strayed into the median. He is a political purist railing against the centre with an idealism forged in the red heat of the sixties. In 1972 he turned his back on the movies for eighteen months and worked full time as the national vice chairman for fundraising in George McGovern's presidential campaign and became one of the Colorado senator's closest advisers. "He has the instincts of a man who has spent a lifetime in politics and a political maturity astounding in someone so inexperienced," said McGovern.

To listen to Beatty this was a golden age. The fact that McGovern suffered a massive defeat at the hands of Nixon is of little consequence. This at least was a time when being leftwing meant something. "The McGovern campaign looked like it would change a lot. I know it is part of the beast of a political party that it just has to keep winning elections to keep some people in jobs. Sometimes you have to be willing to lose elections." So would it have been better if Dole had beaten Clinton in 1996? "I don't think it is about personalities. I voted for Clinton in 1996. It's better the Democrats won but the downside is that there is still not a party that is in opposition to big money. Where's the party of protest? Where's the party Bobby Kennedy was in? What happens to that party if everything goes to the centre?"

Discussing politics with Beatty you are never quite sure if you are talking to a hard-line Marxist or a soft liberal. Poor blacks and poor whites have more in common with each other than they do with the rich, he says. "We have this so-called thriving economy which has missed most people and while the disparity between rich and poor increases we have just one party—the money party, made up of Republicans and Democrats." This is the kind of talk that would get you thrown out of the Labour Party. But call Beatty a socialist and he will run a mile: "I would call myself a liberal Democrat who is very, very

interested in the safety net." Wouldn't socialist be less of a mouthful?
"I'm interested in a government that looks out for people who need to
be looked out for. Ideology seems to be so unfashionable, so why not
take advantage of it and not name oneself with a term that has become
particularly problematic. I don't even like the label 'liberal Democrat.'
If anything sounds archaic then that's it." He is, however, sympathetic
to President Clinton's present predicament, which he believes symbol-
ises a coming of age for the entire country. "America is coming face to
face with its puritanical roots. Sexual hypocrisy is greater in the U.S.
than just about anywhere else. It is interesting that the divorce rate is
higher than anywhere else and that might have something to do with
the level of sexual hypocrisy. If we had a lower level of sexual hypocrisy
maybe it would bring the divorce rate down and that would be better
for families. I'm not advocating bad behaviour but it might be useful."
But the central issue in America is not Clinton's impeachment trial, he
insists, but race. "Race is the unavoidable question," he says. "This was
very apparent to me even at the time I became a movie star." Despite
his status as a Hollywood grandee and Baldwin's wise counsel, he is still
very concerned about what African Americans make of Bulworth. He
can reel off the great and good of the black intelligentsia—Henry
Louis Gates Jr., Nikki Giovanni and Cornell West—who liked it.
"With particular people it really matters," he says.

It is a concern that took him to the land of gangsta rap, culturally a
long way away from mainstream Hollywood, in order to secure an authenticity for the rapping and portrayals of black life within Bulworth.
He met up with most of the big names in hip hop, including Chuck D,
Ice-T, Suge Knight and Snoop Doggy Dogg.

For a liberal who learned his politics in the civil rights era, the encounters left him both inspired and slightly bewildered. "There is a
strong romantic thread between them and the black power generation.
There is also a philosophical thread which is often much more difficult to find. I think I have more in common with people of my generation who are black than with people of my own race who are younger.
It's about cultural style."

Quite how Beatty came by his cultural style or his radical streak is un-
clear. He was born in Richmond, Virginia, in 1939, to a solid, Southern
academic family. His father was a violin teacher and his mother taught
drama. Later they moved to the Washington suburb of Arlington.

His great-great-grandfather, from whom Beatty inherited his name, had been a spy for the Confederate army during the Civil War, although his great aunts, Maggie and Bertie, always referred to it as the "war between the states." "They were from an educated family, not rednecks. They would never admit the war was about slavery. They said it was about states' rights." His parents, both of whom are now dead, raised him and his sister, Shirley MacLaine, to be self-confident. "I would say that both of them encouraged a high level of self-esteem in both kids . . . Shirley and I didn't have parents who were engaged in pointing out limitations." He remained very close to his mother until her death but never really had an emotional connection with his father, although he does think about him every day. "He wrote me a letter on my thirtieth birthday and a few years ago Shirley found it and framed it in glass so that you can see it on both sides. It's hanging in my bathroom. And then, while he was ill, he asked me once if I had tried using shaving gel. He said I should give it a go. So now every morning, when I shave I think of him," says Beatty, slapping his jowls.

It was his parents' academic interests that helped shape his political opinions. "I grew up around people who had an interest in history and you can't be interested in history without being interested in government and you can't know anything about government and go around seriously thinking that government is bad." Their liberal Southern gentility left him with a sense of fair play. "My parents would have been appalled if anyone had accused them of being racist. By the time *Brown* [the Supreme Court decision to desegregate the schools] came along I was just graduating from school and it all seemed like a pretty good idea to me. But I do remember the signs 'Colored' and 'White.' I went to the largest school south of the Mason-Dixon line but there wasn't one black kid there. We thought Catholics were odd."

While he was good at school, and was his high school class president, Beatty excelled at American football—a talent that would earn him ten scholarship offers to colleges around the country. He chose a liberal arts course at Northwestern University in Evanston, near Chicago, but after a year he dropped out, because the education was not serious enough: "I think it was easier for me to drop out of Northwestern than if I had come from a family which had no education. I think my father secretly admired it. He was happy that I would 'do' something. My father spent so much of his life thinking, that he would never have encouraged me to stay in school. My parents never even encouraged me to get married." Beatty went to New York and took acting lessons at the Stella Adler Studio, stayed in a furnished room on West 68th street for $24 a month, and started doing odd jobs to pay his way; washing dishes, digging the Lincoln Tunnel and occasionally playing cocktail-bar piano. He also looked for acting jobs. It was around this time that he earned himself the reputation as the bratty younger brother of Shirley MacLaine that would stay with him for some time. He reportedly walked out on auditions if he did not like the atmosphere.

In 1959 he was finally discovered by Joshua Logan, director of *Picnic*, *Bus Stop* and *Sayonara*, who wanted to cast him for his new film, *Parrish*. Logan flew him to L.A. for a screen test alongside another fresh face—Jane Fonda. But the film was never made.

MGM snapped Beatty up, paying $400, but had no work for him. After a few months he gave them their money back and headed east, to Broadway, where he appeared in William Inge's *A Loss of Roses*. Four months later Elia Kazan cast him alongside Natalie Wood in *Splendor in the Grass*, a film about the unfulfilled passions between two high-school children in southeast Kansas.

The film was a hit. It was 1961; at twenty-three Beatty was on top of the world. "After that movie I was like Leonardo DiCaprio is now. It took me ages to even think of myself as an actor. For years after that I would see 'actor' on my passport and think, 'God, this is odd.'" He went on to secure his position a few years later by starring in and producing *Bonnie and Clyde* and then producing, writing and starring in *Shampoo*, the tale of a hairdresser and gigolo illustrating the immorality of the Nixon years.

His versatility—he has directed four films, produced nine, been involved in writing six—has ensured that his career has remained varied. His ability—nominated for thirteen Oscars, won one for best director (*Reds*); nominated for nine Golden globes, won three—has cemented his role of Hollywood grandee.

But this is all the more remarkable given the few films he has made—just twenty-one in thirty-eight years. For almost a decade now he has been working on a film about Howard Hughes, although he refuses to say when that might appear. He seems in no rush either to complete it or to have his work assessed.

"Nobody asks how many copies of *Crime and Punishment* were sold in the first week or month or even decade," he says. "You know you're really cooking when you don't know what a film is about until ten or fifteen years after it's come out." Since 1981 he has only made five films: *Ishtar* (a spectacular failure), *Dick Tracy*, *Bugsy*, *Love Affair* and *Bulworth*.

"He's not a great director but he's a smart director," said one critic. "He doesn't make the ordinary Hollywood fodder and most of what he does is very relevant to the time and very brave. If you consider when *Reds* came out, it was very courageous stuff, as was *Shampoo* and as is *Bulworth* in its own way." Jeremy Pikser, who shares the *Bulworth* screenplay credit with Beatty, says he is a "great sponge and synthesiser" of ideas. "But with Warren, you have to be ready for a knockdown, drag-out war every day. You'll go off to capture an idea he's had, but when he reads what you've done, he'll say, 'This is awful. What kind of idiot told you to write this?' And if you say, 'You did, Warren,' he'll say, 'Do you really think I'm that much of an idiot?'"

Almost with each film came a highly publicised affair with the leading lady: Natalie Wood, his co-star in *Splendor in the Grass*; Julie Christie (*Shampoo*); Diane Keaton (*Reds*); Madonna (*Dick Tracy*); and Annette Bening (*Bugsy* and then *Love Affair*).

His sexual adventures in the sixties, he says, were a reaction to his puritanical upbringing in the fifties: "I went through exactly the same sexual revolution as the country went through. In the fifties when I was a kid, I was walking around in a mode of behaviour that related to centuries of Protestant repression. Every cell and fibre around you was influenced by religious upbringings of the past. It was a very puritanical time and I didn't act out in the way that I should have. When the sixties came it was different . . ." One friend referred to the transformation in him as a fortuitous awakening: "He suddenly realised that he had this gift to attract women and that was it. He could never resist using it." But Warren Beatty doesn't want to talk about the sex life he lived within the goldfish bowl that is Hollywood—it's private.

He drives me back to my hotel and on the way he recommends fatherhood—"It sounds like you're ready for it," he says in an avuncular tone—and laughs at the commonly held view that the famous are immortal. "You get on a plane with other famous people and one of the other passengers will say: 'Well, this plane isn't going down. Not with those people on it.' And you think: 'Who says it's not going down?' Just because you're famous doesn't mean the plane's not going to crash." He drops me off with a warm goodbye. "If there's anything else you need, just call me—any time. I don't mind at all. Remember, I like talking on the phone."

Harlem—the New Theme Park

October 14, 2000

On Saturday night, Johnny's Recovery Room, a down-at-heel bar on Harlem's main drag, had been marinating in Motown and malt whisky. A woman who had been staring into space for at least half an hour had fallen off her perch on a bar stool only minutes after Gloria Gaynor had finished "I Will Survive." She landed with a thud, remained there for a short while before being picked up and offered another drink. Minutes later an equally drunk man had danced out to "Midnight Train to Georgia" and cheers from the bar.

But now, on 125th Street in the cold light of Sunday morning, the last partygoers are outnumbered by churchgoers. Saints and sinners pass each other as though in different worlds. The faithful, suited, booted and ready to pray, walk purposefully clutching Bibles in small suitcases, while the feckless, in last night's gladrags, sit on stoops holding cans of beer and bottles of whiskey in brown paper bags, watching the coaches go by.

Large, plush, air conditioned vehicles are cruising Upper Manhattan with eager cargoes of tourists. Japanese, Germans, Koreans, British and even some Americans are now regular features in Harlem's Sunday landscape and cast a curious, slightly nervous, eye over the drunks who cast an ambivalent, slightly mocking, eye back. Later the tourists head for one of a select group of churches—to watch rather than worship—and then on to Sylvia's for soul food and a story to tell the folks back home.

"Harlem wears to the casual observer a casual face," wrote James Baldwin, who was born there. "No one remarks that—considering the history of black men and women and the legends that have sprung up about them, to say nothing of the ever-present policemen, wary on the street corners—the face is, indeed, somewhat excessively casual and may not be as open or as careless as it seems."

His essay, "Harlem Ghetto," was written in 1948 but is as pertinent now as it has ever been. For surrounding the church-day nonchalance are signs of fundamental change. Some, like the Gap billboard, the Starbucks coffee shop and the scaffolding around the Abyssinian Baptist Church are comparatively subtle. Others, like the Harlem USA shopping mall, the new buildings and the huge HMV store, are not. All are indications of the economic development pouring into the area over the past five years, a combination of government money and corporate investment that is changing the texture of life here not just commercially but culturally.

To some this marks the second Harlem Renaissance, mirroring the area's heyday early in the last century, when it was home to a new wave of African American literature, art and music that exuded confidence and originality. It presents another opportunity to emerge from a public perception of urban decay and deprivation. "We are only minutes away from some of the most expensive real estate in the world, yet there are still buildings in Harlem that remain vacant," says Darren Walker, chief operating officer of the Abyssinian Development Corporation, a non-profit organisation affiliated to Harlem's biggest church. "Rebuilding and filling them makes us a more attractive neighbourhood." To others the change represents a threat to spiritual integrity—gentrification that will drive out the poor and destroy all that has made Harlem aesthetically distinctive. "It's a corporate takeover," says Leon Griffith, who works in Record Shack, a music shop. "It's all about money. It has always been a place of hustle and now they just want us to look like downtown Manhattan."

What is at stake is far more than the fate of a small patch of real estate: it is the historical legacy that earned Harlem the title of Negro Capital of the World, the urban backdrop for great dramas of the

American twentieth century: where Malcolm X was assassinated, Marcus Garvey marched, reds and blacks rioted, and everyone from Cab Calloway to James Brown performed. This is the place that inspired some of America's finest cultural moments, driving Langston Hughes to poetry, Zora Neale Hurston to prose, and Sarah Vaughan to song.

Harlem is no stranger to change. It was settled by Dutch immigrants in 1658, and by the nineteenth century had become a wealthy suburb for European immigrants, particularly the Irish, Italians and Jews. But as African Americans left the rural poverty and racial oppression of the South and headed north in search of opportunity, a few mostly Jewish and black estate agents with empty buildings and an eye for a profit awaited them. Ralph Ellison's protagonist took that journey in his landmark novel, *Invisible Man*. In a few years just before the First World War, the racial complexion of Harlem was transformed.

The impact on Harlem was huge, and the influence of black politics no less so. The move from country to city and field to factory, at a time of great social turmoil around the globe, inspired both activism and ideology. Revolutions in Ireland, Russia and Germany, and the radicalising effect of the war, forged a new consciousness whose often contradictory strands—internationalism, communism, anti-racism, pan-Africanism—were woven together.

"Hitherto it must be admitted that American Negroes have been a race more in name than in fact, or to be exact, more in sentiment than experience," wrote Alain Locke, a professor of philosophy at the historically black university of Howard in Washington, D.C. "The chief bond . . . has been that of a condition in common rather than a life in common. In Harlem, Negro life is seizing upon its first chances for group expression and self determination."

This change in ideas and the activism it engendered gave rise to the "New Negro"—by self-definition an urban, more radical Northern relative of a down-trodden Southern cousin. Poverty and discrimination may still have been widespread, but now America's black urban population felt politically and culturally equipped to deal with it differently.

The mood was articulated by poet Langston Hughes in 1926: "We younger Negro artists . . . intend to express our individual dark-skinned selves without fear or shame. If white people are pleased we are glad. If they are not, it doesn't matter. We know we are beautiful.

And ugly too . . . If colored people are pleased we are glad. If they are not, their displeasure doesn't matter either. We build our temples for tomorrow, strong as we know how, and we stand on top of the mountain, free within ourselves." The birthplace of this political and temporal construct, said Locke in 1925, was Harlem, which "had the same role to play for the New Negro as Dublin has had for the New Ireland or Prague for the New Czechoslovakia."

This burgeoning spirit of self-assurance and defiance found its expression in the Harlem Renaissance. Although the term is often used, and universally recognised, its definition has always been elusive. Its period roughly spans from the end of the First World War to the beginning of the Depression. This was the era that saw the emergence of some of the greatest names in black American letters.

Jean Toomer's *Cane*, a volume of poems and novella, marked the beginning of the literary renaissance. He had been raised in Louisiana and later abandoned writing for mysticism. Zora Neale Hurston, a flamboyant, spirited young woman from Florida, challenged the sexism and class-snobbery of the renaissance, but did not publish her most famous work, *Their Eyes Were Watching God*, until the late 1930s. She ended her life in poverty, dying in a Floridan welfare home, and was buried in an unmarked grave. Nobel laureate Toni Morrison has since called her "one of the greatest writers of our age." Langston Hughes, "poet laureate of the renaissance," also wrote short stories and novels but made his greatest impact with a book of verse, *The Weary Blues*. Claude McKay, Jamaican-born, racially militant, politically radical, wrote *Home to Harlem*, the first black novel on the bestseller lists. He was the enfant terrible of the renaissance: he converted to Catholicism late in life and moved to Chicago to work in a school.

There were renaissance artworks, too: the sculpture of Meta Warwick Fuller; the paintings of Aaron Douglas, Palmer Hayden and William Johnson; the documentary photography of James Van Der Zee and the photographic portraits of Carl Van Vechten.

The renaissance was literary and artistic, but it was backed by the impressive soundtrack of the golden age of jazz. Louis Armstrong, Jelly Roll Morton and James P. Johnson were in their prime, Duke Ellington and Fletcher Henderson were innovating, applying orchestral discipline to their creativity. The jazz age coincided with the renaissance, but it was not part of it. Artists rarely passed up a chance to play in Harlem, but their geographical axis was further south and west, their following more working class.

Even though the "New Negros" of the renaissance, led by writers and artists, proudly asserted their intellectual independence, they were mostly financially reliant on white patrons. Their talents had to catch the attention of white editors and publishers who introduced the work to the mainstream in books or literary magazines. Beyond that, Harlem was in vogue. Black people lived there, but fashionable white people longed to be seen there, enjoying the success vicariously.

The geographical proximity of all these black stars gave social and artistic momentum to their work. "In those days there were a great many parties in Harlem to which various members of the New Negro group were invited," wrote Hughes in his autobiography, *The Big Sea*. "These parties, when given by important Harlemites were reported in full in the society pages of the Harlem press."

It was a movement and a moment: a literary, artistic and musical expression rooted in a time and place which, because of the nature of that time and that place, flitted between the political and the cultural, the interests of the elite and the needs of the many. "Nothing will do more to change the mental attitude and raise [the Negro's] status," claimed essayist James Weldon Johnson, "than a demonstration of intellectual parity by the Negro through his production of literature and art."

The renaissance ended when Wall Street crashed and its many white patrons withdrew. "That was really the end of the gay times of the New Negro era in Harlem," wrote Hughes. "The white people had much less money to spend on themselves, and practically none to spend on Negroes, for the depression brought everybody down a peg or two. And the Negroes had but few pegs to fall."

The renaissance stalled, and left behind the human, geographical and economic space that had given the renaissance its name. In the dire days of the 1930s, Harlem descended into urban decay and cultural desolation. As early as 1930, in a prophetical essay, "Black Manhattan," James Weldon Johnson foresaw inevitable change of a nature that still resonates today. "Will the Negroes of Harlem be able to hold it? Residents of Manhattan, regardless of race, have been driven out when they lay in the path of business and greatly increased land values. Harlem lies in the direction that path must take; so there is little probability that Negroes will always hold it as a residential section."

At the corner of Frederick Douglass and Martin Luther King Boulevards, there is a huge Disney store on one side and a Kentucky Fried Chicken on the other. The Audubon Ballroom, where Malcolm X was assassinated, the Cotton Club, where jazz heroes made their name, and the Harlem Opera House have all been knocked down. A few blocks up you can see the brick imprint of what was the Teresa Hotel, to which Fidel Castro famously decamped during a U.N. general assembly in 1960, claiming that he was being mistreated in Manhattan, and had more solidarity with the people of Harlem.

The Apollo Theatre, which once hosted Louis Armstrong, Bessie Smith and Aretha Franklin, still stands, although control of it has now been turned over to Time Warner. James Brown made his name on amateur night there, and that night's blend of ruthlessness and playfulness—booing unpopular acts off stage to the accompaniment of a clown-like executioner—continues. So do the step shows and religiously-inspired soul performances. But most of those in the expensive seats are Japanese, Korean and German tourists, not local African Americans.

"It's like we don't exist any more and those of us who do exist are constantly looking for money to survive," says Dr. Barbara Ann Teer, founder of the National Black Theatre. "We need to develop an understanding of what we have begun to call culturenomics. We need to create the kind of cultural expressions that we can sustain here economically. We have to develop a support system of our own."

Harlem is still poor. It maintained a rich cultural life and varied economic existence through the 1950s and early 1960s, though the emergence of a monied black middle class meant that resources and talent left the area, which then become a byword for urban decay and crime. Tours have become popular, but tourism has yet to take off. Since the Teresa shut, it no longer has a hotel, although there are plans to build one. The crime rate has plummeted, but unemployment remains high at 18 per cent, four times the national average.

Harlem will receive almost a billion dollars in public and private funds over the next four years. But Leon Griffith says the money that is coming in goes out again just as fast. Record Shack, which has become a local institution since it started in the 1960s, has been struggling after an HMV opened around the corner. "They may bring jobs to the area, but at the same time they are destroying our businesses," he says. "We can't compete with HMV. I live in Harlem. So the money that used to stay in the community is now leaving it and we are losing control."

According to the president of the 125th Street Business Improvement District, Barbara Askins, only 35 to 40 per cent of retail businesses on the main drag are minority owned. As more corporate fast-food outlets open, small joints whose names are a taste of Harlem life—No Pork On My Fork and Nuff Niceness—will be threatened. Rents are rising; many are moving to the Bronx and Queens. Barbara Ann Teer says: "They are bringing in the corporations and they are employing the workers. But they are not paying the workers enough to live in Harlem."

The coach tourists are received by some—but not all—with mixed bewilderment and contempt. "Sometimes tourism here is handled like it's a jungle safari," says Lloyd Williams, president and CEO of the Greater Harlem Chamber of Commerce: "Like they're in the wild kingdom, looking at the animals running around."

In this atmosphere only the very strong, very big, or very canny survive. Sylvia's soul food cafe has opened Also Sylvia's next door, to cater for the tourist trade. Its thirty-eighth anniversary was sponsored by Rupert Murdoch's local television franchise, Fox Five. ADC, the non-profit wing of the Abyssinian Baptist Church, employs a small army of estate agents, financiers, developers and lawyers. They have helped build a supermarket, day care centre and two schools, but are currently working on a deal with Gap and a chain-restaurant, the International House of Pancakes.

"One of our goals is to ensure longterm sustainability and for this we need to have a balance," says Walker, of the ADC, who interrupts our conversation for an urgent call with his broker. "There is enough opportunity to protect the interests of poor people and the rights of the indigenous community to remain here while allowing for some people to move in. There were lawyers, maids, doctors, bus drivers in the past, and we are striving to make it socioeconomically diverse."

True, much of Harlem's past has been mythologised. The first renaissance may have been culturally black-led, but it was "white-owned" economically, which caused tension, particularly between Hurston and her patron, who wanted her to concentrate on the exotic rather than the anthropological. There was always a significant white presence in the renaissance period, and it was always greeted with a degree of ambivalence. In 1927, author Rudolph Fisher wrote in an essay, "The Caucasian Storms Harlem": "It may be a season's whim, then, this sudden contagious interest in everything Negro. If so, when I go into a familiar cabaret, or the place where a familiar cabaret used to be, and find it transformed and relatively colorless, I may be observing just one form that season's whim has taken."

The issue now is neither should Harlem be economically developed—it already is—nor whether such development would change the character of the area—it has already done so. The issue is more on what terms will change take place and who will benefit as a result? Weldon Johnson said in 1930: "The next move . . . will be unlike the others. It will not be a move made solely at the behest of someone else; it will be more in the nature of a bargain." Many in Harlem wonder now whether they are selling themselves short or whether the price is too high.

Susan Sontag: The Risk Taker

January 19, 2002

The teenage Susan Sontag was lying on her living room floor, book in hand, when her step-father walked over with a warning. "Susan," he said, "if you keep on reading so much you'll never get married." It was just after the war, a time of economic affluence and cultural complacency in America, and from the backwater that was home on a dirt road in Tucson, Arizona, there could have been little evidence that Sontag's readings of Proust would come in handy in later life, let alone be attractive to the opposite sex.

But the young Sontag could barely contain her mirth: "I just couldn't stop laughing," she says.

"I thought, 'Oh gosh, this guy's a perfect jerk. There must be millions of people out there who want to know me.' I knew there must be loads of people just like me, interested in the same stuff. Otherwise who else was writing these books and drawing these paintings, and who were they doing it for? I thought there were two worlds and if I could only get out of this one the other one would be so much more fun."

It is this combustible mixture of self-confidence, optimism and tenacity, so evident in her adolescence, that continues to drive the essayist, novelist and playwright at sixty-nine. "Sontag stands for what is articulate, independent, exploratory: for self as a work in progress," claims fiction writer, Hilary Mantel. "During her four decades as thinker and cultural commentator, as novelist, director and playwright, compliance has not been part of her brief."

"I'm very devoted to the idea of transformation," says Sontag. "It's the most American thing about me and it's what I love most about America; you're allowed to change your life, to reinvent yourself. That's what I look for in art and arts; the willingness to give it up or move on, put it in a closet or put it in storage."

And so it is that after twenty years in storage she has placed her essay-writing skills on display in a collection entitled *Where the Stress Falls*. The book gathers around forty pieces penned between 1982 and last year—prefaces, forewords, afterwords, tributes, articles and talks—in a display case for Sontag's full range of interests and writing styles. The subject matter stretches from her love for Bunraku, a Japanese form of puppet theatre, to her account of directing *Waiting for Godot* in besieged Sarajevo.

The shortest is a four hundred-word note on *Don Quixote*, published in translation for the National Tourist Board of Spain, while other pieces flit from praise for individual artists, authors and filmmakers to broader themes, such as a century of Italian photography or the inherent complications in literary translation. The longest, and the one Sontag is most proud of, is on Roland Barthes: "The single most ambitious essay in the whole collection and the one that took me longest to write," she says. It is also the most emblematic.

If you're preparing for an intellectual journey through her book, then you should not travel light. Her work presumes a shared breadth and depth of intellect from the reader as well as a common singularity of purpose. If dumbing down is indeed a cerebral virus of the modern age, then Sontag has had her jabs. "I guess I think I'm writing for people who are smarter than I am, because then I'll be doing something that's worth their time. I'd be very afraid to write from a position where I consciously thought I was smarter than most of my readers."

She does not read reviews: "I often feel I know what's wrong better than any reviewer does," she once said. Her friends say this is a coping strategy—a means of asserting some power over a situation over which she has no control. So she measures success principally in terms of durability. "Is it an essay that people will want to read thirty or fifty years from now, which is certainly not the case with most essays," she asks. "It works for me if it is saying things which are true, original and saying them in as eloquent, spirited, lively and lucid a way as I can."

It is the essays that have made her famous. Over the past forty years her voice has been marked, first and foremost, by a supreme intellectual confidence, a tone evident from the first line of the first essay ("Notes on Camp") that made her name in 1964: "Many things in the world have not been named. And many things that have been named, have never been described." From then on she became best known for the occasional declamatory remark: "America is founded on genocide"; "the quality of American life is an insult to the possibilities of human growth"; and "the white race is the cancer of history" are just three sparky sentences she threw into the tinder box of an America at war with the world and itself in the mid-sixties. But more common was a subtle, if strident, tone that preferred complexity to simplicity and met intellectual and emotional challenges head on. Her account of a trip to Hanoi in 1968 reveals an individual both politically dedicated and personally conflicted at a time when loyalty was supposed to be determined by the camp you were in rather than the ideas that you held.

Susan Rosenblatt was born in 1933 in New York City. Her parents, Mildred and Jack, spent most of their time in Tientsin, China, where her father was a fur trader, leaving Susan, and later her younger sister, Judith, to be looked after by her Irish-American nanny Rosie, whom Sontag remembers as "an enormous, benign elephant." When Susan was five, her mother returned from China on her own, saying Jack would soon follow. A few months later, when he still had not arrived, her mother took Susan aside during lunch break and said he had died of tuberculosis. She then sent her daughter back to school.

The episode is illustrative of Sontag's emotionally spartan childhood, which produced a self-contained but not insular child. "The most meaningful relationship I had as a child was in my head. I adored my fragile, withholding mother, who was not very maternal. I had a sister who I was not close to, whom I belatedly befriended at my mother's death-bed. There was no support or encouragement. I experienced childhood as though it were a prison sentence. I never wanted to look back because there was nothing I wanted to take with me."

The family was always on the move: to New Jersey, then Florida and then Tucson, Arizona. When Susan was twelve her mother married Captain Nathan Sontag, an army air corps pilot. The children took his name, but her stepfather never formally adopted them. Sontag still refers to him as "Mr. Sontag." She finally escaped at a precociously early age: at fifteen she went to study for a semester at Berkeley. While waiting to register, she overheard a conversation between two older students about Proust that confirmed her arrival in a world in which she would be more comfortable. "I thought, 'That's how it's pronounced.' I'd been saying it all wrong. I thought, it's all going to be great."

The responsibilities of adulthood came on suddenly. By seventeen she had married a sociology lecturer, twenty-eight-year-old Phillip Rieff. By nineteen, she had given birth to a son, David, who is now a journalist and to whom she remains very close. "The most meaningful relationship I've had in my life was with my child," she says, describing parenting as "an upgrading experience." They moved to Boston, where Sontag studied philosophy at Harvard and let her mind marinate in the work of the great philosophers. Herbert Marcuse stayed with them for a year. "The culture I was involved in had absolutely no relation to anything contemporary. My idea of modernity was Nietzsche's thinking about modernity."

With her late teens taken up with books, marriage and motherhood, she had bypassed the traditional joys of adolescence. And it was in search of them that she divorced Phillip and headed for New York at twenty-six, with her seven-year-old son. The end of her marriage marked the beginning of her adolescence. She says: "I had a very enjoyable adolescence from twenty-seven to about thirty-five, which coincided with the sixties—I enjoyed them in a way people much younger experienced them. I was practically thirty and I learned to dance. I became a dancing fool." She took a series of editing and lecturing jobs, thus starting a financially precarious and intellectually enriching career.

While she is best known for nonfiction, it is fiction that she most enjoys writing. Roger Straus, a close friend and editor at Farrar, Straus & Giroux who in 1963 published her first novel, *The Benefactor*, says fiction interested her most from the beginning, "perhaps, because the writers she admired most were novelists. I remember her then as very intense, very pretty and very interested in absolutely everything."

The Death Kit, her second novel released four years later, received mixed reviews and modest sales, which Straus says "she took in her stride."

But in between came *Against Interpretation*, which included "Notes on Camp" and outlined a theory of her own artistic sensibilities—railing against "interpretive criticism and mimetic art" in favour of an appreciation of artistic work for what it is rather than what we would like it to be. "Suddenly, she had a very high profile," recalls Straus. "From then on Susan Sontag was a name to be conjured with." It is from this reputation that she has long been trying to escape and why this current collection of essays has been so long coming. She says it represents a longer span of work than any of the previous collections "and the reason is that I've been trying to kick the habit of writing essays. From the beginning they received what was, in my eyes, a surprising amount of interest, which was disorienting. But it was also seductive.

"The fiction for several reasons fell to the side. I lost confidence. I knew how to write essays. I was at the top of my form and maybe at the top of the form but I didn't feel I was the best fiction writer in the world or in my country or the English-speaking world." But then came two novels which were released to widespread if not universal acclaim. First, in 1992, *The Volcano Lover,* the fictionalised account of the triangular relationship between Lord Hamilton, his wife Emma and her lover, Horatio Nelson, and then, in 2000, *In America*, the tale of a Polish actress who gives up her career and resettles in California hoping to set up a commune, for which Sontag won a National Book Award. "It was only when I'd written two novels I really liked that I thought I could permit myself to collect the essays I felt were worth saving. I do forgive myself for waiting that long."

Never having had a regular job she has not had to negotiate the constraints of an institution. She has no regular working regime or timetable, no structure other than that which she imposes episodically on herself. "I don't feel the need to write every day or even every week. But when I get started on something I just sit for eighteen hours and suddenly realise that I have to pee. Many days I start in the morning and suddenly it's dark and I haven't gotten up. It's very bad for the knees."

But nor has she known the security of a regular pay check. "Money was always a problem," says Straus. "It's only in the past fifteen years that she's really been comfortable."

Sontag says, "It was okay because I didn't look on it as a sacrifice. I could get along without doing things I didn't want to. I was helped by a series of fellowships and grants—I had two Rockefellers, two

Guggenheims and a MacArthur Fellowship. But I didn't want a car or a television set, or a house in the country. I just wanted to pay the rent and make sure David had what he needed."

In her top floor flat on Paris's Left Bank, overlooking the raging high tides of the Seine, she strides purposefully through the sparse living room. She is a tall, commanding physical presence dressed in comfortable, casual black. A conversation with Sontag is a breathless event, a narrative operating under its own steam. Continuous in its logic, it careers off on endless and lengthy diversions without ever quite losing sight of the main path.

"Everything makes me think of something else," she says. "It's the story of my life." But it is nevertheless a conversation. Rare among high-profile thinkers, Sontag does not simply bombard you with anecdotes or even appear to enjoy holding court. She is interested in engaging and being engaged. You will leave with a book list ("I know you're gonna love this"), but more importantly with the impression that she would be even happier if you left her with one too. "She's a very grounded person," says actress and long-time friend Vanessa Redgrave. "Probably Sarajevo has been part of her grounding."

She loves going to the cinema where, says her friend and Italian translator Paolo Dionardo, she insists on sitting in the centre of the third row. "They are usually small art house cinemas, so it actually makes sense because you feel you're part of the film," he says.

"Susan's like a brilliant older sister," says writer and friend Darryl Pinckney. Sontag has little patience with the journalistic shorthand she believes often either distorts or disfigures meaning. She has described herself as bisexual but remains guarded about her private life. Pinckney says, "I think people get annoyed when they can't get her to talk in terms they want her to talk in. Nobody makes her use words she doesn't respect." Dionardo first met her after she had rejected the first Italian translation of *The Volcano Lover,* not done by him, and asked if he would do another one. He went to New York to work on it with Sontag, who reads and understands the language. "We worked on the book together word by word," he recalls. "She loves language. She can discuss the meaning of just one word for hours."

The result is a woman often depicted as formidable, arrogant and doctrinaire. Many people who knew her reputation before they actually got to know her admit feeling apprehensive about their first meeting. At the beginning of their friendship Pinckney recalls her saying: "Look, you've got to stop being scared and say what you think." She is far less intimidating than her image would suggest. True, she peppers her sentences with highbrow references, but they are always there to illustrate her point rather than illuminate her brilliance. She is sufficiently confident about her own intellect not to make you feel self-conscious about your own. She doesn't expect you to know what she knows because she presumes you know something else that she doesn't.

And alongside her intellect she has an acute emotional intelligence, equally at home talking about feelings as well as ideas, but very aware that feelings can inform ideas, and vice-versa. "I feel that my public persona is just an accumulation of misunderstandings and misperceptions, and my impulse is just to flee," she says. "How in the world would I begin to correct it?"

But while her public perception is unfair, it does not come from nowhere. Some of it stems from more awkward aspects of her personality. Even her friends describe her as "proud" and occasionally "severe." "She doesn't suffer fools, and she'll meet an argument head on," says Alan Little, a BBC reporter who met and befriended Sontag in Sarajevo during the Bosnian conflict.

A review of *Where the Stress Falls* in the *Washington Post*, accused her of a haughty writing style: "Her manner now is virtually indistinguishable from that of George Steiner in his lugubrious moments as Last Intellectual, striking that solemn pose as embodiment of high seriousness—perched atop the Nintendo ruins of western civilization," wrote Scott McLemee.

She is not averse to self-praise, saying things of herself which are true but which others might leave for someone else to point out. "I'm one of the very few essayists still in print," she says. "My collected essays have been around for twenty years and never gone out of print. They've been translated into twenty-eight languages. That's unusual."

"She doesn't have guile," says Pinckney. "In some ways she's strikingly innocent. In this day and age of celebrity, when people want to be talked about and written about, she wants to be known for her work but not for herself. She comes from a different tradition." But much criticism stems from who she is, rather than what she has ever said or written. Some of it is undoubtedly rooted in sexism. "Being a woman is a cliche," she says. "If you are or were good looking, as I was when I was young, then it's a double cliche. Being a smart woman is just fair game. With intelligent women there is a feeling that it is inappropriate."

One of the worst things, she believes, that was ever said about her was supposed to be a compliment from Jonathan Miller, who remains a good friend. "He said in an interview that I was the 'smartest woman in America.' I just felt covered in shame and humiliation to be described in this way. First of all it's so offensive and so insulting. It so much assumes that you're doing something which is not appropriate for the category that is being named, namely being a woman. Secondly, it isn't true because it can't be true because there is no such person."

Her transatlantic lifestyle, shared between New York, Paris and, to a lesser extent, Berlin and London, seems to be born from a deeply ambivalent attitude to the United States, which many American commentators understand as a sign of her aloofness. "I don't like America enough to want to live anywhere else except Manhattan," she says. "And what I like about Manhattan is that it's full of foreigners. The America I live in is the America of the cities. The rest is just drive-through."

And she is an intellectual member of what she describes as "that obsolete species—an old-fashioned liberal democrat" in a country that has little love for either liberals or intellectuals. It is a tension that propelled her into the public eye following a short article she wrote in the *New Yorker* following the attacks on September 11. The article questioned the use of the word "cowardly" to describe the attacks, accused commentators of infantilising the public, and ended with: "Our country is strong, we are told again and again. I for one don't find this entirely consoling. Who doubts that America is strong? But that's not all America has to be."

Sontag says: "I hope I'm not getting timid in my older years. I thought I was writing centrist, obvious mainstream commonsense. I was just saying, let's grieve together, let's not be stupid together." The reaction was ferocious; she received hate mail, death threats and calls to be stripped of her citizenship. For a few days she was part of the story. The *New Republic* ran an article asking what did Osama bin Laden, Saddam Hussein and Susan Sontag have in common. The answer: they all wish the destruction of America.

Sontag says: "I still think mine was the right response. But I was quite astonished. It all goes very, very deep. The American way of looking at themselves is that the U.S. is an exception and doesn't have a destiny like other nations. Anytime anything happens in the States, people are indignant. Americans are always talking about losing their innocence, but then they always get it back again. They say 'Before, we were innocent; before, we were naive, trusting, gullible. But now we realise that it can happen here and we too are vulnerable.' My deepest fear is that this time it's true. The country does feel different. The forces of conformism and mindless acquiescence to authority have certainly been strengthened."

Friends most commonly describe her as generous—with her time, contacts, intellect and money. "When we were both living in Berlin and I had no money," recalls Pinckney, "there was a time when Susan took me to dinner thirty nights in a row." *Where the Stress Falls* is itself a huge act of generosity. Around half the collection is made up of tributes to other writers, artists and filmmakers. She has singlehandedly saved a number of less-well-known writers from extinction by championing their work and pushing for their publication. "She's very interested in other writers," says Straus. "She brought us a number of important authors we would never have heard of."

Sontag says: "I'm very ambitious. But I don't think I'm competitive. I feel that everybody who is still doing good things is part of an informal association or company that strengthens others. One wouldn't want to be the last good writer or the last serious writer or the last serious person on the planet. You have to feel that there are people out there who are doing things that you admire and respect."

Sontag is lucky to be alive. In 1976 she was diagnosed with metastatic breast cancer. "I was supposed to be in stage four, which was terminal," she says matter-of-factly. "I sought good treatment when doctors were telling me to go on a trip and enjoy myself." She had no medical insurance, but friends had a collection so that she could find the best treatment available.

"They told me I had two years, they told David [her son] I had six months. I said, 'I just wanted to see if there was a possibility.' I sought experimental treatment here in Paris and it worked. So back in New York I'm called the miracle patient." Her response was not just medical but intellectual. In 1978 she published *Illness as Metaphor*, in which she argued that society has obscured and mystified its relationship to sickness by transforming it into a metaphor for social, cultural or moral decay. In what is probably her most widely read work, she used her own experience as a starting point for understanding the issue. The essay never strayed into the self-indulgent or autobiographical, but looked out to the sense of listless inertia that blights patients when what is needed is aggression and energy.

Once again she has been struck, this time by a rare form of uterine cancer, diagnosed in 1998, for which the survival rate is only 10 per cent after five years. For several months, a couple of years ago, she was in great pain, unable to walk, and living on morphine derivatives. "A few times I seriously thought we were going to lose her," says Andrew Wylie, her literary agent. "This time, it's a different cancer," says Sontag, "but I'm in an early stage."

Facing down apparently certain death, only to confront it again in a similar form but a different place, she says, forces a permanent re-evaluation of your sense of self. "There is something about facing a mortal illness that means you never completely come back. Once you've had the death sentence, you have taken on board in a deeper way the knowledge of your own mortality. You don't stare at the sun and you don't stare at your own death either. You do gain something from these dramatic and painful experiences but you also are diminished. There's something in you that becomes permanently sad and a little bit posthumous. And there's something in you that's permanently strengthened or deepened. It's called having a life."

It was this mindset that took her to a besieged Sarajevo in the early nineties to direct Beckett's *Waiting for Godot* to the sound of bombing and sniper fire. Alan Little, who attended the opening night, described her presence there as being of "tremendous symbolic importance at a time when symbols really mattered. She didn't just swan in for three days and then leave. She stayed and worked." But she says few of her American friends understood her commitment.

"I would come back and my friends would say, 'How could you be in a place that could be so dangerous?' And I thought, it's okay. I didn't think I was invulnerable, because I had a couple of very close calls, and I don't think I'm a thrill-seeker. I just thought it's okay to take risks, and if ever I get to the point when I don't then take me to the glue factory."

Sadly, Susan Sontag finally succumbed to cancer and died on December 28, 2004.

Maya Angelou: No Surrender

May 25, 2002

Maya Angelou does not like to fly. So she made it to the West Coast from her home in North Carolina by bus. It is 2,152 miles as the crow flies. But she more than trebled the distance, coming via Toronto and the Rockies, on her five-week book and lecture tour. It's not a Greyhound, she quickly explains, but a serious tour bus, complete with a double bed, spare rooms, shower, cooking facilities and satellite television.

The first one she had, which she rented from Prince, had a washer-dryer, too. She herself designed the interior for the next one, which will be delivered before the end of the year. It will be decked out in kente cloth—the hand-woven fabric of Ghana's Ashanti region that has become an aesthetic signifier of black America's African heritage. In the thousands of miles that they have travelled around the country in this bus, she has bumped into Lauryn Hill and passed BB King.

Angelou gave up flying, unless it is really vital, about three years ago. Not because she was afraid, but because she was fed up with the hassle of celebrity. One of the last times she flew, her feet had not made it to the kerbside at the airport before an excitable woman started shouting her name. "It's Maya Angelou, Maya Angelou," she screamed incessantly.

Angelou looked around her and asked the woman. "Are you with someone?"

"No," the stranger replied and continued shouting.

"So who are you calling to?" asked Angelou.

"People over there who maybe haven't seen you yet," says the woman.

"Well, that was a non sequitur," recalls Angelou. "So I just kept walking."

Heading down an escalator a few minutes later, she was met by a woman who thrust a baby into Angelou's arms, while the stranger rummaged in her bag for a pen and something for Angelou to sign.

On the plane, a flight attendant crouched beside the author and confessed her intimate woes. Angelou listened politely until the plane took off. With seat belt still buckled, sitting 45 degrees to the earth, climbing at great speed, the pilot came out to pay his respects. Angelou almost choked. "Who's minding the store?" she spluttered.

Angelou often gets treated as public property. People think they know her. Not surprising, given that she has told them so much about herself. For, probably more than almost any other writer alive, Angelou's life literally is her work.

She has just released the sixth and final tranche of her autobiography—*A Song Flung Up to Heaven*. It is the culmination of more than thirty years' work that started with her bestselling debut, *I Know Why the Caged Bird Sings*, a title taken from the first line of Harlem Renaissance poet Paul Laurence Dunbar's poem "Sympathy."

The first book tells how her father sent her and her elder brother, Bailey, to live with her paternal grandmother in the tiny Southern town of Stamps, Arkansas, after her parents divorced. Aged three and four, the two children arrived at the station wearing wrist tags reading: "To Whom It May Concern." At eight, she was raped by her mother's boyfriend. Soon after she had identified him as the rapist, he was found murdered—the police said he appeared to have been kicked to death. For the next five years, the young Angelou went mute, thinking that her voice itself had killed him and that if she spoke again she might kill someone else. Later, she would move to California and, while still a teenager, give birth to her only son, Guy.

The huge array of experiences that she managed to pack into her first sixteen years presages a life of ceaseless, albeit occasionally calamitous, adventure. In later years and subsequent autobiographical works, she became a waitress, madam, prostitute, singer, actress and activist, a dancer in Paris, an editor in Egypt and a lecturer in Ghana.

She will not say how many times she has been married for fear of
sounding frivolous, but it is at least three.

A Song Flung Up to Heaven takes its title from the last line in the
same Dunbar poem. It starts with her returning to America to work
for Malcolm X, who had just changed his name to Malcolm Malik-
Shabazz and his politics from black nationalism to a socialist version
of Pan-Africanism. It ends with her beginning to write her first
memoir.

Gliding down the freeway in a stretch limousine, Angelou asks for
a whisky.

"Do you want ice and stuff?" asks her assistant, Ms. Stuckey.

"I want some ice, but mostly I want stuff," says Angelou with a
smile, and invites me to join her.

We are heading to a packed house of two thousand eight hundred
in Pasadena. The night before she performed to three thousand in Re-
dundo Beach. It is a peculiar kind of stardom for a poet, writer and
lecturer. It is difficult to think of a contemporary of hers who com-
mands the same popular appeal. When I call 1-800-FLOWERS the
next day to send her a bouquet to say thank you, the young woman
taking my order says she is in awe that I have even met her. "She's a
great philosopher," she says. "That's what I like about her because I
like philosophy. I like thinking, really."

Angelou, like her good friend Oprah, is in the inspiration business.
While the medium may vary from proverb, poetry, metaphor to
mantra, the message is the same. You only have one life, so live it to
the full. Be angry but never bitter. Take risks, love, laugh, acknowledge defeat but do not succumb to it. And while humility is part of the
vocabulary, guile is most certainly not.

"Does my sassiness upset you?" she asks in one of her most famous
poems, "Still I Rise."

"Why are you beset with gloom?
Cause I walk like I've got oil wells
Pumping in my living room."

Alongside and intertwined in her call for emotional uplift is a simple,
humanist, anti-racist message: "We are more alike than we are unalike."
"I could fall in love with a sumo wrestler if he told stories and made

me laugh," she says. "Obviously, it would be easier if someone was African American, and lived next door and went to the same church. Because then I wouldn't have to translate. But if I make the effort to learn the language and respect the mores then I should be able to get along anywhere and with any kind of people. I think I belong wherever human beings are."

As we pull up and make our way through the artist's entrance, a member of the audience shouts that she's driven two hundred miles to see her. We leave Angelou in the green room, alone with her thoughts and the nibbles.

Inside, the audience is gathering. As Angelou predicted, they are mostly white. "Maybe 5 per cent black professional, 5 per cent street." With the exception of the very few Hispanic faces, it roughly reflects the racial composition of the city itself. It is about three-quarters female.

And while more than half appear to be in their sixties or over, many of those have come with either their granddaughters or much younger friends. Whatever city she is in, Angelou insists on doing a signing in an African American–owned bookshop as well. Those, too, are usually packed. In a nation where segregation still defines everything from where you worship to what television show you watch, this level of crossover appeal is rare.

It is a breadth, across age groups, too, that brought her to the attention of Hallmark cards, who approached her to add both her words and her name to a new range. Angelou was interested at first, but sceptical. One of her friends tried to talk her out of it. But what some saw as crass commercialisation, Angelou viewed as an opportunity.

"My friend said, 'Oh no, please. You're the people's poet. Don't trivialise yourself by writing greetings cards.' I thought, 'You're right,' and I hung up the phone. Then I thought about it. I thought, 'Suppose I really am the people's poet? Then the people ought to be able to have my work in their hands. People who will never buy a book will buy a card.' So I thought, 'Oh yes.' I called my friend back and said, 'Thank you so much. Now I'm going to do it.' "

So now her name appears on everything from bookends to pillows and mugs to wall-hangings. Expansive in range and expensive in price, her Life Mosaic Collection offers a "Glorious Banquet Bowl," with the message: "Life is a glorious banquet, a limitless and delicious buffet." Her work and, given the nature of her work, also her life have effectively been branded. The pain of her early years, and the wisdom she has derived from it, has been commodified. It seems a long way from Malcolm X.

Angelou is unapologetic. "I agree with Balzac and nineteenth-century writers, black and white, who say, 'I write for money,'" she laughs. "Yes, I think everybody should be paid handsomely, I insist on it and I pay people who work for me, or with me, handsomely."

The joint venture with Hallmark, she says, is a literary challenge. "It's exciting because it means I have to take two or three pages of work and reduce it to two lines. It's haiku, it's an epigram. So there's this woman I know who's in an abusive relationship—not physically, I don't think, but psychologically—and she accepts it. At work she's a boss to the people under her and is much disliked, so I wrote all of that out and then reduced it to these two lines: 'A wise woman wishes to be no one's enemy, a wise woman refuses to be anyone's victim.' Now it took me a good two days to get that and it's delicious. It's just great."

The politics of commercialisation aside, both Angelou's work and world outlook do lend themselves to the epigram. She was raised on dictums, riddles and rhymes with reason. Once, while directing a film in Sweden, she was having trouble with the actors and the crew. She called for her mother who arrived in Sweden with the words, "Baby, mother came to Stockholm to tell you one thing—cow needs a tail for more than one season." Growing up, her more devout and somewhat prudish grandmother told her: "Wash up as far as possible, and then wash possible."

When she began this current tour in North Carolina, the county commissioner was part of the official welcoming committee. When Angelou noticed he had tried to get her to sign his books ahead of others in the queue, she told the crowd: "In West Africa, in times of famine, in times of drought, the chief tightens his belt first. I ask those of you who are leaders to wait." The commissioner was sent scurrying to find someone in the line to take his books for him.

It is a form, both literary and oratory, that is prevalent in African American life, from politics to publishing, thanks to the dominance of the church. It's a style developed at the pulpit, when the church was the only organisation independent of white supremacy, and combines charismatic delivery with a mixture of truism and teaching, parable and polemic.

This is her language. And this, in Pasadena, is her audience. Witnessing Angelou on stage is like watching stand-up comedy, a university lecture and a poetry recital all in one. With stories, quips and poems—both her own and those of African American poets both dead and living—she has them laughing, gasping and listening for over an hour.

At seventy-four, she has no intention of retiring. "I wouldn't know how," she says. With her skin of cinnamon, cane of silver and earrings of pearl, she has reached this point with grace, good humour and relatively good health. Her breasts, she told Oprah recently, "are in an incredible race to see which one will touch [her] waist first." Arthritis, she informs an audience in Pasadena, plays tricks on her knee. She may pause to catch her breath mid-sentence. And her six-foot frame may move hesitantly and with a stoop. But beyond the inconveniences of time and gravity, she is in fine form.

Ask how she deals with people's responses to old age and she answers by singing the final verse of her poem, "On Aging":

"I'm the same person I was back then
A little less hair, a little less chin,
A lot less lungs and much less wind.
But ain't I lucky I can still breathe in."

Her voice is slow and rich—so deliberate she seems to be tasting words before she lets them leave her mouth. Her speech is peppered with Southern courtesies. You may introduce yourself with your first name, but she will address you with your second. Everybody, in her presence, becomes Mr., Mrs. or Miss—legacy from a time when African Americans were denied those basic signifiers of civility by whites, and so demanded it within their own community.

"I insist upon that," says Angelou. "I did it and do it still. I do it still to Dr. Dorothy Hyde, who is ninety. I'm still the young kid and very respectful."

Later this year she'll direct the movie version of Bebe Moore Campbell's novel *Singing in the Comeback Choir*. She teaches a course at Wake Forest University in North Carolina on the philosophy of liberation, is writing a cookbook, and will continue to pen poems and essays.

For all her optimism, there have been times, she admits, when she has believed that the political equality and personal happiness she sought during the 1960s might never come. Her latest book spans the four crucial and painful years—1965 to 1969—both in her life story and America's racial history, when that pessimism had most firmly taken root. A period when two of black America's greatest leaders, Martin Luther King and Malcolm X, were both murdered. An era when the focus of black politics in America shifted from civil rights to economic rights, rural to urban, South to North, and from peaceful protest to violent retribution. It was also a time when she had to cope with the guilt of leaving her then troublesome teenage son, Guy, in Ghana, and the end of a long-term relationship with an African man whom she has never named.

Normally she submits herself to an eccentric, if apparently effective, work regime: to avoid distraction, she rents a motel room, and asks for it to be stripped bare of any decoration; then she fills it with a thesaurus, a dictionary and a bottle of sherry, and starts writing longhand. But, for this book, a disciplined routine was not enough: "I went down to Florida for a different mood, a different atmosphere," she says. "It was a very difficult book to write. In all my work, I try to say— you may be given a load of sour lemons, why not try to make a dozen lemon meringue pies? But I didn't see how I could do that with this book, dealing with Malcolm's murder, Martin's murder, the uprising in Watts, the end of a love affair-marriage-cum-something. It took me six years to write this book, and it's the slimmest of all the volumes."

Within a week of her arrival from Africa, Malcolm X had been assassinated. "After Malcolm was killed, the hope and I were both dashed to the ground," she says. A few years later, Martin Luther King Jr. asks her to help organise the poor people's march on Washington. Soon afterwards, he, too, was assassinated.

The men had more in common, both politically and personally, than most people recognise, she says. "They were men of passion, exquisite intelligence, great humour, shattering courage. I don't mean the courage to stand up against the possibility of being assassinated. I mean the courage to stand in front of a hostile world and say, 'I was wrong.'

"Malcolm X, after having gone to Mecca, said, 'I've met some blue-eyed men who I can call brother, so I was wrong. All whites are not blue-eyed devils.' Now that was courage. It took courage to say that."

It is her personal connection to these political events that makes them so evocative. Her own narrative is closely interwoven into black

America's political and cultural fabric. She was there in *Roots*, as Kunta Kinte's grandmother, a role for which she was nominated for an Emmy. Her character is there in the film *Ali*, being introduced to the boxer by Malcolm X while in Ghana. She was there in 1997, at the bedside of X's widow, Betty Shabazz, when she died of multiple burns caused by a fire started deliberately by her grandson.

The year before, she had been instrumental in getting together Coretta Scott King, Shabazz and Myrlie Evers-Williams, three women who had been widowed by the civil rights movement. "They went to the Doral in Miami. And they asked me to come," she recalls. "And I said, 'I'm not coming, I'm nobody's widow.' I made them laugh. I said, not one of you knows how to tell a good story, and only one or two of you will have a half a glass of white wine."

But the following year, when the three women repeated the meeting, she accepted the invitation. "On Thursday, Betty had called me at my apartment, and told me she had wanted me to cook something. And I cooked it and she came and it was the two of us and it was great." On the Sunday, the day Angelou was supposed to meet her again in Florida, she got a call from Coretta Scott King to say that Shabazz had been seriously injured in a domestic fire. "She said, 'Sister, our sister.'" And then her gift for storytelling dissolves in pain.

The delinquency of Shabazz's grandson and the tragedy of her death seemed, in a sense, emblematic of not so much how little had changed in black America, but of how deeply some things had regressed. Just as when civil rights icon Rosa Parks was attacked in her home in Detroit by a black burglar, here, yet again, we saw the embodiment of political purpose bludgeoned by the arbitrary fallout of social disintegration.

Ask her what she thinks King's or Malcolm X's agenda would be now, and she releases a long, helpless breath. "I can't," she says. "I can't. So many things have happened since they were both assassinated. The world has changed so dramatically."

But significant progress, insists Angelou, has been made, and must be lauded in order for more progress to be forthcoming. "I think that, as one looks at Watts, one must look at the Academy Awards. As one looks at the drug epidemic, one has also got to look at General Colin Powell and Ms. Condoleeza Rice and the mayor of Washington and the mayor of Atlanta. I mean, there are changes. It's not nearly what has to happen . . . One has got to say there are changes, and the reason for that is this. If we suggest that there are no changes, then young people must say, 'Well, damn, with the lives and deaths of Martin King, Malcolm X, the Kennedys, Medgar Evers, you mean all of that and they weren't able to effect any change—then there's no point in me trying. So we've got to say, yes, there have been changes, minimal changes, but there have been some. And you must try." Yet the successes that she points to are all individual, while the setbacks are collective. What connection is there between those who have got on and those who have been left behind, if the successful do not lift others as they rise? "Some didn't, some don't, some won't, some forget, some have really short memories. They suggest that 'I've got mine—too bad about you. Give me the million-dollar contract for the baseball team or the basketball team. Give them my nothing and I'll take their everything.' There is that, yes. But that is not general. Usually, black people do try to serve the race and try to serve the nation, really."

With poems entitled "Phenomenal Woman," "Poor Girl" and "A Good Woman Feeling Bad," she has always been outspoken on gender issues. But race provided the prism for her analysis of the women's movement in America. "The white American man makes the white American woman just a little kind of decoration," she once said. "He can send his rockets to the moon, and the little woman can sit at home. Well, the black American woman has never been able to feel that way. No black American man at any time in our history has been able to feel that he didn't need that black woman right against him, shoulder to shoulder—in the cotton field, in the auction block, in the ghetto, wherever. That black woman is integral, if not a most important part of the family unit."

This mixture of race pride, rugged individualism and realpolitik has made for unpredictable political standpoints over the past twenty years. Angelou backed the nomination of arch conservative Clarence Thomas to the Supreme Court in 1991, following allegations of sexual harassment. At the time, she argued in the *New York Times*: "Because Clarence Thomas has been nearly suffocated by the acrid odor of racial discrimination, is intelligent, well-trained, black and young enough to be won over again, I support him."

Several negative decisions on affirmative action and a court-assisted election victory for George W. Bush later, does she still believe that?

Angelou laughs. "It's hard for me to say that. I thought so when I wrote the piece. And I may have been right even then. I said let's co-opt him. Don't let's wait for somebody else to co-opt him. Let African Americans co-opt him, let's surround him with so much camaraderie and friendship, and don't let him forget, let us do it rather than fall victim to Machiavelli's dictate, separate and rule, divide and conquer. I still think if we had done that at that time we might have had him. But people laughed at me, rather than consider what had been suggested."

She spoke at the Million Man March, supporting Minister Louis Farrakhan, who nine years earlier she had branded as "dangerous."

"I think he has become more and more wise. Sixteen years ago he may have still have been talking about a state apart, I haven't heard him say that in many years. As he speaks of education and self-respect and self-love and race pride and hard work and loyalty, he speaks of the needs of the people. And he has the following; and if they listen to him and are taught by him, follow those teachings, then it will be a better country and there will be a better future."

She addressed the nation, and the world, at President Clinton's inauguration in 1993 with a poem full of hope. Does she feel the hope was satisfied?

"No. But fortunately there is that about hope: it is never satisfied. It is met, sometimes, but never satisfied. If it was satisfied, you'd be hopeless."

So was it met? "Some of it, yes."

There are many Americans who supported Clinton, Thomas or Farrakhan. But there are few who supported all three. While she is undeniably liberal, if not radical, on most issues, it is her support for black people who do not necessarily espouse issues commonly regarded as in the interests of black people that often places her outside America's traditional liberal/conservative spectrum. This eclectic approach to race, she says, she learnt from Malcolm X.

"Malcolm once said to me, 'Well, you would be upset if the NAACP [referring to the oldest, most conservative civil rights organisation] had a party at the Waldorf Astoria. You wouldn't go, would you?' I said, 'No, I wouldn't go.' He said, 'Think of racism as a mountain, now cut it open. Now, on all the strata we need people. We need people to support the NAACP. Some of the scholarships they give may be given to the young Malcolm X, the young MLK, the young Septima Clark, so we need people on all the levels.'"

What some may view as inconsistency she regards as intellectual rigour. "I insist to be myself, wherever I am. I have enough of the language to try to explain myself, to convey what I'm really thinking. I'm not always successful, but I try. I've lived long enough to see some things. I have enough courage to try and say what I see. If I'm taken out of context, then I say I've been taken out of context."

Only in her response to September 11 has this approach eluded her. "I don't want to be dodgy, but I have to be careful, because if only some of what I say is published then I might have to go on television and lay it out." She was in her apartment in New York on the day and saw it unfold. "When the second one hit I thought terrorism. My second thought was for the people in the buildings on those floors. My God. And my next thought was retribution."

She agreed to do only one or two interviews with people she trusted, for fear of being given insufficient time to explain her views. "We should regard it as a hate crime," she says, arguing that it should be both comprehended and condemned within the context of all hate crimes, wherever they are committed and whomever they are committed against. "It has made Americans more American—that is to say, protectors and defenders of the country. It has, I think, made a number of Americans more inquisitive about our foreign policy, too. More concerned about what are we doing in other parts of the world, and how did we come so late and lonely to this place.

"Living in a state of terror was new to many white people in America, but black people have been living in a state of terror in this country for more than four hundred years."

As our car leaves the Pasadena civic centre, Angelou rolls down the window and waves, thanking those in the audience who have stopped to cheer her. Back on the freeway, the whisky is out again. "I don't talk down to whites. I don't talk up to whites. I just talk to them," she says.

She asks Mr. Schaeffer, the chauffeur, to drop me at my hotel. It is one of those aggressively trendy places, where the name on the front is upside down and there is a live model asleep in a cabinet behind reception. When I told her about it earlier, she screwed up her nose in mock disapproval. As the car pulls away, she winds down the window and shouts, "That's swanky!" and laughs. And then they're off. A white driver and his elderly black female patron. As though someone pulled out the negatives from *Driving Miss Daisy*.

Michael Moore: The Capped Crusader

October 4, 2003

During the commercial break in this year's Oscars, the floor director approached the nominees for best documentary to tell them that their category was up next. Until then, the issue of an acceptance speech had not entered Michael Moore's mind because he didn't think he had a chance of winning.

But this was no regular ceremony. Taking place just three days after the United States launched its attack on Iraq, the red carpet had been abandoned, a number of actors had dropped out, saying they thought it would be "inappropriate" to attend, and those who did show up dressed down for the event.

Moore's wife, Kathleen Glynn, the producer on his film *Bowling For Columbine*, whispered, "Have you thought about what you are going to do?"

"No, because we're not going to win," replied Moore.

"But what if we do?" she said.

"I went into this panic," recalls Moore. Going from self-doubt to presumptuous generosity, he leaned over to the other nominees, who were all wearing peace pins, and said he'd like them to join him on stage if he won. "Come up with me and celebrate the whole thing. I just want to warn you I may want to say something about what's going on. I don't know, because I haven't prepared anything. Just so you know."

When *Bowling For Columbine* was announced the winner, Moore came on stage, with fellow nominees in tow, to a standing ovation and still no idea what he was going to say. "I look out and I can see Martin Scorsese, Meryl Streep . . . all these people. And there's the devil on one shoulder and an angel on the other. The angel's saying, 'Mike, just thank them, blow them a kiss and walk off the stage.' And the devil's saying, 'No, you have a job to do.' And then the angel says, 'But it's your moment, it's your Oscar moment, it happens once in a lifetime, most people don't win the Oscars. Just soak up the love.' Every bone in me just wanted to say thank you and walk off," says Moore.

Still in a quandary as he approached the microphone, he decided to repeat the speech he'd made the night before at the Independent Spirit Awards (the "alternative" event for indie filmmakers), where he'd won a similar prize. To the din of boos and cheers, he said nonfiction films were important because, "We live in a time when fictitious election results elect a fictitious president. We live in a time where we have a man sending us to war for fictitious reasons."

"Then it really explodes," recalls Moore.

But he continued: "We are against this war, Mr. Bush! Shame on you, Mr. Bush! Shame on you!" The microphone was being lowered and the orchestra starting up as he delivered his last line: "Any time you've got both the Pope and the Dixie Chicks against you, you're not long for the White House."

The notion of Moore as a reluctant controversialist is a difficult one to swallow. This is the journalist who held a mock funeral of a dying man outside the offices of the health care provider that had denied him the transplant that would save his life. (The man got his transplant.) He is the filmmaker who turned up at Kmart's headquarters in *Bowling For Columbine* with two young boys who'd been shot, asking if they could return the bullets still in their bodies and demanding that the store stop selling handgun ammunition. (Kmart finally complied.) In short, political tumult is not something that gatecrashes Moore's otherwise quiet life. He courts it, flirts with it, engages it and is ultimately wedded to it.

As an activist, polemicist and journalist, Moore occupies a unique space in the U.S. media and politics. He does so not because he is dissident—America has many dissenting voices, even if most are rarely heard—but because of the combination of what he says, and the way he says it, on television, film and in books. He is a choir of one with little in the way of back-up vocals.

He has equivalents on the right in America, such as the columnist Ann Coulter and the radio shock jock Mike Savage, but they have a rightwing administration, Congress and media to back them up. He has equivalents on the left in Britain, but they have a long-established liberal network and a public understanding of satire to sustain them. Moore has no such tradition to fall back on. He is like Mark Thomas in a journalistic culture that has produced no John Pilger or Paul Foot; like Tony Benn in a political culture that never produced a Labour Party; at his most scathing, he is like Julie Burchill in a nation that couldn't cope with *Spitting Image*. Then, suddenly last year, he had lots of company. *Stupid White Men* became the bestselling nonfiction book of the year and *Bowling For Columbine* became a hit. Through them, he bypassed the cultural and political gatekeepers, and established a link with a huge swath of Americans whose voices were not being heard.

For Moore, this is not just a personal achievement, but a political triumph. "Only that British woman, J.K. Rowling, has sold more books than me this year," he says gleefully. "Think about that. It's Harry Potter and it's Michael Moore. In fiction it's her and in nonfiction it's me. So the American public, during a time when everyone was supposedly rallying behind George Bush, was buying something called *Stupid White Men*, which essentially trashes George Bush." His detractors have branded his work "Chomsky for children," but my guess is that he would consider that a compliment. Chomsky reaches thousands, maybe tens of thousands. Moore reaches millions, maybe tens of millions.

If his speech on Oscar night tells us a lot about Moore, the response to it tells us even more about the political mood in America, particularly shortly after the beginning of the war. His only concern after the ceremony, he says, was not that he made a fool of himself, but that he compromised the safety of those closest to him. "I felt like I'd put my family in danger. In the weeks and months after the Oscars, there wasn't a day went by without someone trying to pick a fight with me in the street, coming right in my face, screaming at me, calling me an asshole, telling me to fuck off." A woman in a business suit approached him at New York's LaGuardia airport and told him he should be exiled. A man refused to sit next to him on a plane. His home in Michigan was vandalised and traitor signs tacked up on the trees outside his house.

But for all that, looking back on it, he does not see how he could have not said anything. "I did not make a film about birds or insects. I made a film about American violence. Let's turn the clock back and it's 1936 in Berlin and you got a theatre award: would it be inappropriate if you say something then, or do you just accept the award because 'You don't mix up politics and theatre'?"

Berlin in 1936 is a fairly good analogy for where Moore thinks America is at the moment. Not that he is comparing Bush to Hitler, but because he believes America's democracy is in peril, as Germany's was in the years following the burning down of the Reichstag. "Since 9/11, the Bush administration has used that tragic event as a justification to rip up our constitution and our civil liberties. And I honestly believe that one or two 9/11s, and martial law will be declared in our country and we're inching towards a police state." He admits "it's not happening tomorrow," but some well-placed suicide bombs or terrorist attacks, he believes, could change everything. "At that point, you will find millions of Americans clamouring for martial law. I'm not talking about a takeover by Bush and his people. They won't have to fire a shot. The American people will be so freaked out they will demand that the White House take action, round up anyone and everyone. That's what I fear. It won't happen with a bang but with the whimpering sound of a frightened nation."

Moore believes such extreme circumstances demand moderate measures. In *Stupid White Men*, he urged the Democrats to merge with the Republicans, so that they could carry on representing the interests of the rich while "the working people of this country will finally get to have their own party." The presidential election between Al Gore and Bush he characterised as a contest between "Tweedledum and Tweedledumber."

September 11 and the Bush administration's response to it changed his mind. In the current climate, Moore believes defending democracy against Bush is a far greater priority than revitalising it through a third-party candidate. In 2000, he backed Green candidate Ralph Nader; for 2004, he has been desperately trying to draft talkshow host Oprah. "Now we have a crisis, we have to consider doing things we otherwise wouldn't do. Tweedledum wouldn't lead us to a police state. Tweedledumber would. This year, there are enough good Democrats running, some of whom give us 80 per cent of what we'd like to see happen in this country. It's not a huge compromise to stop the eventual formation of a police state."

While the strategy may differ, Moore's overarching political take on
America remains the same and can be summarised thus: the American
people are a decent and basically fair-minded nation who are either ill-
informed or misinformed and certainly misled into behaving otherwise.

In his new book, *Dude, Where's My Country?*, in a chapter entitled
"Liberal Paradise," he points to polls showing that the majority of
Americans are pro-choice "in all or most cases," agree with the goals
of the civil rights movement and the environmental movement, believe health insurance should be provided to everyone, and that gays
and lesbians should enjoy equal opportunity in the workplace. "You
live in a nation of progressive-thinking, liberal-leaning, good-hearted
people," he writes. "Let's take a victory lap together and then get to
work on fixing the Great Disconnect—how is it that, in a nation of
lefties, the right hand controls everything?"

There is more to this than many liberals on either side of the pond
would dare to admit. And yet there are two major problems with it,
too. The first is that there are many other polls that suggest Americans
are pretty rightwing. Almost half (48 per cent) believe the U.S. has
had special protection from God for most of its history. More than
half (57 per cent) oppose abortion solely to end an unwanted pregnancy "if the mother is unmarried and does not want the baby." And
while Bush may have got fewer votes than Gore, he was still the choice
of nearly half the country who voted.

The second problem is that Moore's answer to his own question con-
cerning the source of this "Great Disconnect" suggests that the American public have been infantilised and can no longer think for themselves
or work out their own interests. "There's a gullible side to the American
people," he says. "They can be easily misled. Religion is the best device
used to mislead them. People are easily manipulated . . . and we have disastrous media."

It is not difficult to see why Moore would think this. The U.S. media
have ill-served their readers, viewers and listeners; political and religious leadership is poor and, with more than two-thirds of the country
believing that Iraq had something to do with September 11, people are
ill-informed. But they are not stupid. Could it not be that, as residents of
the most powerful nation in the world, they believe it is in their interests
to dominate weaker countries and pilfer their natural resources, so they
can have cheap oil and maintain a relatively high standard of living? Is

it not true that, if the world were fairer, most Americans would be poorer? One may disagree with their assessment, but that is different from saying they came to it because they are misled.

The line between paternalism and idealism on the left is a thin one. On the one side lies the belief that the left knows best. At its root is the notion of false consciousness, meaning that those who act in a certain way do so because they are unable to perceive the objective nature and source of their oppression. On the other side is the hope that we can build a better world if people look beyond their individual interests to the collective good. At its root is the evangelical notion that a better world is possible if people would only have the confidence to fight for it.

Moore straddles both, but leans towards the latter. With a laugh bordering on the maniacal, he relates how rightwing talkshow hosts accuse him of instigating class warfare. "Like that's some horrible thing. I always take it as a compliment. I say, 'Thank you. I don't have to instigate it, though. It already exists. And it's going to get greater and you're going to lose. And next time could you please just introduce me as America's bestselling author, because I want all your rightwing buddies to know that we're coming.'"

Suddenly the laughter stops and he becomes deadly serious. "It's not just Michael Moore. There are millions who think like I do. They just don't know where to go or what to do yet. The Democratic Party has failed them. And so they don't have anything to grasp on to politically. But we'll figure it out."

Does he say that because he actually believes it, or because he has to believe it just to keep on going? "I absolutely believe that. Like most people, I'd much rather slide into cynicism and despair," he says, the laughter returning. "Just reach for another Budweiser and forget about it all. I am truly optimistic, because when people are given the information and given leaders who will truly lead and have the courage of their convictions, the majority will go with them. It's not a large majority, it's a slim majority. But it's a majority nonetheless."

In his landmark book, *Democracy in America*, the nineteenth-century French intellectual Alexis de Tocqueville makes reference to the often shrill tone that can characterise American political discourse in a chapter entitled "Why American Writers and Speakers Are Often Bombastic." "I have often noticed that the Americans whose language when talking business is clear and dry . . . easily turn bombastic when they attempt a poetic style . . . Writers for their part almost always pander to this propensity . . . they inflate their imaginations and swell them out beyond bounds, so that they achieve gigantism, missing real grandeur."

A hundred fifty years later, little has changed. America's most popular polemicists, on the left or the right, have little use for subtlety or nuance. The titles of the bestselling diatribes say it all. The last two books by Al Franken, who is liberal, were called *Lies and the Lying Liars Who Tell Them* and *Rush Limbaugh Is a Big Fat Idiot*. The most recent two by Ann Coulter, who is on the right, were called *Treason* and *Slander*.

Coming from this tradition, the title *Dude, Where's My Country?* sounds positively conciliatory. Open the cover, though, and Moore once again delivers a tirade worthy of the genre. At one point he writes: "These bastards who run our country are a bunch of conniving, thieving, smug pricks who need to be brought down and removed and replaced with a whole new system that we control."

His arguments, however, are for the most part lucid and powerful, and his humour effective. But just in case you ever miss the point, he often draws attention to it with the use of capital letters, italics, bold type and exclamation marks. Reading his prose, there are times, in the words of Hugh Grant, when he seems to have gone "shouty crackers."

Between the man in print and the man in person, there are definite similarities. Face to face, Moore is funny. When I mention his Arsenal cap, he breaks into an impersonation of the Clock End singing opera tunes in praise of Patrick Vieira (he's been to a match or two at Highbury). He is also passionate about his politics and determined in his activism. But in everything but his size—Moore is big in all three dimensions—he is not overbearing. For a start, he listens. Even though he is the one being interviewed, he is very ready to engage in a dialogue. Even though the opinions in his book are forthright, they are not finished. He is still thinking. And so—and this is rare among male opinion-formers of his age—he does not consider being challenged an act of insolence. In fact, you get the impression that he really rather enjoys it.

When I ask why he did not write more in the new book about Israel and America's relationship to it, he pauses. The issue receives a couple of passing mentions and the book is dedicated to, among others, Rachel Corrie, the young American who was crushed by a bulldozer while trying to defend Palestinian houses from being demolished. But, considering its centrality to America's actions in the Middle East, it gets relatively little space. "That's interesting," he says. "The only piece of criticism I got from my publisher about this book are the pieces about Israel. She thought they were too harsh. So the parameters of the debate are different in this country than they are in Britain, and there is a lot of pressure to toe the line."

A little bit later, he comes back to the question of his own volition. "I think it's a good point, because, as much as I think I've done, I haven't done enough. I feel that one of the big flaws in *Bowling For Columbine* is that I go through the history of American violence around the world and completely miss out what we've done in the Middle East when it comes to the Israelis and the Palestinians."

All in all, given that he is a millionaire celebrity sitting in an armchair in a spacious eighteenth-floor office with a panoramic view of Broadway, Moore is pretty grounded. He puts this down to the fact that he has kept the same circle of friends that he had in Flint, where he grew up. "Maybe the lucky part of this for me is that this so-called success didn't happen until I was thirty-five, and by that age you're kind of set in your ways. I'm in the same relationship I was in when I was twenty-two. I have no friends in this business. I don't go to movie premieres. I like the life I always had."

Moore, now forty-nine, was raised in a working-class Irish-American family. He is not a professional dissident—for most of his life he has done it for free. At eighteen, he ran for the Flint school board on the platform of firing the headmaster at his high school. He succeeded. Later, he would drop out of college to work for a leftwing paper, *Flint Voice*. After that came a short—and by all accounts unhappy—stint as editor of the radical monthly magazine *Mother Jones*. "I was one of these people who would sit around saying, 'Somebody should do a film about this,' and then I got to thirty-five and I thought, 'OK, nobody's gonna do it.'"

So he did it himself, in 1989, with *Roger & Me*, a documentary about how General Motors destroyed the manufacturing base of Flint when it laid off thirty thousand workers; fourteen years later, he is worth millions. In *Dude* there is a chapter called "Horatio Alger Must Die," in which he rails against the American dream of social mobility (Alger, a nineteenth-century author, wrote improving tales of lads who rise from rags to riches). "Listen friends," Moore writes, "you have to face the truth: you are never going to be rich. The chance of that happening is about one in a million." It is a good argument, but Moore, being one of those one in a million, is probably not the best person to be making it. "There is great irony in the fact that, by my railing against the wealthy, I have had the good fortune of this financial success."

Perhaps as a result of his Catholic upbringing—at one stage he wanted to be a priest—he couches his relationship to money, celebrity and politics in ascetic moral terms. "It would be a sin" to use his tax break in any other way than to defeat Bush.

One of the main consequences of being rich, he says, is that he feels a greater responsibility. "Instead of creating a feeling of, 'Ooh, I've made it, let's go sailing,' in my conscience it forces me to a place where I feel I have to work harder and do more to make things better. It's a very dangerous thing to give someone like me a lot of money. Because I have so few material needs and so little desire for things [this is a man who doesn't drink coffee, let alone alcohol], if you put that much money in my hands I am going to do a lot of damage with it. It's like handing me a Molotov cocktail."

The other things it gives him is political and journalistic independence. "Because I have this money now, nobody can tell me this has to be taken out of the movie. Nobody can say to me again, 'This has to be taken out of your book'—I'll just go publish my own damn book, I'll make my own movie. I don't need your money. This is every working-class kid's dream. You have the money to tell the boss to fuck off. You don't have to take an ounce of shit from anybody."

There is a price he pays for that. In his personal life he claims to be introverted, but in his professional life he is on the cover of all his books and on the posters promoting his films. Like Martha Stewart and Puff Daddy, he is the person become product. Moore is aware of this even as he tries to resist it.

He does fewer interviews now, and even once he agreed to this one he was hell to pin down. He confides in me that he's hoping the interview runs on so long he'll have no time for the photographer. But Moore is consumed by his message. "I really don't like doing interviews. I have no control over what you're going to write. But somewhere I hope you're going to say that I hold Blair more responsible than Bush for this war. Because Bush doesn't know better, Blair does. Bush couldn't have gotten away with this without Blair. It is my challenge to the British public to get up off the couch and find another way."

Jayson Blair: The Man Who Took the *New York Times* for a Ride

March 6, 2004

Jayson Blair plans to write fiction. "Not literary fiction," he says, "but commercial fiction. Telling stories that people read and feel like they're real. It'll be like journalism without the stamp of nonfiction on it."

As I raise my eyebrows, Blair senses a race to the punchline. "I'm not going to tell my bad joke," he says but, with the minimum of encouragement, he does: "Maybe my first fiction book could be a compilation of my last few *New York Times* stories."

Around this time last year, Blair's interpretation of the difference between fact and fiction was no laughing matter. For most, it still isn't. Following a complaint from the *San Antonio Express-News* in Texas that Blair had plagiarised one of its stories, an internal *New York Times* investigation into his work revealed a litany of deception and inaccuracies relating to half the articles he had written between October 2002 and April 2003. "I started with attempts to garner the truth," he says, "and then just started cutting corners when I couldn't get the truth."

Before long, Blair had cut so many corners, he had reshaped the very notion of journalism into a pattern of pure fantasy. He described scenes he had never seen, invented quotes from people he had never spoken to, assured his editors he was in several different states at different times when he almost never left his flat in Brooklyn.

His resignation on May 1 last year was followed ten days later by a mammoth correction of almost fourteen thousand words, spanning four broadsheet pages of the *New York Times*. "The widespread fabrication and plagiarism represent a profound betrayal of trust and a low point in the 152-year history of the newspaper," read the first paragraph of the front-page story. "His tools of deceit were a cellphone and a laptop computer." Over the next month, the paper slowly imploded under the weight of institutional rancour and individual animus. Pulitzer Prize–winning writer Rick Bragg resigned after admitting that an unpaid assistant had done virtually all of the reporting for a story on oyster fishers in Florida for which he took full credit. It also emerged that the paper's bioterrorism expert, Judith Miller, had relied on the Pentagon's favourite Iraqi, Ahmad Chalabi, for her stories on weapons of mass destruction and was accused of having toed their line uncritically.

Attention soon turned to the management style of executive editor Howell Raines. At a staff meeting at the Astor Plaza Theatre, near the *Times* offices, to discuss the crisis with staff, Joe Sexton, a deputy editor of the Metro section, said, "I believe that at a deep level you guys have lost the confidence of many parts of the newsroom . . . I do not feel a sense of trust and reassurance that judgments are properly made. People feel less led than bullied."

Business reporter Alex Berenson asked Raines if he had considered resigning. Raines said no—or at least not unless he was asked to do so by the publisher, Arthur Sulzberger Jr., who was sitting next to him. Sulzberger said he would not accept the resignation even if it were offered. Three weeks later, Raines, as well as his deputy managing editor, Gerald Boyd, had gone. Blair had set off a train of events that would claim two of the biggest scalps in American journalism.

Standing at 5 feet 2 inch and only twenty-seven years old, Jayson Blair looks altogether too small and too young to have triggered such an earthquake. He's never more than five minutes away from a giggle and fifteen from a huge foghorn of a laugh. You are left with the impression that he's barely got started with adulthood, yet the first line of his obituary may have already been written. "It's never anything I intended, expected or wanted," he says of the calamity that befell the *Times*. "I view what happened as a personal self-destruction and personal crisis for me that blew up into something that was much bigger than my personal, individual story. And I wish it was something that could have happened in private. I wish I was in a profession where it would never have made the news."

It is difficult to know where to start with Blair's personal crises. There was the sexual abuse as a child that is referred to several times in the book but is never fully explained. "I cut out that chapter," he says. "It was a family decision. It deals with people who are still around." Then there is the drink and drugs. At times, his story reads more like that of a Fleet Street hack in the 1970s than a young journalist in the far more sober world of American journalism today. Blair bounced from bar to bar, scoring cocaine, snogging colleagues, abusing the company car and coming in to work wrecked or high as though he had only days to live. "I did coke when I was sad and then I needed alcohol to go to sleep," he explains. "There was no fun about it. Towards the end, it was maintenance of life. I had to have the bottle of scotch in the apartment to make it to sleep at night, then I had to have the cocaine so I could make it through the day."

Rehab cured the abuse. But the abuse, he now believes, was a form of self-medication to cure his undiagnosed manic depression. With drugs and booze out of the way, the mania took over. "For the first six months, I was just focused hard on keeping sober and not doing any drugs, and the fact that I felt like shit didn't matter so long as I was going to my meetings and my outpatient programme. Then I reached this plateau. Without the self-medication and the therapy, mental illness just whupped my ass."

And then the descent into deception began. Not a headlong freefall, but a slow, steady slide—a degradation by increments. The first few slips are explicable, if not justifiable. But his lies had an exponential quality—each one, once he had got away with it, simply created more space for, and less ethical angst about, the next. "It starts with you needing just one quote. It's in AP [the wire service used by most US newspapers]. Then you read something and rewrite the whole thing off the wires. Then a story breaks really, really late and I don't want to go back, so I call my sources and ask if it's true and then ask them to give me some facts that nobody else has and then I write it. But I'm not there and I say I am. So that's the trick there. And I don't give credit to the *Washington Post*, which broke the story. So I'm blurring the lines, more and more and more and more."

Soon, there is no saying where the line is at all. With the boundary between fantasy and reality breached, he just cannot stop. In a desire to look as though its reporters were not just all over a story, but all over the country, the *Times* paid particular attention to datelines and employed freelancers to help reporters on stories on the ground. This, alleges Blair, led to a practice known as the "toe-touch," which he defines as "a popular and sanctioned way at the newspaper to get a dateline on a story by reporting and writing it in one location, and then flying in simply so you could put the name of the city where the news was happening at the top of the story." A committee set up to review the paper's practices in the wake of the Blair scandal recommended that reporters "skip the trip" and settle for a "stale dateline" when the "toe-touch" serves only to justify a dateline artificially beneath the byline.

Working on the Washington sniper case, Blair got a call to make one such trip. "After making all these back and forth trips, I got another call to go down and I just didn't want to go. I thought, I'll call the AP correspondent, I'll call my sources, I've got a stringer there who's working for me, so what does it matter if I'm there? He's in the courtroom. Then it becomes, what does it matter so long as the AP guy's in the courtroom? And finally, what does it matter if anyone's in the courtroom? By then, you're into fiction."

At times, it seems as if he almost wanted to get caught. "At the time, I would have told you that, as soon as I felt better, I was going to get back out on the road. My doctors believe that I was really crying out for help. It's hard to say, because I don't have enough time away from it. But by the end I was out of touch with reality."

Reality got back in touch with Blair in the most brutal fashion. As the net closed in around his deceptions, he became increasingly desperate. He was chasing his tail, lying to back up the lies he had already told. At one stage, he got up from his table at a cafe in Greenwich Village and went into the toilets, mumbling, "Dead man walking." In the toilet, he tied his belt around his neck as though to kill himself, took a look at the metal hinge up above, and then relented. "That was the moment," he recalls of the time he realised he had to come clean and face the music. "I thought, I'm lying to people who care about me. They wanted to know the truth, but they also wanted what was best for me. I realised I was fighting at that point to hold on to something that I lost a long, long time ago. Having that weight lifted off me was probably the happiest moment in the entire thing."

Blair counts one of his most serious character flaws that contributed to the scandal as his willingness to please. As failings go, there are far worse, but it does not take long to see his point. His first words to me are, "Can I help you with that?" as I ineptly juggle my bag, his new book, a tape recorder and batteries while trying to shake his hand. He banters with the waiter. When I order the lobster club sandwich, he says, "Good call, go for it." When he goes for his coat, I go to the loo. When I come out, he is engrossed in conversation with the cloakroom attendant, who is showing him a room in the restaurant he never knew was there.

If he really wanted to please a lot of people, however, he would have swapped his raucous laugh for a hangdog expression to prove that he has learned the humility to accompany his humiliation. When it comes to Jayson Blair, people do not just want to hear remorse, they want to see it. To many, including several of his former colleagues, his tales of sexual abuse, addiction and mental health problems are little more than flight from responsibility for his actions. If there is a blurred line between fact and fiction in the case of Blair, then there might be an equally fuzzy one between explanations and excuses.

On this, he is clear. "It's deadly dangerous, because however much I say explanation, people will interpret it as an excuse. The reasons for my actions are my own bad choices. Bottom line. Was my judgment impaired? Yes. Did mental illness and substance abuse and the pressures of the job affect my choices? Yes. Were my character flaws the key reason why things went wrong? Yes. I made bad choices. It would be a disservice to anyone who has been through sexual abuse or substance abuse and come through it OK to say otherwise. There are people who go through much more difficult things and make much better choices."

It is about as complete a statement of individual responsibility as you can get. The trouble is, he is still only five minutes from his next giggle. He can sound penitent, but he refuses to look pathetic. There are times when it sounds like he just might break out into a Gloria Gaynor track. "There's an inherent piece of me that loves beating the odds," he says. "Some people fall into the abyss or the deep, dark hole and get shunned there and can't fight any more. But that's the fight I was born for.

"I'm twenty-seven years old. I can live two more lifetimes on top of this one. This is not the end of it. The important part for me isn't what the public view of me is, but what good can I actually do and what do my friends and family think of me, what do I think of myself. If the public or the media want to bury me as Jayson Blair the fabricator, that's perfectly fine. The important part is to take this opportunity I've been given and make the most of it."

Others would have disappeared. Within a year, however, Blair has a book coming out, *Burning Down My Masters' House*, and is holding forth on the ethics of journalism. "It's an innate part of my personality that I didn't consider for a moment the idea that I wouldn't share my own story. That shouldn't be misinterpreted as me not being ashamed. But I just don't believe that because you're ashamed about something, you don't have the right to speak. I think it would have been cowardly to crawl into a hole and not share the lessons that people could learn from my situation simply because it was going to cause discomfort for me. This whole process has been measurably more uncomfortable for me because I have chosen to speak."

One of the lessons he thinks we should learn is that journalists are not mini-gods and the American public should be far more sceptical and questioning about the role of the media. "In some ways my scandal could do for journalism what Watergate did to the presidency. It shows that there should be controls, there should be ombudsmen at papers . . . It's not exactly what I wanted my lasting legacy to be, but the part of my brain that puts critical analysis to it says it's true."

One of the lessons he thinks should not be drawn from the scandal is that affirmative action does not work. "I have yet to see one example where racial preferences or affirmative action played any role in my rise or my fall," he says. "I think more than race, at the *Times* class plays a role. A lot of the power is consolidated with heiresses and Ivy League grads who were in secret societies together and socialise in the same circle. It's very hard to break into those groups."

All good points, but none of them is best represented by Jayson Blair. Tackling his credibility deficit will take a long time, he says, and right now he is happy to be sober and sane. "Dealing with the mental health issues is the real struggle right now. We're still working on the right medication. The right combination. I feel immensely better. I haven't had bouts of psychosis or extreme mania. I've dealt with some rough depressions, but it's better than it was being out of control."

In the meantime, there is the book to promote and the inevitable brickbats that will come from all angles as he and his former colleagues relive the trauma. On February 23, the *New York Times*'s new executive editor, Bill Keller, issued a memo to staff about its release. "The book pretends to be a mea culpa," he writes, "but ends up spewing imaginary blame in all directions. Some of you may find the smears hurt, even if they are utterly lacking in credibility."

"Redemption comes a long, long way down the road," admits Blair. "It needs a lot of work. I think the book is the beginning of the process. But it may only enhance that pariah status. I have no idea how it's going to pan out. It's just the truth."

Sesame Sans Frontières

October 14, 2002

In the beginning there was Big Bird, and children saw him and said he was good. And in one of those rare moments of intergenerational concord, parents saw him and said he was good too. And so it came to pass that Ernie, Bert, Mr. Snuffleupagus and the other characters of *Sesame Street* were welcomed into liberal homes and hearts, first in America and then around the world.

Progressive parents who denied their boys access to toy guns and forbade their daughters Barbies, only to find their offspring escaping to friends' houses to play war and dress dolls, finally found a tool for ethical and educational child-rearing that worked. Unlike broccoli and piano lessons, here was one of those rare things that parents thought was good for their children and that their children actually enjoyed. Recently, however, even this simple relationship has been violated. In the past year *Sesame Street* has come under fire in the Middle East, been subject to intense criticism and scrutiny in the U.S. Congress from rightwing Republicans, and is struggling to make itself understood within the sectarian atmosphere of Northern Ireland.

A tragic indication that even the most noble attempts to inculcate children with the basic principles of universal humanism—that, whatever our differences, we are more alike than unalike—will founder against the rocks of deeply held prejudices of their parents. Proof, at the very simplest level, that while culture can confront prejudice, only changes in the material conditions that gave rise to it can ever eliminate the discrimination that feeds it.

If the Golden Arches Theory of Conflict Prevention claimed that no two countries that had a McDonald's had ever gone to war with each other, then this is the Sesame Street Theory of Conflict Resolution: that no two communities can claim peace unless a locally specific format of *Sesame Street* can be screened to their children.

It is, admittedly, a major claim for a children's programme, launched in America in 1969 with particular attention to disadvantaged pre-school children in urban areas. But its remit soon widened. It intertwined the effective teaching of basic literacy and numeracy with values, such as sharing and tolerance, which do not make their way to school league tables.

By dealing directly, yet sensitively, with issues like death and divorce, it encouraged emotional intelligence as an essential part of a child's education. By deliberately but unselfconsciously involving children of different races and abilities, it demonstrated that different did not mean worse and bigger did not necessarily mean better.

It soon went global and is now screened in more than 140 countries. Unlike McDonald's, here was one form of U.S. cultural hegemony that liberals could embrace because it involved America exporting its best rather than its worst. Not the military, economic and political power that repels, but the diversity, humour, creativity, energy and optimism that attracts.

Even more so because, while they were anxious to preserve the integrity of the Sesame Street brand—two actors dressed as Ernie and Bert were arrested in the Netherlands last year because they did not have permission from the creators—they have not tried to impose uniformity on how the show might be tailored to local needs.

So in Egypt there is Khokha, the education-eager puppet who encourages girls to go to school; China has Xia Mei Zi, the assertive toddler who promotes self-esteem among girls; and the Russian version has Zeliboba, the ancient tree spirit who teaches children there is much to learn from Old Russia. Last month the South African version, *Takalani Sesame*, was introduced to Kami, a five-year-old orphan with HIV who lives with a foster mother.

As it has spread in influence so has it risen in stature. Last year the U.N. secretary general, Kofi Annan, appeared on the show and said diplomats could learn a thing or two from its cast. In April one of its characters, Elmo, testified before legislators on Capitol Hill in favour of music teaching in schools. But as its friends have become more powerful so have its enemies. Plans to introduce a similar HIV character into the American version were dropped in August after Republican politicians objected with the veiled threat of cutting the partially state-funded show.

But the *Street*'s most thorny problem has been applying its format to areas of conflict. To discover why, we need look no further than Northern Ireland where they are looking to develop a local version. In a recent study, conducted by the University of Ulster, children were shown pictures and objects relating to different communities and asked what they thought of them.

The results were staggering. Almost two-thirds of three-year-old Catholics preferred the Irish flag, while 59 per cent of Protestants preferred the Union Jack. One four-year-old Catholic girl said: "I like the people who are ours. I don't like those ones because they are Orangemen. They're bad people." A Protestant girl of the same age said: "Catholics are the same as masked men. They smash windows." Little wonder then that *Sesame Street*, which is aimed at precisely that age group, is having trouble setting up there. "It won't be easy. The issues [in Northern Ireland] are extremely complex and we don't pretend to have all the answers. It'll be about finding the right partners," says Gary Knell, the president and chief executive of Sesame Workshop.

For the sake of the region we must hope he succeeds. Research in the Middle East showed that the prejudicial attitudes of children who watched *Sesame Street* towards those on the other side of the divide softened. In 1993, in the warm glow of the Oslo accords, an Israeli-Palestinian co-production set up a joint venture to screen the show. But, an intifada, several suicide bombers and Israeli military incursions later, the name has been changed to *Sesame Stories*—the notion of a street in the region where people and puppets could mix freely was regarded as untenable, as has the notion that Arab and Israeli children might even become friends. With separate programmes to be made from now on, this illustrates how the show's success is contingent on the political context in which it is shaped.

"Children in Palestine today will not appreciate, understand, absorb and react in a positive way to the goals we want to accomplish," said the Palestinian executive producer, Daoud Kuttab, whose studio in Ramallah was damaged by Israeli soldiers. "You're telling them to be tolerant to Israelis when Israeli tanks are outside their homes."

The best thing parents who want their children to grow up with liberal values can do is make sure there is a liberal world for them to grow up in. Where progressive standards lead, Ernie, Bert and the rest of the crew are sure to follow.

This column was brought to you by the letters P, E, A, C and E, tragically complicated by the numbers 9 and 11.

On Tour with the Harbingers of Doom

April 1, 2004

Robin Bales has seen the signs—war, terrorism, microchips in animals and corporate logos tattooed on the foreheads of the young. As prophesied in the book of Revelation, she explains, the end of the world is nigh.

"A lot of what is written down is literal and a lot of it is happening today. I definitely believe that," she says. "The seasons are meshing together. One day in January it was 75 [Farenheit] and the next day it snowed. The world has gone down so quickly."

Impending doom notwithstanding, Ms. Bales is delighted. She got to the South Carolina Christian Supply store early on Tuesday to buy her copy of *Glorious Appearing*, the twelfth book in the bestselling Left Behind series, based on a fictionalised account of the apocalypse, on the day it came out.

The first eleven Left Behind books have sold more than 40 million copies, making the authors, Tim LaHaye and Jerry Jenkins, bigger sellers than John Grisham.

Orders for the *Glorious Appearing (The End of Days)* were so strong that the publishers started a second printing two weeks before the first copies had reached the shelves. According to the publishers, a survey last year showed that one in eight U.S. adults has read some of at least one book from the series.

So Ms. Bales, who has read all eleven, booked her place in line early, thus avoiding the queue of eight hundred people snaking around the shop and out into the rain, waiting to meet the authors on Tuesday night. And now she is clutching a signed copy of one of the most startling literary sensations of our time. "I'm going to read the eleventh one again before I start this," she says.

Coming in the wake of the success of Mel Gibson's *The Passion of the Christ*, which details Jesus' last twelve hours before crucifixion, the Left Behind series is the latest example of the huge impact religious themes are having on popular culture in the United States, as well as the vast amounts of money that can be made from them.

Scan the Christian Supply store in Spartanburg and you will see everything from *The Bible's Way to Weight Loss* to Bible Bingo, along with T-shirts, keyrings, CDs and toys bearing scripture and car registration plates asking: Got Jesus?

"Americans don't just have to rely on the Bible anymore," says Sarah Golightly, one of the few African Americans who came to the launch. "God is showing himself in many ways through movies, books and audio."

Ms. Golightly, who has read only the first three of the Left Behind series, found Gibson's film hard going but rewarding: "It was two hours of rough beating. But it was good."

The Left Behind series is not all easy reading either, with long passages both vivid and violent. It starts with what evangelists call the Rapture—the moment when, they believe, those who have been born again will disappear and ascend to heaven. The first book opens with a 747 heading to Heathrow from Chicago. The flight attendant finds half the seats empty as the faithful are whisked away into the firmament, leaving behind only their clothes, fillings and wedding rings. Several thousand feet below husbands and wives are waking up next to piles of pyjamas, and cars, suddenly deprived of drivers, crash as the righteous rise.

The next ten books—with titles including *Assassins*, *Armageddon* and *Desecration*—detail the seven-year period of upheaval in which those left behind have their final chance to find Jesus. The authors committed themselves to portraying at least one "believable conversion" in each book. As the series progresses, the antichrist becomes the head of the U.N. and triggers the second coming after he signs a peace treaty with Israel, while 144,000 Jews convert to Christianity.

Glorious Appearing should be the final episode, in which Jesus returns—although the publishers plan a postscript (with the final judgment of Satan after Jesus' thousand-year reign on earth) and a prequel (which will introduce the characters sent to the Rapture before the first book began).

It was all LaHaye's idea. The seventy-seven-year-old creationist and religious-right stalwart had been preaching and writing self-help books for decades when he got the idea for a fictional series about the end of time. When he realised he couldn't write it himself he drafted Jenkins, fifty-four, a former journalist and prolific religious novelist. LaHaye provides the scripture; Jenkins moulds it into drama.

Some Catholics and conservative Protestants have charged that the Left Behind novels are anti-Catholic because they depict a future pope establishing a false religion linked to the antichrist.

"Dr. LaHaye believes we should treat the Bible literally where we can," Jenkins says. "For people who disagree with us, we say, 'Write your own books.' We're just glad we can live in a country where we can compete in a marketplace of ideas."

And with that they start their twelve-city, six-day tour through the South—home to almost half of their readers—from Spartanburg through Georgia, Alabama, Mississippi, Louisiana and Texas. The book's core reader is a white, Southern, female homemaker in her mid-forties, who is a college-educated, born-again Christian.

When LaHaye first pitched the idea publishers did not think it had much of a future outside of the Christian market. It was a hard sell, according to Ron Beers, the senior vice president and publisher of Tyndale fiction, which published the series. The production team asked why anybody would "want to buy a book when they know what the ending's going to be?"

But with each edition word of mouth grew. More than twenty thousand volunteers formed a Left Behind "street team," to introduce the books to family, friends and neighbours. When the fifth book, *Apollyon*, was released in 1999 it hit number two on the *New York Times* fiction hardcover list and the novels have remained in the mainstream ever since.

If the series's success illustrates the high degree of religious feeling in the U.S., it also offers a glimpse of how evangelism and fundamentalism are shaping the national mood after 9/11.

A *Time*/CNN poll eighteen months ago found that 59 per cent of Americans believe the events in the book of Revelation are going to come true, while nearly 25 per cent think the Bible predicted the September 11 attacks. Little wonder then that sales jumped 60 per cent after 9/11 and *Desecration*—the ninth book, released in October 2001—was the bestselling novel of the year. "The tragedy of 9/11 made everything so much more real and believable," Jenkins says.

Referring to Mel Gibson's film, LaHaye said: "I think the world is waking up to the fact that there are a great many people who support wholesome movies and maybe we'll have a whole new field of faith-based movies.

"People complain that *The Passion* is violent and wonder if children should see it . . . But they're used to violence. Good grief, television and the Internet abound with it. But that's senseless violence. This is purposeful violence. Children end up asking why Jesus was committed to go through that."

Jon Stewart: Such a Tease

October 1, 2005

Back in early 2003, as Democrats discussed setting up a liberal talk radio station to counter the right's supremacy in the culture wars, there was concern that progressive values were inherently unsuited to a popular format. "Progressives have this problem: they sound too erudite, it's like eggheads talking at you," Thomas Athans, co-founder of Democracy Radio, Inc., told the *New York Times*. "Most liberal talkshows are so, you know, milquetoast, who would want to listen to them?" said Harry Thomason, a Hollywood producer close to Bill Clinton. "Conservatives are all fire and brimstone."

Meanwhile, over on the cable TV channel Comedy Central, Jon Stewart appears to have cracked it, albeit in another medium. His nightly formula of spoof news, sarcastic asides, satirical swipes and teasing interviews on *The Daily Show* has since 1999 been hammering away at political elites in general and, since his election, the Bush administration in particular. In that time it has gained cult status and audience figures climbing to around 1.5 million. Last month *The Daily Show*—a British equivalent would be somewhere between *Have I Got News For You* and *The Fast Show*—won Emmy Awards for best comedy and best writing. Stewart's book, *America*, a jokey guide to democracy, was the year's nonfiction bestseller. (Sample discussion question: "Which of the following is the best combination of reasons to vote for a candidate? a) Issues and eyes; b) Party affiliation and hair; c) Background and teeth; d) Religious zealotry and tits." Sample classroom activity: "Hold a mock election. If you can't do this, mock a real election.") Less blunt than Michael Moore, but more politically engaged than late-night hosts Jay Leno or David Letterman, Stewart, forty-two, combines the irreverence of Chris Evans with the wit of Armando Iannucci. His show is anything but milquetoast.

While Stewart and his team will often lampoon Democrats and liberals, the show's staple diet is the gaffes, contradictions, hypocrisy and hubris of the Bushites, and the pomposity of the mainstream media. He makes no secret of his liberal leanings, but his duty as a comedian, he insists, is first and foremost to be funny. "People's sense of humour typically goes as far as their ideology," he says, "but I don't particularly think of ourselves as ideological here. I don't mean in the sense that we're equal opportunity offenders—we're not. I think we consider those with power and influence targets and those without it, not. But we're not a liberal organisation, we are still clearly selfish observers. We do not have a dog in the race. And that is to our discredit, but to do what we're doing, it's also natural and necessary."

Stewart did not come from a particularly politicised family. "When I was younger, I considered myself more of a socialist. But I came from a very suburban family of middle-class Jews who joined the great migration from the city to the suburbs during the early sixties. There's nothing in there that's particularly activist. We didn't sit around the table and debate, we much more followed the *I'm OK, You're OK* paradigm." His mother was a teacher, his father a physicist. Born Jonathan Stewart Leibowitz, he started using his middle name as his surname in 1987. "I'm not a self-hating Jew," he once said. "Actually, to borrow a line from Lenny Bruce, I just thought Leibowitz was too Hollywood." He started his career doing stand-up (his first big gig was as the opening act for Sheena Easton in Las Vegas) and still goes on the road from time to time. But the tone of *The Daily Show* is less a gagfest than a repertoire of shrugs, smirks, rolling eyes, raised eyebrows and damning asides, expressing frustration and despair at the powers that be. Relating Bush's decision to have a day of prayer following Hurricane Katrina, Stewart frowned. "OK," he said, followed by a long pause and plenty of laughs, "but—and I don't want to be crass here—isn't a hurricane an act of God? Shouldn't we have a day of shunning?"

When Condoleezza Rice admitted to the Senate that she had seen a presidential daily briefing in August 2001 . . . "I believe the title was 'Bin Laden Determined to Attack Inside the United States' " . . . Stewart just stared at the camera for twenty seconds. Then he covered his face in his hands, lifted his head up and moaned. "You're fucking kidding me, right? Please say, please say, you're fucking kidding me."

Stewart began on *The Daily Show* just before the 2000 election. The debacle of the Florida recount and the Supreme Court intervention provided ideal material. The country was shifting. With the brief respite of national unity following the September 11 terrorist attack, political discourse plunged to its most rancorous for more than a generation. Into this culture war came Stewart—a nightly reminder, principally for the urban and urbane American liberal, that their leaders, not they, were insane. In an era in which, having lost the presidential election and both houses of Congress, liberals have little to laugh about, he offers release.

Asked to compare his work with Michael Moore's, Stewart says: "He's an activist. We travel in the same sorts of manipulations to some extent, but we are more passive editorialists. He's an active editorialist. I would go so far as to say that I don't necessarily agree with a lot of the stuff that he says. But I admire the fact that he puts himself out there and tries to change things."

Despite bleeped-out expletives and single entendres about blow jobs and soft drugs ("Dude, I totally want to smoke a bong with you," Stewart told a Christian fundamentalist who had been explaining the theory of intelligent design), Stewart secures high-level interviews. Over the past few years his guests have included former Democratic presidential hopeful John Kerry, Bill Clinton, former Republican presidential challenger Bob Dole, counterterrorism chief Richard Clarke and Bush adviser Karen Hughes—and vice presidential hopeful John Edwards announced his candidacy on the show. Stewart has become a player, appearing on the covers of *Newsweek*, *Rolling Stone* and, most recently, *Wired*.

It's just gone three o'clock and on the street outside *The Daily Show*'s offices on the West Side of Manhattan, the day's audience has started a two-hour queue to see the show. They are young, mostly white and an even mix of men and women. One man wears a T-shirt stating: "I bet God's cock is huge."

"It's a short cut to the real news," says another audience member,

Shaun Field, twenty-seven, explaining why he likes Stewart. This is Stewart's base. Two-thirds of *The Daily Show*'s audience is aged eighteen to forty-nine. Fox News host Bill O'Reilly has described them as stoned "slackers," but on election night the show attracted almost as many viewers in the eighteen to thirty-four category as Fox.

Stewart knows his fans are out there, but . . . "One of the things we try not to do is to fall in love with the audience." He understands, to an extent, why he is popular—"If you feel like your philosophy is not being served by either the government or the media, then you will find comfort in a point of view that sounds or feels familiar"—but to pander to it would be counterproductive, he says. The criteria are: "Is that funny? Is that smart? Is that good? Not will those people be mad at us, will they like it." In short, Stewart is self-conscious about being unselfconscious. "The only skill I have is writing jokes," he says. "Like anything if you have an ability, ultimately you want to apply it to something you care about. Otherwise, you're just jerking off in your cage . . . which also has its advantages."

The show is produced by a team whose influences are *The Simpsons*, *Late Night with David Letterman* and *The Onion* (a spoof newspaper that blends the best of *Viz* and *Private Eye*), which is where both Ben Karlin and head writer David Javerbaum worked. The show begins with Stewart summing up the top story of the day. Then comes a spoof news segment in which a "reporter" stands against a fake, newsworthy landscape—a rubble-strewn street in Iraq, say—and pretends to be sending in a dispatch, usually as much a joke on journalists as it is on politicians. Occasionally, they really do take to the road, carrying out Ali G–style interviews in which the reporter asks outrageous questions of people so bound up in their own agendas they are apparently unaware they are the object of ridicule.

From the vantage point of New York, it can look as if the "reporters" have gone in search of a backward foreign country to patronise and have pitched up in Middle America. "You could run a *Daily Show* from Dayton, Tennessee," says Stewart. "People from Dayton could come to New York and cover the gay pride parade and they'd also be covering a foreign country. So much of what we do is deconstructionist and reductionist." Off-screen he sounds more like a funny academic than a brainy comedian.

After the "reports," there are more skits on regular themes such as

"Mess O'Potamia," the slugline for anything to do with Iraq, or "Evolution, Schmevolution," a recent week-long series on the debate over creationism. Finally, Stewart has an interview with an author, politician, journalist or actor. Regardless of whether it's a rightwing ideologue just days after the election or Kurt Vonnegut offering a stream of consciousness, Stewart's tone is the same—polite and mildly mocking rather than abrasive. He says he's not comfortable being more than two minutes away from a joke.

That was the image most people had of him until October 15 last year, just a couple of weeks before the election, when Stewart appeared on CNN's *Crossfire*. This is a show that pits a Democrat commentator against a Republican; they raise topical issues in rapid succession and bellow over each other in an attempt to score cheap points and earn applause from the studio audience. Stewart was clearly invited on for some light relief. But alongside Democrat Paul Begala and Republican Tucker Carlson (who are regulars), he instead started to berate the two hosts for their "partisan hackery," substituting bluster for political discourse.

"Wait. I thought you were going to be funny," said Carlson. "Come on. Be funny."

"No. No," said Stewart. "I'm not going to be your monkey."

Carlson went on to chide Stewart for putting lame questions to Kerry when he appeared on *The Daily Show*, insisting *Crossfire* would have given the Democrat a grilling.

Stewart responded: "If you want to compare your show to a comedy show, you're more than welcome to . . . You're on CNN. The show that leads into me is puppets making crank phone calls."

Carlson concluded: "I do think you're more fun on your show."

Stewart shot back: "You know what's interesting, though? You're as big a dick on your show as you are on any show."

In a highly-scripted election, during which mainstream news rarely departed from the storyline set by the two main parties, the clash between Stewart and Carlson was electric. Supposedly the election was a battle royal between Republicans and Democrats, and *Crossfire* was a symbol of it. Stewart's intervention—and the wide support he received—suggested there was an even deeper divide between political posturers and the public at large. A few months later, CNN decided to take *Crossfire* off the air.

"Ultimately, people would respond a lot better to being treated like

adults . . . if politics wasn't treated like marketing," Stewart says. This
sounds like a great American fantasy. Every few years Hollywood pro-
duces a film, whether it is Warren Beatty's *Bulworth* or Chris Rock's
Head of State, in which a presidential candidate goes off-message, tells
it like it is, and the voters respond warmly. The last time we saw anyone try this was Howard Dean and he was dismissed for his lack of
polish. "But who said that?" asks Stewart. "The polishers. So much of
what these guys do is an attempt to consolidate power because they
feel it slipping away. They think Dean's out there. But George Gal-
loway came here and completely blew away our congressmen. We're
just not used to unvarnished rhetoric."

If the parties and the media serve the country so badly, why do
Americans put up with it? "Because for the majority of Americans life
is pretty tolerable," says Stewart. "It's very hard to organise reasonable
people with moderate views. Reasonable people with moderate views
don't usually light their torches and head out to town with pitchforks
shouting, Be reasonable. Shit has to get really bad before people stand
up and take notice."

And Stewart clearly regards himself as one of those reasonable
moderates. Indeed, for a man hailed as a liberal standard-bearer, he
can sound rather complacent. "In general, the more egregious flaws of
our country have, over time, become less egregious," he says. "That's
not to say that we don't have enormous problems of poverty and race,
but they are no longer so clearcut as during the times of slavery, segregation or when women couldn't vote. In our big ticket items we're down
to gay people getting married. That's a lot of progress over the past few
hundred years, considering where we came from." Two close elections
may have given the impression of a divided America—a nation riven
between blue and red states, the secular and religious, town and
country—but Stewart believes the divisions have been exaggerated.
"For the amount of ultimate difference in the country, it is remarkably
stable. Only one civil war in two hundred years? Boy, that's something
to be proud of."

The big picture from outside America looks somewhat different,
and Stewart recognises that. "The thing that probably upsets the
world more than anything is the sense of American exceptionalism,"
he says. "But it is important to keep perspective. Whatever response to
9/11 that was ham-handed or arrogant or larger than may have been

required by our government, it was in many respects, regarding our history, pretty restrained. In the Second World War, we interned our Japanese citizens on the West Coast. Right after the revolution they had the Alien and Sedition Acts. We dropped an atomic bomb on a country. As much talk as there is about over-reaction in our history, this has been a mild form of that. Iraq probably being an exception."

The thing that surprises him about the election last year is not that the Democrats lost, but that they came so close to winning. "Americans are loth to abandon the captain in a time of war. It's almost remarkable that Bush had to fight so hard to get re-elected, given the fact that the worst attack on American soil happened three years earlier; one hundred thousand votes in Ohio and the Democrats would have won it. They absolutely could have won it. It is shocking."

Stewart voted for Kerry, although he hardly seems enamoured of the Democratic Party. "I don't really know what they want. The Democratic Party appears to be the party of reaction. The difference between the Democrats and the Republicans is the difference between driving towards a brick wall and trying to avoid hitting a deer. The Democrats appear to try to avoid hitting things that might dart out in front of them. Whereas the Republicans clearly have plotted a road and if there's something in their way, they're just going to blow it up. Sometimes literally."

The key dividing line in America, he says, referring to the New Orleans flood, is poverty. "I have to say poor is poor. And in this country that's where people really get screwed. If that had been in Appalachia (a poor white area of West Virginia), it would still have been a real fuck-up because they're the people that people think about last."

So, as the host of *The Daily Show*, does he think about those people first? "Us, no," he says without skipping a beat. "We're thinking about jokes."

Urbane, Not Urban

October 17, 2005

There's fabulous. And then there's ghetto-fabulous. When it comes to
societal approval these two expressions of ostentatious chic are supposed to be polar opposites. Fabulous is meant to be desirable—
classic, classy, pricey and proper. Ghetto-fabulous is meant to be
deplorable—crude, crass, vulgar and vile. Fabulous is for the urbane,
who buy gold by the ounce and call it jewellery; ghetto-fabulous is for
the urban, who buy their gold by the pound and call it bling. The
twain were never supposed to meet.

Take Martha Stewart and Lil' Kim. Stewart is the domestic diva
whose name is her brand and whose brand means all that is blissful,
serene and homely—fabulous. Lil' Kim is the hip-hop diva whose out-
fits left little to the imagination and whose lyrics filled whatever gaps
were left—ghetto-fabulous. Stewart will tell you all you want to know
about how to use flowers to decorate your table; Kim will show you
everything you want to see about how flowers can adorn a naked breast.

But increasingly, while the faces, fashions and forms of the fabulous and the ghetto-fabulous may differ, their functions resemble each
other like never before. Rarely has a business culture, which purports
to be led by the most upright people with the most proper values, been
so full of gangstas and players. Meanwhile, never has a street culture,
which stakes its claim on reflecting the aspirations of the poorest, produced so many dandys. Ghetto-fabulous set out to be a parody of the

fabulous, but in the end it seems to have just reproduced it: a pale imitation with darker skins.

In the words of Diddy (the artist formerly known as P. Diddy before he decided the "P was getting between me and my fans"): "It's all about the Benjamins." Benjamin Franklin's face is on $100 bills; Diddy—who counts Martha Stewart among his role models—means business.

Which brings us back to Stewart and Kim. Their names were never destined to share a sentence. But prison does strange things to people. In March, Stewart was released after spending five months inside for conspiracy, obstruction of justice and lying about a stock sale. Three weeks ago Kim went in for perjury, after a CCTV camera showed her witnessing a shooting she said she knew nothing about.

But even before either one went in, they were well on the way to morphing. Kim, like Martha, went to court carrying a $6,000 Hermes Birkin leather handbag from Paris. Both asked if they could serve time in a far less harsh facility in Danbury, Connecticut, so that they could be close to their ailing mothers. Both were denied.

Indeed, at times they seemed to have undergone a complete role reversal. Stewart (who was known as M. Diddy on the inside) was recently seen rapping with the actual Diddy on her show, referring to herself as "Miss Martha." Kim (whose real name is Kimberly Jones) spent her last night of freedom driving around Manhattan in a Bentley coupe, quaffing Cristal from a flute.

These parallels are not just understood. In a world where celebrities are their own brands, they are actively promoted. Three days before Kim went to prison, a young man handing out flyers at Utica station in Brooklyn offered me a "last chance to see Kim before she becomes Martha Stewart."

The crossover seemed complete when Kim told the *New York Daily News* that she considered Stewart a role model. "Her courage and strength is definitely encouraging," said Kim, adding that Stewart "came out [of jail] looking better than when she went in."

The contradictions look stark, but the sense of kinship is nothing if not consistent. Despite all the profanity and claims to rebelliousness, the bling of gangsta rap is really little more than rapacious free-market capitalism set to beats and rhymes. With huge record companies selling millions of units that promote the acquisition of high-priced material goods as a core human value, its culture is as corporate as an office Christmas party organised by David Brent.

"First the culture came to influence the boardroom and now the boardroom's influencing the culture," says Greg Tate, author and cultural critic of the *Village Voice*. "There's probably more money at stake in hip-hop now than when the battles were for turf between the different drug gangs. 50 Cent is probably making more money than the whole crack industry on the Eastern Seaboard."

50 Cent, one of the hottest names on the rap scene, sings about shootouts in the Bronx, where he grew up, but now lives in a custom-built mansion in Connecticut. Likewise, despite the facades of both decorum and civility, the white-collar world, which has seen such a huge rise in high-profile crimes in recent years, looks like a bunch of gangstas in suits. Enron and Worldcom are just the two best known examples of the kind of brazen, lawless behaviour that makes Eminem look like a choirboy.

Recently, Dennis Kozlowski, the former chief executive officer of Tyco, was sentenced to up to twenty-five years in prison for looting the company of $150 million. The jury saw a video of a lavish $2 million Roman-themed birthday party thrown for his wife, partly charged to the company, complete with scantily clad models and ice statues dispensing drinks that would not have been out of place on MTV. Kozlowski also charged to the company a $6,000 gold-threaded shower curtain and a $2,900 set of coat hangers for his apartment. That is serious bling.

But while the worlds of the fabulous and the ghetto-fabulous are analogous, they are neither identical nor equal. The world of the fabulous, while much respected, is the one that deprives people of their pensions and livelihoods while buying huge political favours and protection through lobbyists. The world of the ghetto-fabulous, while much reviled, makes money for the fabulous by exploiting the culture of deprived people who are marginalised from the political system. The fabulous donate huge sums to political campaigns; the ghetto-fabulous are usually the subject of those campaigns.

For all their similarities, Kim and Stewart remain worlds apart. Kim is a young, black, working-class woman—the kind for whom America's prison-industrial complex was built. Stewart is a white, upper-class woman for whom prison came as a shock. Black women are almost five times as likely as white women to end up in prison. While sentencing Kim, District Judge Gerard Lynch said he had considered the public perception of sending a young black entertainer to prison for a far longer term than Stewart. Stewart was sent to Alderson—nicknamed Camp Cupcake—which has dormitories and scenic grounds. She came out with two new shows and a lot of public sympathy. Kim was sent to a far more miserable facility in inner-city Philadelphia for a year and a day.

"Why are we going to an inner-city federal prison when others like Martha Stewart simply go to camps?" asked Kim's lawyer, Londell McMillan. "Not fair. Not fair." Not fabulous. Just ghetto.